CHRISTIANITY CORRUPTED

CHRISTIANITY CORRUPTED

The Scandal of White Supremacy

JERMAINE J. MARSHALL

ORBIS BOOKS
Maryknoll, New York 10545

Founded in 1970, Orbis Books endeavors to publish works that enlighten the mind, nourish the spirit, and challenge the conscience. The publishing arm of the Maryknoll Fathers and Brothers, Orbis seeks to explore the global dimensions of the Christian faith and mission, to invite dialogue with diverse cultures and religious traditions, and to serve the cause of reconciliation and peace. The books published reflect the views of their authors and do not represent the official position of the Maryknoll Society. To learn more about Maryknoll and Orbis Books, please visit our website at www.maryknollsociety.org.

Manufactured in the United States of America

Library of Congress Cataloging-in-Publication Data

Names: Marshall, Jermaine J., author.
Title: Christianity corrupted : the scandal of white supremacy / Jermaine
    J. Marshall.
Description: Maryknoll, New York : Orbis Books, [2021] | Includes
    bibliographical references and index. | Summary: "Examines the
    development of oppressive Christian theologies and the normalization of
    white superiority and white privilege in the United States"-- Provided
    by publisher.
Identifiers: LCCN 2021008351 (print) | LCCN 2021008352 (ebook) | ISBN
    9781626984332 (trade paperback) | ISBN 9781608338962 (epub)
Subjects: LCSH: Racism--Religious aspects--Christianity. | Racism--History.
    | Race relations--Religious aspects--Christianity. | Christians,
    White--United States--History. | African American Christians--Social
    conditions. | Racism--United States. | United States--Race relations.
Classification: LCC BT734.2 .M25 2021 (print) | LCC BT734.2 (ebook) | DDC
    277.73089--dc23
LC record available at https://lccn.loc.gov/2021008351
LC ebook record available at https://lccn.loc.gov/2021008352

To the Christian (formerly Colored) Methodist Episcopal Church
that has nurtured me in the authentic Christianity of Christ
from the cradle, especially the following congregations:
Central Metropolitan CME Church (Jacksonville, Florida)
Williams Tabernacle CME Church (Jasper, Florida)
Murray Temple CME Church (Anniston, Alabama)
Mount Olive CME Church (Orlando, Florida)
Williams Institutional CME Church (Harlem, New York)

Contents

Acknowledgments

This book began as my dissertation for the Regent University School of Divinity. I'm indebted to my dissertation committee, Dale M. Coulter (chair), Kimberly Ervin Alexander, David D. Daniels III, and Love Henry Whelchel Jr., for their wisdom, knowledge, academic guidance, and scholarly fortitude. I'm especially grateful to Dale Coulter and Kim Alexander for their courage, perseverance, and commitment during a time in which the nature of my scholarship was not in accord with the ethos of the institution. They did not cave into the duress of political expediency but were dedicated to seeing my dissertation through despite the potential repercussions.

I'm grateful to the scholars, colleagues, and friends who were conversational partners and offered imperative feedback, especially Aaron Sheehan-Dean, Dianne M. Stewart, Néstor Medina, Dale Irvin, Lynn M. Hargrow Jr., Jeremy Williams, and Cassandra G. Perry.

I'm grateful to the many professors who challenged and helped me to shape the treasure of academic scholarship in this earthen vessel and to fuel in me the passion I have for academic excellence and the study of history and theology. I'm particularly grateful to Henry M. Thomas, Elizabeth Daniell, Julie Ingersoll, and the late Carolyn Williams, all of whom challenged and inspired me during my undergraduate studies at the University of North Florida, and also to Lisa Allen-McLaurin, Love Henry Whelchel Jr., Randall Bailey, Riggins Earl, and Wallace S. Hartsfield who challenged and inspired me during my master of divinity studies at the Interdenominational Theological Center. I'm particularly grateful to Dianne M. Stewart, Emmanuel Lartey, Noel Erskine, E. Brooks Holifield, Rex Matthews, Russell Richey, Randall Balmer, and Jonathan Strom for challenging and inspiring me during my Master of Theology studies at Candler School of Theology (Emory University). I appreciate each of you for your role in ensuring that I answered and fulfilled the divine calling to the academic vocation.

I'm grateful to my many friends and colleagues who encouraged and supported me throughout my doctorate program, especially to Zena Fleming, Valerie Landfair, Lisa Allen-McLaurin, Candy Gunter Brown, Sylvia E. Williams, Kendra Hammond Williams, Erika Rembert Smith, Jonathan Alvarado, David Ricci, Alton McGriff, Freeman McKindra II, Kornelius Neal, Clarence Kelby Heath, Ricky Helton, Loretta Helton, Roscoe McKinney

III, Walt Gessner, Rodolfo Estrada, Daniel Davis, Brandon Badcock, Lynn Hargrow Jr., Jeremy Williams, Cassandra G. Perry, Jamie L. Capers, and Ericka S. Dunbar. Thank you all for your love and encouraging words during some of my most vulnerable times, especially during the writing of my dissertation, which materialized into this book and gave me the fortitude and perseverance to complete this mammoth task.

I am especially indebted to my entire church family for your love, support, patience, and compassion. I know that there have been some shortcomings in my pastoral work due to my academic commitment, and yet the church has believed in this work and invested in me at every level and every step of the way. The doctorate degree is our degree, and this is our book.

I am grateful for every member and officer of every church that I have had the honor and privilege of serving as senior pastor. Without each of you this work would not be possible. I'm grateful for each presiding bishop under whose episcopal supervision and leadership I have had the privilege and pleasure of serving as a pastor and without whose unfailing love and unwavering support this academic work would not have been possible. This includes Senior Bishop Lawrence Lewis Reddick III, the late Bishop Wallace Edward Lockett, Bishop Teresa Elaine Jefferson-Snorton, and Bishop James Bernard Walker. I'm grateful for each presiding elder under whose supervision I have had the privilege and pleasure of serving and without whose love and support this academic work would not have been possible. This includes Lilly A. Rainey, Roscoe C. McKinney Jr., and Frederick Douglas Belcher. I'm grateful for every associate minister who has served under my pastoral leadership and faithfully fulfilled any pastoral voids. This includes the late Shirley Jamieson, Marcus Walker, Tyree Anderson, Diane Hinton, Charlotte Woods, Cassandra G. Perry, Linda McFall, and Glennie Van.

I'm especially indebted to Paul McMahon of Orbis Books, whose masterful editing of my work made this a much better book. Paul is truly a gem and a rare gift to the publishing world. His wisdom and guidance greatly transcend what is expected. I'm eternally grateful for the honor and privilege of working with him on this writing project. And I'm especially indebted to Lisa Allen-McLaurin, who was a great source of strength and encouragement from the book proposal to publication.

Whatever I am and whatever I do is made possible by my family. I'm especially indebted to my loving and faithful parents, Carolyn Ann Webb Walthour and Freddie Lee Walthour Sr., whose love, nurture, support, encouragement, and many sacrifices have fostered the fulfillment of all my dreams and goals in life. I'm grateful for my siblings Carla Smalls and Freddie Lee Walthour Jr. Finally, I'm especially indebted to Dr. Natalie Walker, without whose unwavering love, unceasing support, and perpetual encouragement over the years this book would not have been possible.

Foreword

The Heretical Ontology of "Americanity"

In his National Book Award-winning history, *Stamped from the Beginning*, Ibram Kendi chronicled how racist ideas have been used from the beginning of the American story to justify the policies of white supremacy. Another of our great contemporary writers, Ta-Nehisi Coates, has written that "race is the child of racism, not the father."[1] These are not simply the individual insights of great minds, but rather an articulation of collective wisdom that has been distilled over generations. To get to the root of racism, we have learned, is to trace the genealogy of a lie.

We are living in a moment when that fundamental lie of racism is being exposed in mainstream American culture. Antiracist books and courses invite Americans to reassess their own stories and daily habits even as major public initiatives like the 1619 Project and the National Memorial for Peace and Justice invite us to reimagine the story we tell about how our nation came to be. These cultural shifts have accompanied social movements for racial equity that have renewed a national conversation about reparations for the descendants of enslaved people and compelled political leadership to examine the impact of a range of policy decisions on racial equity.

But this shift to antiracist thought and praxis has also inspired a backlash. As public challenges to racism have threatened the individual's self-understanding and whole communities' political assumptions, many who feel threatened have gone on the attack, attempting to ban certain books or ideas from public school curricula and supporting voter suppression efforts that target African Americans, as one federal court ruled, "with surgical precision."

The book you now hold in your hands recognizes that the lie of race is one rooted in and sustained by how we talk about God. At the moment when

---

1. Ta-Nehisi Coates, *Between the World and Me* (New York: Random House, 2015), 7.

racism sired race through the legal codes of the American colonies, theology was queen of the sciences. White supremacy could neither have been claimed nor defended without an appeal to divine sanction and a case that God's will was being fulfilled as people created in God's image were bought and sold as property. Though the Constitution was amended and Jim Crow laws were struck down, the heretical ontology that was contrived to sanctify American injustice lives on. One of my teachers, C. Eric Lincoln, called this distorted theology, distinctive to the American experience of indigenous genocide and race-based chattel slavery, "Americanity."

Jermaine J. Marshall is a scholar who sees the need to trace the genealogy of Americanity's lie to its source. But he is also a pastor and teacher of the church who wants to help free souls from the heretical ontology of the idolatry that is too often confused with the religion of Jesus in this land. I thank God for him, and I commend his work to you with this prayer:

> *Spirit of the Living God,*
> *Fall fresh on your people.*
> *Grant us courage to face the lies we inherited.*
> *Grant us wisdom to follow those who followed your Way before us.*
> *Grant us hearts on fire for justice, love, and mercy*
> *As we work for the new world you give us grace to imagine. Amen.*

Bishop William J. Barber II
President, Repairers of the Breach
Co-chair, Poor People's Campaign

Introduction

Between the Christianity of this land and the Christianity of Christ, I recognize the widest possible difference—so wide, that to receive the one as good, pure, and holy, is of necessity to reject the other as bad, corrupt, and wicked. To be friend of the one, is of necessity to be the enemy of the other. I love the pure, peaceable, and impartial Christianity of Christ: I therefore hate the corrupt, slaveholding, women-whipping, cradle-plundering, partial and hypocritical Christianity of this land. Indeed, I look upon it as the climax of all misnomers, the boldest of all frauds, and the grossest of all libels.

—Frederick Douglass

In 1845, African American abolitionist Frederick Douglass (1818–1895) published his autobiographical account of life as an American slave.[1] A major part of this account consists of Douglass reflecting on the disconnection between the Christian faith and the American institution of slavery. In his reflection, Douglass dichotomizes American Christianity, concluding that there existed two distinctly different brands of Christianity in the United States during the nineteenth century: one, reflective of the faith discovered in the gospel of Jesus Christ possessing the true Christian virtues of love, purity, peace, and impartiality, which he identified as the Christianity of Christ; the other, the religious tradition that dominated the British colonies and the early American republic and characterized as a "slaveholding religion." Douglass expressed his utter disdain for the latter brand of Christianity and asserted that this religion of the American enslavers possessed the vices of corruption, abuse, oppression, partiality, and hypocrisy.

Douglass's dichotomy demonstrates how slaveholding religion constituted a distortion of true Christianity, which reflected the teachings of Jesus Christ. This dichotomy exposes the effects of a scandalized Christian faith. Slaveholding religion indeed scandalized the Christian faith through the teachings and practices that were antithetical to those of Christ. The

---

1. Frederick Douglass, *Narrative of the Life of Frederick Douglass, an American Slave* (New York: Literary Classics of the United States, 2014) [Frederick Douglass, *My Bondage, My Freedom* (Lexington, KY: Odin's Library Classics, 1855)].

correlation between modern racism and oppressive Christian theologies is pivotal to this scandal.

In 1964, Fannie Lou Hamer declared, "I'm sick and tired of being sick and tired," from the pulpit of Williams Institutional Christian Methodist Episcopal Church in Harlem, New York. In her speech, Hamer was expressing her extreme anguish over the pervasiveness of racial injustice in the United States and its failure to keep its beloved democratic principles and promises. Almost sixty years later, Hamer's cry remains the cry of the African American community in the United States. After over four hundred years of the dehumanization of Blacks in this country, racism is still a chronic disease pervading the very fabric of American society. I'm sick and tired of feeling the clear and present danger of bringing a Black child into this world. I'm sick and tired of feeling that having black skin is a crime in America. I'm sick and tired of feeling that having black skin means having some form of leprosy. In Scripture, leprosy was a skin disease, and persons suffering from the disease were automatically considered social outcasts and socially destitute (see Lev 13:1–45). This reality is evident in the racist tropes that have become common nomenclature in American society. For example, following the historic election of the first African American president, "take our country back," declared by adherents of the Tea Party movement, became a rallying cry for white people who viewed the election of a Black man as anti-American and a literal threat to their way of life—as if Black people had hijacked the United States through the election of President Barack Hussein Obama. Another racist trope, "Make America Great Again," became the proclaimed sentiment that propelled the election of Donald Trump, translated in the African American community as "Make America White Again" because of the clandestine way that it asserts that the restoration of whiteness constitutes the restoration of greatness. Such racist tropes express the feelings of white supremacists in America, who see only lepers when they see people of color.

As a pastor, it grieves my heart that the racism in the United States is being perpetuated, aided, and abetted through spiritual wickedness in high places and religious hypocrisy. White evangelicals have cultivated a culture in America through which they claim to possess a monopoly on the Christian faith and morality. Yet they have scandalized the gospel of Jesus Christ and corrupted the Christian faith through their religious hypocrisy. The Gospel asks, "For what will it profit them to gain the whole world and forfeit their life?" (Mark 8:36). While white evangelicals today pride themselves on belonging to Christ, the awful reality is that many of them have sold their souls to the cult of Trump. While some of these white evangelicals would argue that their undying loyalty to Trump results from their attempt to protect what they believe are endangered moral values in America society, the reality is that there are covert and overt racial motivations that are just as prominent in their political allegiances.

In 1989, Trump took out $85,000 in op-eds in the *New York Times*, *Daily News*, *New York Post*, and *New York Newsday* titled "Bring Back the Death Penalty, Bring Back the Police" and suggested that there was no more law and order in New York City. This was in response to five boys of color (four Black and one Latino) being made the prime suspects by two white women, one the assistant district attorney at the time and the other the head of the Sex Crimes Unit of the Manhattan District Attorney's Office. The charges against these five boys of color were related to the case of a white woman jogging in Central Park who was attacked, raped, and beaten so severely that when she awoke from her coma, she had no memory of the attack. Even after a confession from the person who actually committed the crime and the exoneration of the five men of color, thirty years later Trump refuses to apologize and admit any wrongdoing. During the 2008 presidential campaign, Trump fostered the emergence of the birther movement—a racist attempt to perpetuate the myth and conspiracy theory that Barack Obama was not a natural-born citizen of the United States, which, based on constitutional law, would have invalidated his candidacy. Trump even had the audacity to question the intellectual capacity of Barack Obama, a Harvard trained constitutional lawyer, demanding that Obama release his college and graduate transcripts to prove his academic success after Obama had served as the head of the *Harvard Law Review*. In 2015, Trump announced his candidacy for the presidency, further promoting racist tropes. During the campaign, he characterized Mexicans as rapists and asserted that Blacks should vote for him because they had nothing to lose. Trump's dehumanization of people of color was further solidified when he characterized African nations as "shithole countries." Unfortunately, Trump's racist tropes and behavior have refueled the evil spirit of white supremacy and antiblackness supremacy in the United States.

African American church historian Love Henry Whelchel Jr. often exclaims that African American history is "too painful to remember and too dangerous to forget."[2] Exposing the trajectory of the theological scandal that resulted in white superiority and white privilege requires an examination and interrogation of history. At this writing, the United States is at a watershed moment in the wake of the multiracial and multicultural protests against racial injustice. Protests are occurring globally in the wake of the brutal killing of many Black people in America; most recently, the killings of Ahmaud Arbery, Breonna Taylor, Tony McDade, George Floyd, and Rayshard Brooks. The protests reflect an awakening to the truth of

---

2. Love H. Whelchel Jr., *The History and Heritage of African American Churches: A Way Out of No Way* (St. Paul, MN: Paragon House, 2011).

racial injustice. James Cone once said, "If we cannot recognize the truth, then it cannot liberate us from untruth."[3] I'm an alumnus of and currently teach at the Interdenominational Theological Center (ITC), which is a Christian Africentric ecumenical seminary committed to liberation theology and social justice. The curriculum at ITC is based on the symbolism of the Sankofa bird. Visually and symbolically, "Sankofa" is expressed as a mythic bird that flies forward while looking backward with an egg (symbolizing the future) in its mouth. This indicates that to understand our present and ensure our future we must know our past. Post-traumatic stress disorder (PTSD) from racial injustice would be a luxury for Black people in the United States because, though stressed, it would suggest that racism has at least been eradicated. However, racism in America is still very much alive, and therefore the trauma of racism continues. It is imperative, therefore, that we look back and examine the theological scandal of Christianity that has produced antiblackness and white Christian supremacy.

In the sixteenth century, the Protestant Reformation developed in reaction to the theological superiority of Catholicism, in addition to its institutional corruption and abuses. French theologian John Calvin became the systematic theologian of the Protestant Reformation and popularized the notion of election. Calvin's doctrine of election was pivotal in the development of covenantal theologies—the covenant between God and the elect—especially in the context of British colonial America and the early republic. Portrayed as covenants of grace but operating as theologies that oppressed and marginalized the nonelect, these covenants secured through supposed divine election proved that they were not grounded in grace but grounded in negative concepts of race.

In the eighteenth century, the Enlightenment emerged as a movement of ideas situated primarily in Europe. This era of intellectual inquiry formed in differing contexts, particularly British, French, and German. The Enlightenment has been identified as a continuation and enhancement of the philosophical and intellectual work of philosophers from the previous era, such as René Descartes, John Locke, Francis Bacon, and Baruch Spinoza. These philosophers fostered the emergence of Modernity, which attacked tradition and eradicated that which was considered old. During the seventeenth and eighteenth centuries, religion was the only institution that emphasized the old over the new.

Due to the conclusion by thinkers of the Enlightenment that the attainment of truth was possible only through the source and norm of reason, the Enlightenment has been characterized as the "Age of Reason." Most historians have situated the origins of Modernity in the work of French philoso-

---

3. James Cone, *God of the Oppressed* (Maryknoll, NY: Orbis Books, 1997), 28.

pher René Descartes (1596–1650), the father of modern philosophy. In 1637, Descartes published his essay "Discourse on Method," in which he famously declared, "I think, therefore, I am," which became central to the prioritization of reason.[4] In other words, Descartes concluded that in order to think it was necessary to exist. This new epistemological focus, with its emphasis on doubt, became the major threat to the orthodox Christian church. To combat the impact of this new focus on certain theological concepts, the orthodox Christian church needed to develop oppressive theologies that, unfortunately, were grounded in negative concepts of race rather than covenants of grace.

Enlightened thinkers were European men who equated whiteness with perfection, and whiteness became the criterion for determining the individual thinker. Whiteness became transcendent because white was not a color; therefore, whiteness constituted the absence of color. African American philosopher Cornel West has asserted that the idea of white supremacy developed because of the powers within the structure of modern discourse.[5]

Enlightened thinkers saw a dichotomy between the epistemological capacity and ontological worth of human beings based on racial classifications. West contends that the initial basis for white supremacy was situated in these racial classifications. In 1648, French physician François Bernier (1625–1688) was the first to devise a classification of races through which he categorized humanity: Europeans, Africans, Orientals, and Lapps.[6] Human beings, and particularly men with white skin color, therefore, were characterized as upper class, individual thinkers (*cogito*), and subjects. Human beings failing to meet this biological criterion were characterized as lower class, racial other, and objects. Consequently, the upper class were light, rational, self-sufficient, civilized, transcendental, and therefore possessed individual rights; the lower class were dark, emotional, dependent, uncivilized, immanent, and therefore lacked individual rights. In addition to these supposedly distinct differences in characteristics based on racial classifications, other theories based on skin color were presented about the cultural aspects and civilization of human beings.

Prior to the Enlightenment, race had been a political category rather than a natural category; however, the racial classifications devised during this period naturalized race. Enlightenment thinkers viewed Europe as the civilized continent in the Age of Light and simultaneously condemned

4. Rene Descartes, *Discourse on Method and Meditations*, trans. Laurence J. Lafluer (Upper Saddle River, NJ: Prentice Hall, 1952), 25.

5. Cornel West, *Prophesy Deliverance: An Afro-American Revolutionary Christianity* (Louisville, KY: Westminster John Knox Press, 2002), 49.

6. West, *Prophesy Deliverance*, 55.

Africa as the Dark Continent.[7] They considered Europe as culturally and racially superior to all other peoples and geographical lands. Therefore, other non-European continents besides Africa such as Asia—and even the American continent—were considered strange lands.[8] African American religious historian Charles H. Long declared that the locus of the problem with Modernity and therefore Enlightenment philosophy was the dichotomy between the idea of primitives and the civilized. Long stated that "the primitives operate as a negative structure of concreteness that allows civilization to define itself as a structure superior to this ill-defined and inferior other."[9] He further contended that the civilization of Western Europe could not have been defined apart from the empirical existence and exploitation of the primitive cultures.[10] African philosopher Emmanuel Chukwudi Eze argued that the European Enlightenment was built on Greek antiquity. The Greeks dichotomized human beings as either cultured and civilized or barbaric, primitive, and suffering from savagery.[11] Race was constructed to keep all other races subjected to one race (whiteness) through oppression. Thus, race was not so much a biological construction as a political construction.

Geography was a pivotal factor in these racial classifications. Enlightenment thought was the catalyst for determining geographical designations by race rather than by space. In 1748, the French naturalist Georges-Louis Leclerc, Comte de Buffon (1707–1788), published an essay in which he devised a geographical and cultural distribution of the human race based on climate and biological differences. Buffon suggested that the natives of the civilized cold climate countries are the most handsome and beautiful people of the world. He identified these civilized countries as "Georgia, Circassia, Ukraine, Turkey, Hungary, the south of Germany, Italy, Switzerland, France, and the northern part of Spain."[12] German philosopher Immanuel Kant (1724–1804) also concluded that heat was the cause of blackness.[13] Kant correlated the intellect of European dogs that immigrated to Africa with blackness. He asserted that "all dogs that are brought from Europe to Africa

---

7. Emmanuel Chukwudi Eze, *Race and the Enlightenment: A Reader* (Malden, MA: Blackwell Publishing, 1997), 5.

8. Eze, *Race and the Enlightenment*, 5.

9. Charles H. Long, *Significations: Signs, Symbols, and Images in the Interpretation of Religion* (Minneapolis: Fortress Press, 1995), 101.

10. Long, *Significations*, 101.

11. Long, *Significations*, 4.

12. Georges-Louis Leclerc, Comte de Buffon, "A Natural History, General and Particular," in Eze, *Race and the Enlightenment*, 26.

13. Immanuel Kant, "On the Different Races of Man," in Eze, *Race and the Enlightenment*, 62.

become dumb and bald and produce only similar offspring thereafter."[14] In his treatise on the geographical distribution of races, Buffon demonized the people of the African continent and condemned their blackness. He argued that Negroes are confined to the African continent due to the heat, which produced their blackness and preserved them in their blackness.[15]

With this brief historical background of the modern concepts of race, we will now set out to explore and expose the trajectory of the theological scandal that resulted in white superiority and white privilege. We will also examine the resistance to this theological scandal and the impact that it has had on religion in general, but in particular, in the United States of America. Our exploration will be benefitted by suggesting potential ways forward where a true understanding of Christianity can be restored and the corruption laid to rest.

The Scandal

Our first part begins by analyzing the roots of the scandal embodied in Enlightenment theories of race and demonstrates the continuity of these roots within Puritanism and Anglicanism. This continuity shows how the Puritans and Anglicans were progenitors of oppressive Christian theologies in British colonial America and the early republic. We will then outline the three factors that contributed to the corruption of American Christianity: (1) the integration of Enlightenment theories of race with the Reformed notion of election; (2) the belief in the ideal of Black inferiority; and (3) the development of proslavery Christian theologies. This theological scandal within the roots of the Puritans and Anglicans formed the praxis for the spiritual oppression of these Christian faith traditions and became a major catalyst for white supremacy and white privilege. Both Christian traditions possessed a distinct oppressive theological identity: Puritans possessed a theology of white superiority; Anglicans a theology of white privilege. Both these theological identities resulted in the adoption of the Enlightenment term "racial others" for those who were nonwhite and their condemnation as heathens.

In the first chapter, we examine the theories of race that developed within the three major European theaters of the Enlightenment era—Britain, France, and Germany. We analyze the philosophical views of British philosopher John Locke and Scottish philosophers David Hume and Adam Smith, demonstrating how Locke's natural law theory, Hume's notion of Black inferiority and destined enslavement, and Smith's postulation of the invisible hand of God were situated in racist ideology and theological contradictions.

---

14. Kant, "On the Different Races of Man."
15. Buffon, "A Natural History, General and Particular," 23.

We also examine various racist philosophical notions. These include those of German philosopher Immanuel Kant that were designed to reduce the value of humanity to geography and climate conditions and the attempts of German philosopher G. W. F. Hegel to construct the ideology of racial superiority of Europeans over other human races. We focus on the dehumanizing definitions of blackness devised by French philosopher Denis Diderot, the notion of Black degeneration as proposed by French naturalist Georges-Louis Leclerc and Comte de Buffon, the notion of white intellectual superiority as postulated by French political philosopher Baron de Montesquieu, the attempts of French historian and philosopher Voltaire to dehumanize people of African descent as heathenistic and subhuman, and the classification of indigenous people (non-Europeans) as noble savages by Genevan philosopher Jean-Jacques Rousseau. Finally, we interrogate Thomas Jefferson's ideology of racial inferiority and the problem of otherness.

From this development, it is clear that the notion of white superiority becomes the theological identity of Puritanism. How this impacts the different branches of the Puritan faith related to enslaved Africans in early American history is our focus in chap. 2. Old Calvinists, in particular, regarded themselves not only as superior to racial others but also to people of other Christian traditions. Consequently, we consider the New Light revival tradition of Jonathan Edwards, which emphasized the experience of conversion and dominated the First Great Awakening. Finally, we consider the theology of disinterested benevolence and abolitionism of New Divinity theologians Samuel Hopkins and Jonathan Edwards Jr. that adopted the scheme of *Christianization-civilization-colonization* that lay the foundation for the formation of the American Colonization Society.

Just as the notion of white superiority became the theological identity of Puritanism, the notion of white privilege, which stemmed from the beliefs of British colonists in the antebellum South, became the theological identity of Anglicanism and is the focus of chap. 3. Here, we engage the work of American historian Rebecca Ann Goetz, who argues that Anglicans in early Virginia connected the skin color of enslaved Africans with the notion of hereditary heathenism, which, she suggests, was the catalyst for these Anglicans, concluding that enslaved Africans were incapable of Christian conversion. We also examine the work of American historian Katharine Gerbner, who argues that "Protestant supremacy" was the forerunner to white supremacy, which shifted the dominant concern of the Christian faith from religion to ethnicity. We analyze the scholarship of American historian Charles F. Irons on the development of proslavery Christianity in colonial Virginia and examine George Whitefield's imperial project in the southern colonies.

The Resistance

The second part of the book explores the scandalous dehumanization of Africans in the early American context that became the catalyst for their spiritual resistance and the development of Christian theologies of liberation. While there are different and competing theories of race, modern racism is the product of human beings whom the Enlightenment thinkers classified as racial others, particularly people of color, being categorized as irredeemable, redeemable and child-like, or redeemable with proper education. These classifications were most evident in certain Christian traditions of the Puritans and Anglicans who created a colonial church based on race as opposed to grace.

For example, baptism, the primary symbol and action of becoming a Christian, had a different significance for racial others in that it became the way through which they could achieve a form of whiteness by being washed in the white blood of Jesus. In other words, baptism made racial others honorary white people, yet it did not change their social status because race trumped grace. In response to such oppressive theologies, enslaved Africans devised a theology of spiritual resistance mediated through their liberative pneumatology that was empowered by grace.

Chapter 4 examines what led to the oppressive theological affinity of Black Calvinist evangelicals of the eighteenth century that was rooted in the integration of their religious training and the appeal of George Whitefield's revivalism. Phillis Wheatley, for example, was enslaved to New England Puritans, who encouraged her to condemn her African spirituality in exchange for Calvinist predestination piety; Jupiter Hammon was shaped by his Anglican enslavers who possessed a Calvinist understanding of divine sovereignty and providence; John Marrant experienced his conversion through the evangelical ministry of George Whitefield and became a Calvinist Methodist; and Lemuel Haynes, a New England indentured servant, was influenced by the New Divinity form of Calvinism and the republican ideology of the revolutionary era. Each of these Black religious figures was influenced by some form of Calvinism, possessed its view of what constituted freedom for enslaved Africans, and theologized from the perspective of the empire theology that shaped their spiritual resistance.

Unlike these Black Calvinist evangelicals, there were the Black radical evangelicals, such as David Walker and Nat Turner, who are the focus of chap. 5. These Black radical evangelicals possessed a liberative pneumatology that informed their theology of spiritual resistance. This liberative pneumatology is clearly evident in Walker's treatise, *An Appeal to the Coloured Citizens of the World*, where he urges enslaved Africans to listen to the Holy Spirit and concludes that they are the property of the Holy Spirit.

Turner's own pneumatic experiences and spiritual gifts, particularly the gift of prophecy, fuel his spiritual resistance against the oppression of white enslavers. The spiritual resistance of Black radical evangelicals mediated through their spiritual experience of the Holy Spirit functions as the foundation for the development of Black liberation theologies designed to combat oppressive forms of classical Christian theology that corrupt the Christian faith.

The Impact

The third part of the book focuses on the historical and theological impact of the scandal and the spiritual resistance to it. Chapter 6 considers the historical trajectory of the theological scandal evident in the theologies of antebellum evangelicalism. Chapter 7 then explores the theologies of post-bellum evangelicalism, such as the rise of Jim Crowism and the emergence of the Ku Klux Klan, and the 1896 landmark Supreme Court decision that legalized racial segregation in the United States. Chapter 8 examines the theological scandal of white American fundamentalist evangelicalism, including the revivalism of Dwight Moody, the rise of the Moral Majority and Religious Right, highlighting the anti-interracial relations policies of Bob Jones University, Jerry Falwell's opposition to the civil rights movement, and the Reagan Revolution fostered through the 1980 presidential election. Chapter 9 explores the racial motivations of the Tea Party movement, the bigotry behind the birther conspiracy, and the complicity of white Christian evangelicals in their loyal support in the election and presidency of Donald Trump, who has promoted and empowered white supremacy and legitimized white American Christian nationalism through racism, sexism, and xenophobia.

The Way Forward

Finally, in light of the theological scandal that has corrupted Christianity through white supremacy, and the resulting resistance and impact, we provide a way forward theologically and socially. Chapter 10 examines the theologies of the white social gospel, particularly in its systematized form, emphasizing the theology of Walter Rauschenbusch. We also explore the theologies of the Black social gospel, analyzing the theologies of Mordecai Johnson, Benjamin Mays, and Howard Thurman.

Chapter 11 explores the social resistance to the ongoing corruption of Christianity, especially the civil rights movement and the influence of Martin Luther King's theology. It also examines the influence of Black theology and the rise of the Black Power movement, which has given rise to the more recent social resistance of the Black Lives Matter movement.

Through this way forward, in Chapter 12 we note the contributions of current scholars. For example, American Catholic theologian and ethicist Katie Walker Grimes identified antiblackness supremacy as a form of racial evil and defined the ideology as the phenomenon through which "non-black people, especially white ones, amass both power and privilege at black people's expense."[16] Antiblackness supremacy reflects the condemnation and criminalization of blackness through assimilation of non-Blacks to whiteness. Black theologian James Cone identifies whiteness as the symbol of the Antichrist, asserting that "whiteness characterizes the activity of deranged individuals intrigued by their own image of themselves, and thus made unable to see that they are what's wrong with the world."[17] African American historian Ibram X. Kendi defines an assimilationist as "one who is expressing the racist idea that a racial group is culturally or behaviorally inferior and is supporting cultural or behavioral enrichment programs to develop that racial group."[18] We emphasize this phenomenon as the problem of neo-whiteness and explore the eradication of white Christian supremacy, which consists of both Catholic and Protestant supremacy and reflects the aesthetic, cognitive, ontological, and spiritual dimensions of racism.

We propose a theological solution for the eradication of antiblackness supremacy and white Christian supremacy. The nucleus of the solution stems from the Wesleyan doctrine of Christian perfection and "entire sanctification," which consists of possessing perfect love of God and perfect love of one's neighbor mediated through the sanctification of the heart. The proposed theological solution involves a *decolonial love* that eradicates the evils of imperial and colonial powers.[19]

Ultimately, this decolonial love is achieved through a liberative pneumatology—the theological solution to the corruption of Christianity by theologies of white superiority and white privilege—and results in the reawakening of Pentecost, the New Great Awakening, which is reflected in the multiracial and multicultural protests for racial equality and racial justice.

16. Katie Walker Grimes, *Fugitive Saints: Catholicism and the Politics of Slavery* (Minneapolis: Fortress Press, 2017), xvii–xviii.

17. James Cone, *A Black Theology of Liberation*, Fortieth Anniversary Edition (Maryknoll, NY: Orbis Books, 2010), 8.

18. Ibram X. Kendi, *How to Be an Antiracist* (New York: One World, 2019), 14.

19. American theologian Joseph Drexler-Dreis cultivated the soteriological nature of decolonial love embodied in the literary works of James Baldwin.

Part I

THE SCANDAL

I

Enlightenment Theories of Race

Our civil rights have no dependence on our religious opinions, any more than our opinions in physics or geometry.[1]

In 1786, Thomas Jefferson authored the Virginia Statute of Religious Freedom, which established religious freedom as part of the freedom of human conscience. This statute was in reaction to the religious establishment in Virginia. Ironically, Jefferson was a member of the Church of England, the established church of the Virginia colony. By situating religious freedom within the realm of human conscience—the divinely ordained freedom of the human mind through the divine creation—Jefferson presupposed that religious belief emanated from human reason and, thereby, postulated the philosophical idea that religious freedom was an antecedent to any governmental rights.[2] Despite Jefferson's philosophical presuppositions, which resulted from the context of his white privilege as a wealthy white male in the eighteenth century, we will demonstrate how Enlightenment thinkers fostered the origins of a religion of white supremacy and the disenfranchisement of civil and human rights for people of color in the United States.

Enlightenment thinkers in the three major European centers of theology and philosophy—Britain, Germany, and France—contributed to the rise of modern racism through the development of white supremacy achieved through the condemnation of blackness as an inferior racial reality. Furthermore, such theories of race had a profound influence on Thomas Jefferson, who was one of the most prominent American thinkers of this period. This chapter explores the injustices of Jefferson's ideology of racial inferiority and the contradictions of his enlightened ideas for the new American empire. The external appearance of Africans, specifically the dark skin and presup-

---

1. Thomas Jefferson, "Act for Establishing Religious Freedom," in *Notes on the State of Virginia* (New York: Penguin Books, 1999), 231–33.

2. Thomas E. Buckley, *Establishing Religious Freedom: Jefferson's Statute in Virginia* (Charlottesville, VA: University of Virginia Press, 2013), 58.

posed wickedness of the African soul, resulted in the European devaluation of the physical, ontological, and spiritual work of African people.

The British-Scottish Enlightenment

In her seminal work *The Roads to Modernity: The British, French, and American Enlightenments*, Gertrude Himmelfarb characterized the thinkers of the British-Scottish Enlightenment as moral philosophers.[3] Historically, British political philosopher John Locke (1632–1784) has been venerated as a proponent of natural law and natural rights and has been characterized as the father of the modernist theory of natural rights.[4] Natural law constitutes the moral law that has been divinely situated in the hearts of human beings naturally and universally from birth. Natural rights stem from natural law and constitute inherent rights divinely tailored to human beings due to their human nature. Philosopher S. E. Frost asserted, "Locke held that the original and natural state of all men is one of perfect freedom and equality. Since all men are free and equal, no one has the right to take away another's life, liberty, or possessions."[5] However, in her study on Locke and race in America, social theorist Theresa Richardson concluded that Locke equated the principles of civilization with natural law, and yet Locke's philosophical presuppositions implied that some individuals and groups were naturally civilized (whites) while others (nonwhites) became members of civil society by consent of a social contract.[6]

Racist Ideologies

At the heart of Locke's political philosophy are contradictions based on racist ideologies. While Locke has been celebrated as a proponent of natural law and the progenitor of modern natural rights, his philosophical theories proved inadequate because he failed to apply these theories to people of African descent.[7] Locke's failure stemmed from his involvement and investment in the Atlantic triangular slave trade. Historically, philosophers have

---

3. Gertrude Himmelfarb, *The Roads to Modernity: The British, French, and American Enlightenments* (New York: Vintage Books, 2004), 25.

4. Craig A. Boyd and Don Thorsen, *Christian Ethics and Moral Philosophy* (Grand Rapids, MI: Baker Academic, 2018), 87.

5. S. E. Frost Jr., *Basic Teachings of the Great Philosophers* (New York: Anchor Books, 1989), 196.

6. Theresa Richardson, "John Locke and the Myth of Race in America: Demythologizing the Paradoxes of the Enlightenment as Visited in the Present," in *Philosophical Studies in Education* 42 (2011): 111.

7. Robert Bernasconi and Anika Maaza Mann, "The Contradictions of Racism: Locke, Slavery, and the Two Treatises," in Andrew Valls, ed., *Race and Racism in Modern Philosophy* (Ithaca, NY: Cornell University Press, 2005), 102.

attempted to preserve Locke's reputation as a philosopher of liberal free-dom utilizing political and economic justifications. Locke's political phi-losophy was situated in the early context of capitalism, colonialism, and imperialism, which were the catalysts for his racist contradictions.[8] Phi-losophers Robert Bernasconi and Anika Maaza Mann characterize Locke as one of the primary architects of racialized forms of slavery and contend that his advocacy of and profit from racialized slavery constitute evidence of his racism.[9] Locke believed that Negroes were subhuman and therefore had no equality with the British colonists and, while included under natu-ral law, could not reason.[10] Consequently, Locke concluded that enslaving people of an inferior status (Africans) was the natural right of people who possessed superiority (European males).[11]

During the British Enlightenment, Scottish philosopher David Hume (1711–1776) drew upon Aristotelian philosophy of Greek superiority to argue for the superiority of whites over Blacks. Hume argued that Negroes and all other species of men were naturally inferior to whites. He further expressed the idea that there has never been a civilized nation of any com-plexion other than white.[12] Similar to Buffon and Kant, Hume based his conclusions about his racial classifications on geography:

> If the characters of men depended on the air and climate, the degrees of heat and cold should naturally be expected to have a mighty influ-ence; since nothing has a greater effect on all plants and irrational animals. And indeed, there is some reason to think, that all nations, which live beyond the polar circles or between the tropics, are inferior to the rest of the species, and are incapable of all the higher attain-ments of the human mind.[13]

In 1770, James Beattie offered a rebuttal to Hume's idea of Blacks pos-sessing an inferior intellectual capacity based on Aristotelian philosophy. He argued against the Aristotelian notion of certain racial groups being of little intelligence but possessing great bodily strength, which des-tined them for labor through enslavement. Aristotle had argued that the Greeks were naturally superior and had a right to empire and that the rest of humanity was stupid and destined for slavery.[14] Hume concluded that

---

8. Richardson, "John Locke and the Myth of Race," 104.

9. Bernasconi, "The Contradictions of Racism," 90–91.

10. Richardson, "John Locke and the Myth of Race," 105.

11. Richardson, "John Locke and the Myth of Race," 105.

12. David Hume, "Of National Characters," in Emmanuel Chukwudi Eze, *Race and the Enlightenment: A Reader* (Malden, MA: Blackwell Publishing, 1997), 33.

13. Hume, "Of National Characters," 32–33.

14. James Beattie, "An Essay on the Nature and Immutability of Truth in Opposition to

Blacks were inferior human beings destined for slavery, and his racist philosophy became a major source for proslavery arguments and notions of antiblackness.[15]

Despite Hume's philosophical argument that Blacks were destined for slavery, he did oppose slavery. Silvia Sebastiani, a French historian of early modern history, has examined Hume's opposition to slavery and asserts that "he [Hume] offered a criticism of slavery that was not grounded on the principle of human equality."[16] She identifies Hume as a "neocolonial" philosopher who "criticized slavery chiefly on the grounds of its economic (dis)advantage, irrespective of the equality between men."[17] Hume, in the essay "Of National Characters," identified such characters as local uniformities generated by the universal uniformity of human progress.[18] The purpose of his essay was to demonstrate the diversification of advanced nations in Europe that were in stark contrast to the uncivilized nations of the savages (nonwhites). The contradictory nature of Hume's essay is in its perceived theme of universality.

Political scientist Andrew Valls argues that the universality of Hume's philosophy is a product of his racialism and concludes that since Hume believed that whites (civilized humans) were only intellectually superior not morally superior to nonwhites (savages), Hume was a racialist, not a racist.[19] He justifies this conclusion by arguing that belief in moral superiority constitutes racism and belief in intellectual superiority constitutes only racialism.[20] Valls attempted denial of Hume's racism constitutes an erroneous rationalization.[21]

Definitions of Racism

There are many definitions of racism, a subject that has been debated for centuries. Due to the scope and nature of this book, it is imperative that a relevant definition of racism be presented. American philosopher Barbara Hall defined racism as "the view that some groups of people are

Sophistry and Skepticism," in Emmanuel Chukwudi Eze, *Race and the Enlightenment: A Reader* (Malden, MA: Blackwell Publishing, 1997), 34.

15. West, *Prophecy Deliverance*, 62.

16. Silvia Sebastiani, *The Scottish Enlightenment: Race, Gender, and the Limits of Progress* (New York: Palgrave Macmillian, 2013), 24.

17. Sebastiani, *The Scottish Enlightenment*, 13.

18. Sebastiani, *The Scottish Enlightenment*, 33.

19. Andrew Valls, "A Lousy Empirical Scientist: Reconsidering Hume's Racism," in Andrew Valls, ed., *Race and Racism in Modern Philosophy* (Ithaca, NY: Cornell University Press, 2005), 127.

20. Valls, "A Lousy Empirical Scientist, 130.

21. Valls, "A Lousy Empirical Scientist, 127.

inherently intellectually, culturally, or socially superior or inferior to other groups owing to some biological or genetic characteristic they do or do not possess."[22] Hall's definition of racism solidifies the charge of racism against Hume. African American psychiatrist Frances Cress Welsing defines racism as "the behavioral power system of logic, thought, speech, action, emotional response, and perception, whether consciously or unconsciously determined in persons who classify themselves as white."[23] She further asserts that "the goal of racism is white domination over the vast majority of the world's people whom the whites have classified as nonwhites (black, brown, red and yellow) in order to ensure white genetic survival."[24] Toni Morrison distinguishes between scientific and social racism, defining the former as "an outsider in order to define one's self" and the latter as the process of othering.[25]

Building on these definitions of racism, we will now identify its aesthetical, cognitive, ontological, and spiritual dimensions. Aesthetically, white supremacists connected physical whiteness with beauty and physical blackness with unattractiveness. Cognitively, they connected whiteness with inherent intellectual superiority and blackness with inherent intellectual inferiority. Ontologically, they connected whiteness with civilization and blackness with barbarism. Spiritually, they equated whiteness with innate righteousness and blackness with innate evil. Therefore, racism is defined as one racial group (white) viewing themselves as aesthetically, cognitively, ontologically, and spiritually superior to other races.

Political and Economic Influences

In 1776, Scottish philosopher and economist Adam Smith published his seminal work, *The Wealth of Nations*, which was based on the modern Enlightenment project that contrasted civilized nations with savage nations and became the manifesto for global capitalism.[26] Smith believed that, outside of Europe, the world was mainly populated by savages who remained in the early stages of social development,[27] and he gave an economic justification for European colonialization. German sociologist Wulf D. Hund argues that

---

22. Barbara Hall, "Race in Hobbes," in Andrew Valls, ed., *Race and Racism in Modern Philosophy* (Ithaca, NY: Cornell University Press, 2005), 43.

23. Frances Cress Welsing, *The Isis Papers: The Keys to Colors* (Washington, DC: C. W. Publishing, 1991), 119.

24. Welsing, *The Isis Papers*.

25. Toni Morrison, *The Origin of Others* (Cambridge, MA: Harvard University Press, 2017), 6–15.

26. Wulf D. Hund, "Racism in White Sociology from Adam Smith to Max Weber," in Wulf D. Hund and Alana Lentin, eds., *Racism and Sociology, Yearbook 5* (Berlin: Lit Verlag, 2014), 23.

27. Hund, "Racism in White Sociology, 33.

Smith apparently "preferred the cultural patterns of disparaging others," which he achieved through a Eurocentric philosophy of history.[28]

Historically, Smith has been venerated for his economic influence on the creation and function of global capitalism, yet few scholars have examined his theological influence on certain Protestant Christian traditions. African American theologian James A. Noel challenged the traditional view of Smith's economic influence and concluded that his influence was more theological. He argues that "Smith did not create global capitalism; rather, he identified the laws and principles of what was already becoming the case through their articulation in secular language providing global capitalism with a theological rationale."[29] While Himmelfarb has a completely different viewpoint, she agrees with Noel's contention that Smith did not create global capitalism and, furthermore, concludes that his political and economic philosophy was not designed to promote capitalism but to refute the notion of class.[30] She argues that Smith's progressive economy was designed to help the lower class, as he believed that the wealth of people in the nation determined the nation's strength.[31] Himmelfarb's attempt to exonerate Smith from responsibility for his racially motivated economic philosophy, which in the end proved regressive for non-Europeans, European women, and poor European men, is erroneous and reckless. Smith's economic philosophy has historically promoted the economic oppression of persons in the lower classes of society, which he attempted to justify using Christian theology.

Smith initiated and promoted the notion of the invisible hand of God working in free-market capitalism. Traditionally, Smith's invisible-hand metaphor has been characterized as a teleological enterprise with some kind of benevolent agent working on behalf of the interests of all persons involved in free-market capitalism regardless of their class status. Himmelfarb rejected this traditional characterization and asserted that Smith's notion of the invisible hand was not teleological because there was no external intervention in the market and those involved lacked any conscious knowledge of a teleologically motivated objective toward which the invisible hand was working.[32]

Noel rightly correlated Smith's notion of the invisible hand of God working in the market with John Calvin's doctrine of double predestination. Smith's philosophy proposes a transcendent divine and benevolent agent

---

28. Hund, "Racism in White Sociology," 35.

29. James A. Noel, *Black Religion and the Imagination of Matter in the Atlantic World* (New York: Palgrave Macmillan, 2009), 42.

30. Himmelfarb, *The Roads to Modernity*, 55.

31. Himmelfarb, *The Roads to Modernity*, 59–60.

32. Himmelfarb, *The Roads to Modernity*, 58.

that operates in a clandestine manner and, without any form of consideration for merit, chooses those who will prosper in the free market and those who will suffer. This philosophy, with its theological implications, clearly reflects the theology of election. While the hand is invisible, its election of persons for capitalistic success or failure was based on context: persons within civilized nations would experience success, and persons within savage nations would experience failure. Smith's notion of the invisible hand demonstrates the danger of theologies of divine choice. The correlation of Calvin's doctrine of election and Smith's invisible hand of God reveals the early correlation of racism and capitalism that defined the social, political, economic, and religious structure of American society from its inception. Power struggles, acts of vengeance, acts of violence, persecution, oppression, unjust acquisition of land, colonialism, imperialism, racism, sexism, and xenophobia have been justified through the theological idea of divine choice. Historically, this reality is evident in the Puritan claim of being God's New Israel and the notion of America as the "city on a hill." It is also evident in the ideology of Manifest Destiny, which justified the acquisition of land in the expansion of American territories and the attempt to colonize native peoples. These examples have contributed to the myth of American exceptionalism and to the continued promotion of ideologies of superiority.

The German Enlightenment

The Enlightenment theories of race that had the most profound effect on the development of oppressive Christian theologies emanated from German philosophers, Immanuel Kant and G. W. F. Hegel. Building on his racist argument regarding geographical climate, Kant suggested that the hot climate of African territories resulted in the strong physical growth of Negroes.[33] Despite their physical strength, Kant also argued that Negroes were lazy, because hot climates made them lethargic.[34] In his classification of races, Kant dichotomized the races of both cold and hot climates. He concluded that Europeans and Americans were the races of cold climates and that Africans and Indians were the races of hot climates.[35] Similar to other Enlightenment thinkers, Kantian racial philosophy dehumanized those races connected to hot climates. While Kant classified Africans and Native Americans together, he concluded that, overall, Africans were below Native Americans, contending that "humanity is at its greatest perfection in the race of whites. The yellow Indians do have a meager talent. The Negroes are

---

33. Kant, "On Different Races of Man," in Eze, *Race and the Enlightenment*, 46.
34. Kant, "On Different Races of Man," 64.
35. Kant, "On Different Races of Man," 48.

far below them and at the lowest point are a part of the American peoples."[36] One of the primary tenets of the Enlightenment was the idea of beauty as aesthetic experience.[37] Africans were at the bottom of the Kantian classification, having no feeling of aesthetic experience, which is possible only with those of refined intellect.[38]

Building on the work of Hume that Negroes have no talent concerning art or science, Kant condemned their spirituality and religiosity, accusing Negroes of having a religion of fetishes, which he condemned as idolatry, and also attempted to eradicate their aesthetic experience. These claims further fostered the perpetuation and development of white supremacy in some orthodox Christian theologies.

Christian Supersessionism

In his seminal work, *Race: A Theological Account*, African American historical theologian J. Kameron Carter describes Kant's universalization of whiteness as perfection, which resulted in the problem of Christian supersessionism, which, he contended, became the racial ground of modernity.[39] Christian supersessionism is the theory that since Jesus Christ is the Messiah, the Christian Church has superseded Israel as the chosen people of God. Carter argues that the problem of Christian supersessionism causes white Christianity to abandon its Jewish roots by racializing Jesus and replacing the Jews with the Christian church in the covenant.[40] He accuses Black liberation theologians of failing to eradicate whiteness from modern theology. While I appreciate and commend Carter for his accusation, his theological proposal also proves inadequate. He argues that "only a Christian theology of Israel establishes the framework within which to overcome the theological problem of whiteness"[41] and contends that human identity is determined theologically through the flesh of the Jewish Jesus as related to God's covenant with the Israelites, not race. Carter's solution to the problem of race still does not eradicate the spirit of hegemony because he promotes a theology of elitism and superiority. If the covenant is connected solely to a certain group of people, it denotes the possibility of other groups being underdogs and, therefore, likely being oppressed.

---

36. Immanuel Kant, "From Physical Geography" in Eze, *Race and the Enlightenment*, 63.

37. Aesthetic experience consisted of possessing feelings for beautiful arts and sciences.

38. Immanuel Kant, "Observations on the Feeling of the Beautiful and Sublime," in Eze, *Race and the Enlightenment*, 49.

39. J. Kameron Carter, *Race: A Theological Account* (New York: Oxford University Press, 2008), 82.

40. Carter, *Race*, 420–21.

41. Carter, *Race*, 420–21.

Carter solidified his contentions through his explanation of how Christianity became the cultural property of Western civilization. He explained that "functioning also as a teleologically structured philosophy of history, Kant's theory of race articulates an account of the destiny of the species as coinciding with the global perfection and spread of whiteness."[42] Equating whiteness with perfection became the perceived conduit for the progress of Western civilization among Enlightenment thinkers. Carter described this perfection in aesthetic terms based on the Enlightenment view of black flesh and white flesh:

> If the white race exemplifies humanity on its way to perfection, the black race embodies the departure and failure to attain this perfection. In the Negro race, white flesh observes a race so mired in its particularity as never to be able to speak with universal force and, therefore, as never positioned to be an analogy or index of the universal. Black flesh lacks universal gravitas. It is trapped in its particularity in such a way that it always needs to justify its existence before universal white flesh. In short, the particularity of black flesh reflects an aesthetic, which for Kant is an ethic and a politics, of excess and imbalance—the excess of bodily particularity over rational universality: the imbalance between law and freedom.[43]

Carter concluded that these Kantian ideas of race are what caused Western thinking to be defined by whiteness and its problematic theological developments.

Race and Religion

In his work *Modern Religion, Modern Race*, American theologian Theodore Vial builds on Carter's interpretation of Kant's anthropological presuppositions. His primary argument is that race and religion have a mutual genealogy.[44] He further argues that race and religion are the building blocks of modernity because these factors constitute the sources of the modern self.[45] Therefore, the epistemological understanding of the modern self becomes the product of a new theological anthropology. Vial concludes that the roots of the demonic character of race are situated in the work of Protestant intellectuals of the eighteenth century such as Kant.[46]

---

42. Carter, *Race*, 81.

43. Carter, *Race*, 90.

44. Theodore Vial, *Modern Religion, Modern Race* (New York: Oxford University Press, 2016), 1.

45. Vial, *Modern Religion, Modern Race*, 1.

46. Vial, *Modern Religion, Modern Race*, 4.

In the nineteenth century, the construct of race shifts from its divine and biological bases to that of culture. Kant was imperative in defining and shaping the modern constructs of race and of racism, but they were defective and oppressive to non-Europeans because his theories of race were devoid of cultural awareness.[47]

Historically, Kant has been celebrated as one of the leading figures of moral philosophy. Therefore, some philosophers have attempted to separate his theory of race from his critical philosophy and further subordinate his theory of race to his critical philosophy. These philosophers have failed in their attempt to vindicate Kant's moral character and the supposed beauty of his mind, which has been portrayed as brilliant yet demonstrates a mind ill disposed toward the non-European "other." Despite his primary contention being the universal moral theory that humans possessed reason and the capacity to follow the moral law,[48] Kant still connected rational and moral capacity to his flawed racial classifications.

African American theologian Willie Jennings argues that European Christians connected racial identity with physical bodies, or biology, and geography, which resulted in the characterization of Europeans as superior to other human races. Jennings contends that the European reconfiguration of bodies and space constitutes a theological operation.[49] He characterizes this theological operation as heretical and further concludes that geographical authority played a major role in shaping racial constructions, asserting that "the story of race is also the story of place."[50] Jennings's use of racial identity in the theological operation of biology and geography reflects Kant's preoccupation with biology and his development of the idea of racism and disregard of culture.

Kant preferred Buffon's taxonomy, or method of classification, over that of Carl Linnaeus. While Buffon's taxonomy was based on internal features of human autonomy, Linnaeus based his on sexual organs. Consequently, his racial classifications were connected to features of sexual organs.[51] The latter taxonomy explains the common belief of colonists in British colonial America that the prevalence of the heat on the African continent hypersexualized people of African descent.[52] One of the racist ideas of the colonial era was the notion that the large genitalia of Black men and Black women

------

47. Vial, *Modern Religion, Modern Race*, 13.

48. Vial, *Modern Religion, Modern Race*, 36.

49. Willie Jennings, *The Christian Imagination: Theology and the Origins of Race* (New Haven, CT: Yale University Press, 2010), 24.

50. Jennings, *The Christian Imagination*, 289.

51. Vial, *Modern Religion, Modern Race*, 30–31.

52. Ibram X., Kendi, *Stamped from the Beginning: The Definitive History of Racist Ideas in America* (New York: Nation Books, 2016), 31.

hypersexualized them and functioned as the catalyst for their supposed sexual desire for the superiority of whiteness.[53]

G. W. F. Hegel argued that people of African descent suffered from ontological inferiority, spiritual inferiority, and epistemological inferiority. In the same Enlightenment spirit of Buffon and Kant, Hegel's postulations were based on geographical location. Hegel identified Africa as the continent on which cultural backwardness predominated.[54] He further argued that African religion and politics were inferior.[55] Hegel characterized the European race as the race of human beings who possessed racial superiority. His notions of racial superiority were an attempt to solidify the idea of ontological inferiority not solely for people of African descent but also for human beings whose ethnicity/nationality was non-European, arguing that non-European humans were subhuman, that is, less human than Europeans.[56] He characterized Native Americans as unenlightened children and argued that Negroes were more susceptible to European culture than Native Americans and stronger in physique, which justified the enslavement of Africans.[57] Building on his concept of ontological inferiority, Hegel argued that Negroes did not view enslavement as a wrong practice and contended that enslavement awakened more humanity in the African.[58] The idea of ontological inferiority produced the ideology of cultural inferiority through the notion of degeneration.

Hegel attempted to morally justify slavery, imperialism, and colonialism, utilizing the contention that Europeans were civilized and non-Europeans were barbaric.[59] Building on the imperial work of the Portuguese and other early colonial settlers in the New World, Hegel classified African religion as fetishism.[60] This correlation was Hegel's attempt to solidify the idea that people of African descent suffered from spiritual inferiority. Based on his notion that Africans lived in a state of savagery and barbarism, Hegel concluded that Africans had lacked awareness of concepts such as God or the law.[61] Therefore, he argued, the religious capacity even to acknowledge a higher power beyond humanity was unknown to Africans.

The grammar of fetishism developed during the fifteenth and sixteenth centuries. The idea of fetish developed as a part of a social economy that

---

53. Kendi, *Stamped from the Beginning*, 43.
54. Georg W. F. Hegel, "Geographical Basis of World History," in Eze, *Race and the Enlightenment*, 122.
55. Hegel, "Geographical Basis of World History," 109.
56. Hegel, "Geographical Basis of World History," 109.
57. Hegel, "Geographical Basis of World History," 116.
58. Hegel, "Geographical Basis of World History," 134.
59. Hegel, "Geographical Basis of World History," 149.
60. Hegel, "Geographical Basis of World History," 131.
61. Hegel, "Geographical Basis of World History," 127.

identified fetish religion as the religion of Blacks. Sylvester Johnson has argued that fetish religion constituted a colonial production of race and concluded that colonialism, not slavery, was the primary context for racialization.[62] Fetishism became the racial concept of primitivism. The Portuguese as the first European enslavers concluded that fetishism and idolatry were normative in the religion of Blacks. Johnson contends that imperialism and colonialism utilized materiality to devise ontological claims related to religion and other races.[63] Europeans utilized the Christian ideology of idolatry to develop their discourse on fetishism and identified the religious materials of Africans as idols or fetishes.[64] Therefore, Portuguese settlers in West Africa condemned West African religion as witchcraft and diabolism.[65] Fetish religion constituted heathenism in the Christian imagination.[66] Johnson argues that there were parallels between what became characterized as fetish religion and Western Christian materiality, specifically Roman Catholicism.[67]

African people were not the progenitors of fetishism; this was a characterization imposed on their spirituality by the Portuguese and other European colonists. Through this European colonial imposition, fetishism became the characterization for the entire cultural system in the western part of central Africa.[68] Yet, what European colonists apparently failed to realize was that this characterization of west-central African religiosity was very problematic for their own European Christianity. Roman Catholicism fostered the relationship between Africans on the west coast and European colonists. Catholic missionaries, for example, cultivated Christianity in the Kingdom of Kongo from the end of the fifteenth century, and many of the Africans from the Angola region, having been educated by Jesuit missionaries, spoke Portuguese and professed Roman Catholicism as their faith.[69] The problem with condemning the spirituality of west-central Africans as fetishism, particularly the spirituality of the Kongolese Christians, constituted the condemnation of the Roman Catholic faith of the Portuguese.

There is extreme irony in the condemnation of west African spirituality as fetishism because the ideal of materiality in European Christianity

---

62. Sylvester A. Johnson, *African American Religions, 1500–2000: Colonialism, Democracy, and Freedom* (New York: Cambridge University Press, 2015), 89.

63. Johnson, *African American Religions*, 83.

64. Johnson, *African American Religions*, 60.

65. Johnson, *African American Religions*, 66.

66. Johnson, *African American Religions*, 91.

67. Johnson, *African American Religions*, 78.

68. Johnson, *African American Religions*, 86.

69. Mark M. Smith, "Account of the Negroe Insurrection in South Carolina," in Mark M. Smith, ed., *Stono: Documenting and Interpreting a Southern Slave Revolt* (Columbia: University of South Carolina Press, 2005), 109–24.

developed with a focus on objects as living things. The true nature and function of fetishism consisted of European colonists connecting materiality or determining how objects are conceived with the empire project of Atlantic colonialism.[70] The idea of fetishism originates with European colonists' fascination with African objects such as charms and amulets. Yet their own Christian religiosity reflected this ideal of fetishism in their prayers to saints, which included daily communion with the living dead, physical contact with holy water, and partaking of the Eucharist with the belief in transubstantiation, through which the elements of bread and wine in the sacrament became the actual body and blood of Christ. Based on the European colonists' ideas of fetishism, these religious practices could constitute a European Christian fetishism in that the spirits of the dead and religious objects become living things.

Western European thinkers constructed the language of fetishism to establish theological and intellectual barriers between the West and the racial others. African American historian James Young asserts that "the fetish represented a temporal, theological, and intellectual barrier between the West and others and reflected a Western presumption that if backward peoples were ever to enjoy the fruits of civilization and enlightenment, if they were ever to become modern, they must first do away with the ritual remnants of the past."[71] African philosopher-theologian F. Eboussi Boulaga viewed fetishism as the Western condemnation and localization of African rituals and customs that were deemed paganistic. The purpose of the European missionary enterprise, he concluded, was to utilize their brand of Christianity as the tool of humanization and civilization:

> The black is still a pagan, and rather a child, despite baptism; and the white Occidental is still a Christian, a rational, reasonable being, despite transgressions and straying. The Christianity of the former is a veneer, something adventitious, an accident. The Christianity of the latter is substrate and substance.[72]

He addressed the European colonists' missionary impulse and emphasis on conversion and baptism for the supposed non-European pagan and uncivilized barbarian, which did not constitute social, civil, or spiritual equality for the baptized African.

70. Johnson, *African American Religions*, 84.

71. Jason R. Young, *Rituals of Resistance: African Atlantic Religion in Kongo and the Lowcountry South in the Era of Slavery* (Baton Rouge: Louisiana State University Press, 2007), 106–7.

72. F. Eboussi Boulaga, *Christianity without Fetishes: An African Critique and Recapture of Christianity* (Maryknoll, NY: Orbis Books, 1981), 21.

Hegel identified Europe as the land of spiritual unity and Africa as the land of sorcery. Based on his observations and conclusions about African religion, Hegel condemned all Africans as religious sorcerers. In his reflection on the Greek historian Herodotus's testimony on African religion, Hegel insisted that "we can sum up the principle of African religion in his declaration that all men in Africa are sorcerers."[73] Hegel offered a vivid depiction of what he observed as sorcery in Africa and suggested that "to prepare themselves for their task, they work themselves into a state of frenzy, by means of singing, convulsive dancing, and intoxicating roots or potions, they reach a state of extreme delirium in which they proceed to issue their command."[74] The notion of epistemological inferiority is evident in Hegel's conclusion that Africans are incapable of giving reverence to God because they lack conscious objectivity of a higher being and therefore possess no knowledge concerning the immortality of souls.[75]

The French Enlightenment

In addition to skin color, eighteenth-century thinkers of the French Enlightenment such as Denis Diderot identified Africans as ugly human beings based on their disenchantment with the external appearance of Africans.[76] In the excerpt on the "Negro," the *Encyclopaedia Britannica* states:

> Round cheeks, high cheek-bones, a forehead somewhat elevated, a short, broad, flat nose, thick lips, small ears, ugliness, and irregularity of shape, characterize their external appearance. The negro women have the loins greatly depressed, and very large buttocks, which give the back the shape of a saddle.[77]

The Enlightenment characterization of Africans as barbaric savages engaging in fetishism resulted in Africans being condemned and classified as wicked. Such condemnation is also depicted in the *Encyclopaedia Britannica*, which characterizes Africans not only as savages but also degenerates:

> Vices, the most notorious seem to be the portion of this unhappy race: idleness, treachery, revenge, cruelty, impudence, stealing, lying, profanity, debauchery, nastiness and intemperance, are said to have

---

73. Hegel, "Geographical Basis of World History," 149.

74. Hegel, "Geographical Basis of World History," 131.

75. Hegel, "Geographical Basis of World History," 133.

76. "Negre," in Denis Diderot and Jean le Rond d'Alembert, eds., *Encyclopédie, ou dictionnaire raisonné des sciences, des arts et des métiers* (Paris, 1765), 11:94.

77. "Negro," in Andrew Bell and Colin MacFarquhar, eds., *Encyclopaedia Britannica* (Edinburgh, 1797), 12:794.

extinguished the principles of natural law, and to have silenced the reproofs of conscience. They are strangers to every sentiment of compassion and are an awful example of the corruption of man when left to himself.[78]

Buffon defined race as an expression of degeneration. He argued that Blacks had degenerated from a white prototype before attaining black skin.[79] As a naturalist, he embraced the theory of monogenesis and, therefore, believed in racial reversibility, asserting that Blacks could move to whiteness and whites could move to blackness.[80] Buffon correlated skin color with the effects of climate.[81] Historian George Frederickson offered a historical argument that connected the theories of climate, degeneration, and racial reversibility, asserting that "some racial environmentalists in the early American republic fully expected imported Africans to turn white in the more temperate climate to which they were now exposed, but the process to be taken was a very long time. There was little doubt among whites on either side of the Atlantic that Africans were currently less beautiful than whites, more barbarous in their habits, and probably less intelligent."[82] Due to his theories on climate and skin color, Buffon concluded that the Hottentot were regaining their white skin as a result of the mild South African climate and the skin of Ethiopians was becoming increasing black.[83]

Baron de Montesquieu (1689–1755)

Buffon's theories about the effects of climate and skin color were based on the philosophy of Baron de Montesquieu, which focused on soil, geography, and climate. He argued that "men are ruled by many things: climate, religion, laws, rules of government, precedents set by past events, mores, customs; a general spirit results from these. . . . Nature and climate are nearly the only forces that bear upon savages."[84] Montesquieu further argued that the cold climate produces high-functioning intellectual characteristics, and the hot climate weakens the strength of the human mind.[85] He also

---

78. "Negro," 12:794.
79. Andrew S. Curran, *The Anatomy of Blackness: Science and Slavery in an Age of Enlightenment* (Baltimore: Johns Hopkins University Press, 2011), 111.
80. Curran, *The Anatomy of Blackness*, 110–11.
81. George M. Frederickson, *Racism: A Short History* (Princeton, NJ: Princeton University Press, 2002), 58.
82. Frederickson, *Racism*, 58–59.
83. Curran, *The Anatomy of Blackness*, 110–11.
84. Baron de Montesquieu, *The Spirit of Laws* (Amherst, NY: Prometheus Books, 2002), 19.4, 1:329.
85. De Montesquieu, *The Spirit of Laws*, 14.2, 1:247–248.

contended that only humans in temperate climates (not extremely hot nor cold) could develop a republic or monarchy.[86] Therefore, Montesquieu concluded that persons in cold climates with white skin were intellectually superior to persons in hot climates with black skin, thus influencing the thought of Buffon in favor of white superiority and nonwhite inferiority.

Montesquieu initially professed an aversion to the institution of slavery. However, the contradictory nature of his philosophy undergirded his failure to reject the practice of slavery. Based on his philosophy of civilization, Montesquieu concluded that skin color was the essence of humanity and affirmed civilizations that utilized color in determining how they treated others, especially through the process of enslavement.[87] Therefore, Montesquieu offered proslavery discourse because while he viewed human enslavement as antithetical to the Enlightenment project, he believed that the effects of climate were the exception to the rule and justified the enslavement of Africans.[88]

Voltaire (1694–1778)

Likewise, French philosopher and historian Voltaire rejected the institution of slavery and yet postulated contradictory philosophical presuppositions. Voltaire condemned Christianity for tolerating the institution of slavery but demonstrated his racist disdain for Blacks and argued that the African was essentially different from the European. He shifted the discourse on racial differences from biblical exegesis to history, through which he promoted the theory of polygenesis over monogenesis,[89] rejecting and refuting the view that Blacks constitute a race of whites blackened by climate.[90] Despite these differences, Voltaire was situated solidly in the Enlightenment tradition of modern racism.

Voltaire's racism was most evident in his conception of the African race. American historian Andrew Curran argued that "Voltaire contributed significantly to one of the major transformations that the African underwent in European thought during the eighteenth century: from barbaric heathen (a moral and religious category) who could be redeemed through slavery, to a subhuman (racial category) for whom bondage seemed the logical but regretable extension of the race's many shortcomings."[91] In addition to describing Blacks as being subhuman—an even greater form of dehumanization than being labeled as heathens—Voltaire asserted that the

---

86. Sebastiani, *The Scottish Enlightenment*, 42.
87. Curran, *The Anatomy of Blackness*, 132.
88. Curran, *The Anatomy of Blackness*, 137.
89. Sebastiani, *The Scottish Enlightenment*, 10.
90. Curran, *The Anatomy of Blackness*, 145.
91. Curran, *The Anatomy of Blackness*, 148.

independent categories of black and white are unchangeable regardless of climate.[92] Hence, Blacks would remain in their savage state and whites in their state of civilized humanity. Voltaire epitomized the dual character of Enlightenment rationalism stating that he illustrated "its simultaneous challenge to hierarchies based on faith, superstition, and prejudice and the temptation it presented to create new ones allegedly based on reason, science, and history."[93] He was the first modern racist insisting that an intellectual can be a theoretical racist without engaging in actual discrimination.[94]

Jean-Jacques Rousseau (1712–1778)

Among the French Enlightenment thinkers, Genevan philosopher Jean-Jacques Rousseau was probably closest in espousing a theoretical affirmation for the humanity of nonwhites, yet he still harbored philosophical notions that proved contradictory. Rousseau believed that selfishness and greed corrupted humanity, and he held Europeans accountable for the evils of civilization.[95] While Rousseau did not question the innate rational-biological capacity of natives in the New Worlds, he argued that the natives needed civilization to develop rational human skills.[96] Sebastiani argues that, for Rousseau, "the savage man possessed the seeds of civilized man, in the sense that the civilization process produced nothing that was not already in human nature."[97] Rousseau believed that the prerequisite for natives escaping their natural savage state was adopting the culture and civilization of the West.[98]

Latin American theologian Néstor Medina asserts that Rousseau popularized the idea of the noble savage.[99] Rousseau affirmed the physical abilities of Negroes and other New World natives but characterized them as mentally deficient and intellectually inferior to Europeans.[100] Rousseau believed that intelligence was an acquired faculty that resulted from certain societal conditions.[101] Ironically, despite promoting the civilizing of supposed savages, Rousseau's philosophical proposals are paradoxical:

---

92. Curran, *The Anatomy of Blackness*, 139.

93. Frederickson, *Racism*, 63.

94. Frederickson, *Racism*, 61.

95. Jean-Jacques Rousseau, *A Discourse upon the Origins and Foundation of the Inequality among Mankind* (London: R. and J. Dodsley, 1761), 97.

96. Néstor Medina, *Christianity, Empire and Spirit: (Re)configurating Faith and the Cultural* (Boston: Brill, 2018), 137.

97. Sebastiani, *The Scottish Enlightenment*, 66.

98. Medina, *Christianity*, 139.

99. Medina, *Christianity*, 139.

100. Bernard Boxill, "Rousseau, Natural Man, and Race," in Andrew Valls, ed., *Race and Racism in Modern Philosophy* (Ithaca, NY: Cornell University Press, 2005), 159.

101. Boxill, "Rousseau, Natural Man, and Race," 159–60.

on the one hand, he advocates for their civilization; on the other hand, he discourages their civilization. Medina concludes that such Enlightenment Europeans brought racial superiority to the New World.[102]

The American Enlightenment

Thomas Jefferson functioned as the most robust reflection of the American Enlightenment in British colonial America and the early republic. Officially, Jefferson held membership in the Church of England, which was the established church of colonial Virginia. Despite his Anglican faith, Jefferson's theological presuppositions proved more deistic than theistic. As a Deist, Jefferson viewed God as transcendent rather than immanent and believed that God is known through human reason.[103] Deism was a product of the Enlightenment and functioned as a theological system that constituted the primary expression of religion based on natural law during the eighteenth century. African American Christian ethicist Riggins Earl notes that Jefferson also viewed God as the author of natural law, to which he possessed a divine sense of duty, and that he believed that God maintained and governed the world through the natural law of reason.[104] American historian Gregg L. Frazer, however, argues that Jefferson never claimed to affirm Deism and that he was more interested in revelation, asserting that Jefferson did not dismiss but challenged the biblical text.[105] While there is truth to Frazer's assertion concerning Jefferson and biblical testimony, it is imperative to note that, while Jefferson emphasized the ethical principles of Jesus, he obliterated the divine witness of Christ through the suspension of the supernatural. Furthermore, Frazer's argument concerning Jefferson and Deism is erroneous, for Jefferson functioned as one of the chief philosophers of American Deism, having built on the natural-law philosophy of John Locke in drafting the Declaration of Independence.

Jefferson's Theology and Philosophy

Jefferson believed that true Christianity was reflected in the lives of those who were disciples of the historical Jesus. American philosopher Kerry S. Walters argues that Jefferson admired the historical Jesus but rejected

---

102. Boxill, "Rousseau, Natural Man, and Race," 139.

103. Riggins R. Earl Jr., "Race, Suffering, Slavery, and Divine Providence: Some Black and White Nineteenth-Century Deists' and Theists' Voices," in James O. Duke and Anthony L. Dunnavant, eds., *Christian Faith Seeking Historical Understanding: Essays in Honor of H. Jack Forstman* (Macon, GA: Mercer University Press, 1997), 112.

104. Earl, "Race, Suffering, Slavery, and Divine Providence," 114–16.

105. Gregg L. Frazer, *The Religious Beliefs of America's Founders: Reason, Revelation, and Revolution* (Lawrence, KS: University Press of Kansas, 2012), 128–35.

Christianity as a theological system and religious institution.[106] Walters contends that Jefferson distinguished between real and institutional Christians and viewed himself as a real Christian.[107] American historian David L. Holmes concludes that "like other Deists, he [Jefferson] valued intellectual and spiritual freedom and abhorred organized Christianity's tendency toward dogmatism."[108] Jefferson believed that institutional Christianity constituted "irrational supernaturalism" and viewed doctrinal tenets of orthodox Christianity such as the trinity, incarnation, and resurrection as "unintelligible propositions."[109] Additionally, as a Deist, Jefferson rejected the rituals and sacramental practices of institutional Christianity.[110]

Some religious scholars have viewed Deism as a theological attempt at Christian restorationism, which was reflected in Jefferson's view of Jesus.[111] Jefferson characterized Jesus as a reformer and moral exemplar.[112] His characterization of Jesus is most evident in his reinterpretation of the New Testament from a deistic perspective. Holmes argued that "because Jefferson's God was a God of reason, not irrationality, Jefferson removed from the gospels anything that appeared unreasonable."[113] Jefferson removed biblical material from the New Testament that constituted supernatural phenomena, such as prophecies and miracles, and preserved the ethical teachings of Jesus as revealed in Gospel discourses such as the Sermon on the Mount. In his correspondence to Charles Thompson on January 9, 1816, Jefferson expressed his purpose for devising his own version of the New Testament, called *The Life and Morals of Jesus of Nazareth*, in that he believed that he had removed the corruptions of Christianity from the New Testament.[114] Jefferson eradicated the divinity of Jesus by characterizing him as "a prophet of natural religion."[115] He wanted to demonstrate that the teachings of Jesus on God and morality were superior to ancient Judaism and Greek philosophy.[116] He believed that the original teachings of Jesus reflected primitive Deism.[117]

---

106. Kerry Walters, *Revolutionary Deists: Early America's Rational Infidels* (Amherst, NY: Prometheus Books, 2011), 150.

107. Walters, *Revolutionary Deists*, 155.

108. David L. Holmes, *The Faiths of the Founding Fathers* (New York: Oxford University Press, 2006), 86.

109. Walters, *Revolutionary Deists*, 150–151.

110. Holmes, *The Faiths of the Founding Fathers*, 85.

111. Holmes, *The Faiths of the Founding Fathers*, 83.

112. Holmes, *The Faiths of the Founding Fathers*, 83.

113. Holmes, *The Faiths of the Founding Fathers*, 83.

114. Holmes, *The Faiths of the Founding Fathers*, 84.

115. Walters, *Revolutionary Deists*, 155.

116. Walters, *Revolutionary Deists*, 159.

117. Walters, *Revolutionary Deists*, 161.

Frazer completely rejected the notion of Jefferson's Deism and concluded that Jefferson's theology constituted theistic rationalism. He identified theistic rationalism as the integration of Christianity, natural religion, and rationalism.[118] Frazer's invention of theistic rationalism results from his theological condemnation of Deism as a non-Christian religious system, which, he concludes, rejected God and divine revelation. This theological invention also resulted from Frazer's attempt to shape Jefferson and other founding fathers of the American empire as Christians who theologized from a rational perspective that was nondeistic. To preserve the historical myth that the United States was founded on orthodox Christian principles, Frazer argues that Jefferson was a theistic rationalist, which Frazer claims was a theological system that was indeed Christian and had a greater spiritual value than Deism. He concludes that the God of orthodox Christianity was not adequate for the political desires of the founding fathers.[119] Frazer further concludes that theistic rationalism constituted the political theology of the Declaration of Independence.[120]

Theistic rationalism constituted a theological system that correlated Greco-Roman, republican political philosophy with Christian virtue. This theological system was designed to meet the needs of wealthy political elites who possessed the political authority to impose Enlightenment virtue on nonwealthy common people. Frazer asserts that "largely because natural religion and rationalism were critical components, theistic rationalism was not a popular system but appealed only to the well-educated elite, specifically those versed in Enlightenment thought."[121] The foundational rule of theistic rationalism stated that "reason was the standard and guide to the interpretation and evaluation of revelation."[122] Ultimately, Frazer concludes that Jefferson and other theistic rationalists formulated this theological system as their own brand of Christianity but that it did not constitute Deism.

Contradictions

Despite Frazer's flawed argument, Jefferson's theological and philosophical presuppositions prove that he was indeed a Deist and the most prominent architect of the ideology of racial inferiority. Jefferson viewed Blacks as inferior human beings with physical and mental differences.[123] He believed that the primary difference between Blacks and whites was color and the secondary difference was bodily features and functions. He attempted to

---

118. Frazer, *The Religious Beliefs of America's Founders*, 14.
119. Frazer, *The Religious Beliefs of America's Founders*, 5.
120. Frazer, *The Religious Beliefs of America's Founders*, 163.
121. Frazer, *The Religious Beliefs of America's Founders*, 14.
122. Frazer, *The Religious Beliefs of America's Founders*, 139.
123. Earl, "Race, Suffering, Slavery, and Divine Providence," 115.

prove that the white race was more beautiful than the Black race. African American historian Ibram X. Kendi has suggested that Jefferson was paraphrasing John Locke in this excerpt from his *Notes on the State of Virginia* concerning the beauty of the races.[124] American historian Winthrop D. Jordan argues that Jefferson's view on the beauty of races transcended physical appearance, asserting that "embedded in his [Jefferson] thoughts on beauty was the feeling that whites were subtler and more delicate in their passions and that Negroes conversely, were more crude. He felt Negroes to be sexually more animal—hence the gratuitous intrusion of the man-like ape."[125] Kendi questioned the irony of Jefferson's contention on the superiority of white beauty over Black beauty, alluding to Jefferson's many illicit affairs with enslaved African women. DNA evidence has proven that Jefferson produced offspring from sexual liaisons with some of his enslaved Africans, particularly Sally Hemings, who was the half-sister of his wife, Martha Jefferson. Therefore, Jefferson dehumanized people of African descent, equating them with animals, yet engaged in sexual relations with them. The deafening irony is that given Jefferson's presupposition that people of African descent suffered from some kind of animalistic sexual perversion and deviance, this, coupled with his dehumanization of enslaved Africans, would constitute Jefferson engaging in acts of bestiality.

The paradox of Jefferson's "opposition" to the institution of slavery was the fact that he himself was a slaveholder. His primary dilemma was that "he hated slavery but thought Negroes inferior to white men."[126] His supposed hatred of slavery evolved from his natural-law theory, which influenced his theological presuppositions.[127] However, Jefferson's more robust dilemma was the reality that he could determine if enslaved Africans possessed natural rights only after he determined if they were fully human beings.[128] Jefferson's life and philosophy were full of contradictions. Jefferson supposedly viewed slavery as an evil and an injustice against humanity, but the qualifier is that his concern revolved solely around the effect of African enslavement on white people and not its effect on enslaved Africans.[129]

The primary motivation for African enslavement was the slaveholders' belief that people of African descent were racially inferior to people of European descent and therefore destined for enslavement. Part of Jefferson's ideology of racial inferiority was his belief that enslaved Africans possessed

---

124. Kendi, *Stamped from the Beginning*, 109.
125. Winthrop D. Jordan, *White over Black: American Attitudes toward the Negro, 1550–1812*, 2nd ed. (Chapel Hill: University of North Carolina Press, 1968), 495.
126. Jordan, *White over Black*, 429.
127. Jordan, *White over Black*, 429.
128. Jordan, *White over Black*, 429.
129. Jordan, *White over Black*, 432–33.

a compromised mental capacity and were intellectually inferior to whites. Jefferson dichotomized morals and intellect, concluding that the Creator had created Negroes with a soul, which provided them with the capacity for morality, yet he still affirmed that they suffered from intellectual inferiority to whites.[130] He believed that Negroes were equal to whites in their capacity for memory but inferior to them in their capacity for rationalization.[131] The basis for Jefferson's ideology of racial inferiority was his inability to overcome his belief that Negroes were naturally inferior to whites.[132]

In British colonial America and the early republic, Jefferson reduced three racial classifications (Native American, Black, and white) to two (Black and white). This reduction resulted by making the Native Americans equivalent to the white race. In his 1785 correspondence with the Marquis de Chastellux, Jefferson declared, "I believe the Indian then to be in body and mind equal to the white man. I have supposed the black man, in his present state, might not be so. But it would be hazardous to affirm that, equally cultivated for a few generations, he would not become so."[133] Jefferson had reduced the supposed inferiority of Native Americans to environmental effects, not natural inferiority.[134] Based on Jefferson's view of the races, Jordan concluded that "logically the Indian could retrieve an original equality. But if the Negro was not originally equal he could never become so, not if equality really stemmed from that equal creation from which Jefferson had derived it in the Declaration."[135] Jefferson's presuppositions on racial differences reveal the erroneous nature of his celebrated maxim in the Declaration of Independence, "we hold these truths to be self-evident, that all men are created equal, that they are endowed by their Creator with certain unalienable rights," which based on his racial, social, political, and theological presuppositions should more accurately state that "all men are created unequal, that they are endowed by their Creator with certain alienable rights." The former wording contradicts Jefferson's lived reality as a slaveholder, and the latter wording more accurately reflects his involvement and investment in the American institution of slavery.

Another major contradiction for Jefferson was his promotion of amalgamation and colonization. Jefferson believed that Blacks improved in body and mind as a result of race mixing.[136] British historian Nicholas Guyatt

130. Jordan, *White over Black*, 440.
131. Jordan, *White over Black*, 436.
132. Jordan, *White over Black*, 453.
133. Jordan, *White over Black*, 453.
134. Jordan, *White over Black*, 453.
135. Jordan, *White over Black*, 453.
136. Nicholas Guyatt, *Bind Us Apart: How Enlightened Americans Invented Racial Segregation* (New York: Basic Books, 2016), 129.

asserted that "slavery itself had become a major driver of amalgamation, with masters regularly impregnating their slaves. In a similar vein, white traders in the Indian country took Native wives and fathered mixed-race children."[137] Guyatt argued that Enlightenment thinkers sought or expected the imminent eradication of slavery yet defended amalgamation.[138] Ironically, there were many laws in the British colonies and territories of the early republic that prohibited racial intermarriage and interracial sex.

The notion of interracial sex only applied to sexual liaisons between Negro men and white women. Jordan asserted that "though white women still occasionally slept with Negro men, southern society was as determined as ever to punish rigorously any Negro sexual attack on white women."[139] Any sexual liaison between a Black man and white woman, even when consensual or when by force at the demand of the white woman, was considered an attack. Despite the inevitability of amalgamation, laws were created and imposed to criminalize certain actors who engaged in racial mixing. White men were not affected by the laws prohibiting amalgamation. However, white women and Blacks were subject to extreme consequences. For example, the legislative body in colonial Virginia rejected Jefferson's proposal to repeal the banishing of white women for the child-bearing of mulattoes.[140] Jefferson's proposal could have resulted from the reality of his own production of mulatto offspring. Unfortunately, the conviction behind this proposal was not applied to all aspects of his life, such as his role as a slaveholder and as an architect of the American ideology of racial inferiority.

Racial Segregation

At the very heart of the scheme for the Christianization, civilization, and colonization of enslaved Africans was racial segregation. Guyatt argues that, for enlightenment thinkers, racial segregation did not constitute a racist idea.[141] He concluded that racial segregation was viewed as an act of benevolence.[142] The scheme was devised by proponents of abolition and colonization during the era of the early republic. There were three kinds of abolitionists: humanitarian abolitionists viewed slavery as an evil and all races equal; paternalist abolitionists viewed slavery as evil but viewed non-whites as inferior; and racial purist abolitionists viewed slavery as destined, races unequal, and sought a purely white society. The paternalist abolitionists viewed racial segregation as benevolent. Guyatt challenges the notion

---

137. Jordan, *White over Black*, 117.
138. Jordan, *White over Black*, 125.
139. Jordan, *White over Black*, 473.
140. Jordan, *White over Black*, 472.
141. Guyatt, *Bind Us Apart*, 10.
142. Guyatt, *Bind Us Apart*, 7.

that the scheme, particularly for colonization, was racist and examines "its rhetoric of benevolence and equality."[143] He offers three reasons for the examination of the paternalist abolitionist proposal for colonization:

> First, the fact that the proponents of colonization imagined that blacks and Indians could be settled elsewhere.... Second, the rhetoric of "separate but equal" helps to explain why the antislavery struggle produced such a limited commitment among whites to genuine equality for African Americans.... Third, it's important that we recognize that, alongside its episodes of vicious and open racism, the nation has always incubated a form of racial "improvement" that sees space as a solution to the problem of race.[144]

Guyatt concludes that the origin of the struggle against slavery was not the abolitionist movement but the principle of colonization and foundational principle of "separate but equal."[145]

Jefferson's supposed hatred of slavery caused him to theorize about the abolition of slavery and to insist that emancipated Negroes become racially segregated from white society through colonization. He believed that abolition and colonization constituted the resolution to the moral problem of slavery in the early republic and concluded that even after emancipation, Blacks could not be integrated into white society on equal terms.[146] There were major philosophical and theological contradictions between the founding principles of the American republic and the institution of slavery.

The practice of slavery did not reflect the natural-rights theory enumerated in the Declaration of Independence. Guyatt argues that the notion of "separate but equal" was the foundational principle of the new American republic. However, Jefferson's ideology of racial inferiority reflects the erroneous nature of Guyatt's argument. Furthermore, Guyatt contradicts his own argument by exonerating thinkers such as the French naturalist Comte de Buffon from their blatant racism. He asserts that "banishment of blacks from the Declaration of Independence was an awkward maneuver for educated Americans in the early republic. Science and religion offered little support for the idea of a permanent racial hierarchy."[147] Guyatt postulates that Enlightenment thinkers did not believe in a permanent racial hierarchy but fails to acknowledge that the racial hierarchies of the Enlightenment were the catalyst for the banishment of Blacks from the Declaration

143. Guyatt, *Bind Us Apart*, 10.
144. Guyatt, *Bind Us Apart*, 11–12.
145. Guyatt, *Bind Us Apart*, 11.
146. Jordan, *White over Black*, 436.
147. Guyatt, *Bind Us Apart*, 22.

of Independence. He further contradicts his argument by asserting that liberal whites of the early republic believed that they were enlightened and benevolent but had difficulty imagining a multiracial society committed to equality.[148]

Colonization constituted racial separation but did not affirm the notion of "separate but equal." The US Constitution reflected the erroneous nature of Guyatt's description about the nonpermanent nature of black inferiority. The clause in the Constitution that reduced enslaved Africans to three-fifths of a person essentially solidified the permanence of Black inferiority. Kendi, who categorizes the delegates of the 1787 Constitutional Convention as assimilationists and segregationists, concludes that both groups argued in favor of the three-fifths clause and solidified the notion of Black inferiority to whites.

The three-fifths compromise further invalidates Guyatt's claim that the new American republic was founded on the principle of "separate but equal." Equality for persons other than white wealthy males was not within the worldview of Enlightenment thinkers. Racial separation became the primary objective of the abolitionist movement in America, particularly for the paternalists and racial purists, which was evident in the efforts of the American Colonization Society. While Guyatt's notion of "separate but equal" as a foundational principle of the American republic is erroneous, I completely concur with his view that the efforts for racial separation through colonization as perpetrated through the efforts of certain abolitionists, including the paternalistic proposals of Jefferson, constituted an attempt to engage in ethnic cleansing.[149]

The Problem of Otherness

Womanist theologian M. Shawn Copeland concludes that while the shift and focus on the subject or thinking individual through the European Enlightenment was intended as an emancipatory phenomenon, it actually resulted in an anti-emancipatory outcome.[150] She argues that "the Enlightenment era's 'turn to the subject' coincided with the dynamics of domination. From that period forward, *human-being-in-the-world* has been identified with white male bourgeois European *being-in-the-world*."[151] Characterizing the Enlightenment subject as a "white, male, bourgeois European subject," Copeland concludes that the European Enlightenment legitimized "racism, genocide, expropriation, exploitation, cultural imperialism,

---

148. Guyatt, *Bind Us Apart*, 9.

149. Guyatt, *Bind Us Apart*, 13.

150. M. Shawn Copeland, *Enfleshing Freedom: Body, Race, and Being* (Minneapolis: Fortress Press, 2010), 85.

151. Copeland, *Enfleshing Freedom*, 89.

and colonialism."[152] Therefore, Christianity adopted and employed the spirit of domination situated within the European Enlightenment.[153] Any human being outside the scope of the Enlightenment subject constituted the "other."

The most prominent "other" in British colonial America and the early republic is the enslaved African. The utilization of classical Christian theologies in the process of othering fostered the theological nature of the problem. In addition to geographical, biological, social, cultural, and other factors, theology functioned as a precursor to the development of the othering process. Christian theologies were corrupted in the vilest manner and utilized to justify deluded theological presuppositions designed to subordinate, marginalize, and oppress enslaved Africans, and suppress their physical, social, and spiritual liberties.

In traditional historiography, the Enlightenment is generally characterized as a negative reaction to the dogmatically driven orthodox Christian faith. The Enlightenment is generally viewed historically as an intellectual and philosophical movement designed to prioritize science and reason over doctrine and faith. Therefore, the Enlightenment has generally been identified as a phenomenon that was antithetical to the tenets of the Christian faith. Historically, the Enlightenment and the white Christian church as a movement and an institution have been viewed as completely independent of each other. This traditional historical view, as we will see in the next chapter, is problematic. Indeed, there are discontinuities between the Enlightenment as a movement and the white Christian church as an institution; however, there is theological evidence to solidify the notion that both are more interdependent than independent. This will become evident in the correlation of Enlightenment theories of race and Reformed Christian theologies as reflected in the theologies of American Puritanism.

---

152. Copeland, *Enfleshing Freedom*, 86.
153. Copeland, *Enfleshing Freedom*, 86.

2

Puritanism and White Superiority

The vein of election doth run through the loins of godly parents for the most part and that for many generations successively.

—Increase Mather

In 1678, Puritan cleric Increase Mather preached the sermon "Pray for the Rising Generation" to promote prayer and fasting among godly parents in New England who were known, due to their election, as "visible saints." Puritan theologians identified visible saints as those Puritans who demonstrated evidence of good behavior and commitment to Calvinist doctrine.[1] Puritans viewed the church as "a covenanted community of visible saints,"[2] which stemmed from the Puritan covenantal theologies of works and grace—the hallmark of Congregationalism.[3] Furthermore, American religious sociologist Philip Gorski maintains that Mather's view of election as reflected in his sermon made blood rather than divine law the basis of covenant and racialized Puritanism.[4] Consequently, it cultivated a theology of superiority that sowed the seeds of white supremacy. This chapter critically analyzes four concepts that cultivated this Puritan theology of superiority: (1) the ideology of religious and racial superiority; (2) the theology of providence, exceptionalism, and predestinarian piety; (3) the theology of divine election; and (4) the concept of antiblackness and the justification of slavery. Furthermore, in analyzing these concepts, we must also explore the attempts to renew the Puritan theology of superiority through the development of the Old Light, New Light, and New Divinity theologies.

---

1. Philip Gorski, *American Covenant: A History of Civil Religion from the Puritans to the Present* (Princeton, NJ: Princeton University Press, 2017), 41.

2. E. Brooks Holifield, *Theology in America: Christian Thought from the Age of Puritans to the Civil War* (New Haven: Yale University Press, 2003), 41.

3. Gorski, *American Covenant*, 42.

4. Gorski, *American Covenant*, 55.

The Ideology of Religious and Racial Superiority

The racialization of Puritan theology stems primarily from the ideology of white superiority, a natural consequence of white supremacy. American journalist Robert Jensen offers the following definition of white supremacy:

> By white supremacist, I mean a society whose founding is based in an ideology of the inherent superiority of white Europeans over non-whites, an ideology that was used to justify the crimes against indigenous people and Africans that created the nation. That ideology also justified legal and extralegal exploitation of every non-white immigrant group and is used to this day to rationalize the racialized disparities in the distribution of wealth and well-being in this society. It is a society in which white people occupy most of the top positions in powerful institutions, with similar privileges available in limited ways to non-white people who fit themselves into white society.[5]

Jensen defined white as power and utilized the white/nonwhite binary to demonstrate the depravity of white supremacy.[6] Therefore, by the designation "white Europeans," Jensen identified European imperialists, colonists, and enslavers who oppressed and enslaved people of color. American constructive theologian Jeannine Hill Fletcher argues that the catalyst for white supremacy was Christian supremacy, and American theologian James W. Perkinson characterizes this reality of white Christian supremacy as the "witchcraft of white supremacy."[7] Fletcher postulates:

> White Christians made choices to create the conditions of White supremacy and non-White oppression. White Christians shifted the weight of the world onto their non-White neighbors so that they might enjoy a subject position of superiority. White Christians chose to enslave Black Africans and dispossess First Nations peoples. It was White Christians who established the rules of citizenship and barred any who did not measure up to the standard of "free white persons" of good (Christian) moral standing. White Christians designed a society in which benefits would be shared among citizens, even as these citizens were assessed on the basis of their Whiteness and how close they came to the measures of (White) Christian morality.[8]

5. Robert Jensen, *The Heart of Whiteness: Confronting Race, Racism, and White Privilege* (San Francisco: City Lights Publishers, 2005), 3–4.

6. Jensen, *The Heart of Whiteness*, 2–3.

7. James W. Perkinson, *White Theology: Outing Supremacy in Modernity* (New York: Palgrave Macmillan, 2004).

8. Jeannine Hill Fletcher, *The Sin of White Supremacy: Christianity, Racism, and Religious Diversity in America* (Maryknoll, NY: Orbis Books, 2017), 80–81.

In 1676, before the governor and council of the Massachusetts Bay Colony, Puritan historian and cleric William Hubbard preached his sermon "The Happiness of a People in the Wisdom of Their Rulers," through which he proclaimed that New England was to be an "order established by divine appointment, betwixt superiors and inferiors."[9] Puritans believed that they were superior to all other faith traditions, that is, *Christian supremacy*, and in the context of British colonial America and the early republic, that they were superior to enslaved Africans, that is, *white Christian supremacy*.

African American church historian Joseph R. Washington concluded that the New England Puritans considered themselves superior to all other people, including the English, "whom we discovered considered themselves superior to all non-Englishmen."[10] American historian Richard A. Bailey concluded that they demonstrated white superiority through affective relationships and suggested that "the lives of enslaved New Englanders were similar to those of their counterparts on southern plantations.... The types of labor that slaves performed, as well as the ways in which whites sometimes described this work and these workers, reveal yet again the tendency of white New Englanders to exercise their authority to promote notions of racial superiority."[11] Puritan exceptionalism evolved from the Puritan theology of white superiority, and Puritan exceptionalism was the forerunner to the ideal of American exceptionalism, which is an expression of white superiority, white supremacy, and white nationalism in the United States.

Providence, Exceptionalism, and Predestinarian Piety

The New England Puritans viewed themselves as the American inheritors of God's divine covenant with the Israelites. Part of the divine covenant was the promise of the holy land, which they considered the New World.

The Puritan notion of covenant became the foundation for American civil religion, and the Puritan notion of conquest became the foundation for American nationalism.[12] The initial common objective of the Puritans was the purification of the Anglican Church in England. However, the Puritan movement evolved into a multifaceted theological tradition that attempted to define and preserve orthodoxy.[13] Therefore, there was no monolithic Puri-

---

9. William Hubbard, *The Happiness of a People in the Wisdom of Their Rulers Directing and in Obedience of Their Brethren Attending Unto What Israel Ought to Do* (Boston, 1676), 11.

10. Joseph R. Washington Jr., *Anti-Blackness in English Religion, 1500–1800* (New York: Edwin Mellon Press, 1984), 318.

11. Richard A. Bailey, *Race and Redemption in Puritan New England* (New York: Oxford University Press, 2011), 100–101.

12. Gorski, *American Covenant*, 37.

13. Bailey, *Race and Redemption*, 16.

tanism as differing Calvinist theological traditions such as Old Light, New Light, and New Divinity theologies developed. The idea of exceptionalism was grounded in both religious and racial ideology connected to Calvinist undercurrents, such as the doctrine of election. While differing Puritan traditions developed, they all embraced and promoted the predestinarian piety of the Calvinist theological template that ensured and preserved Puritan exceptionalism based on theology and race.

In 1630, John Winthrop, the first governor of the Massachusetts Bay Colony, delivered his sermon "A Model of Christian Charity" while aboard the *Arbella*, which brought him and other Puritans to the New World. The sermon characterized the anticipated destination of the Puritans as "a city on a hill," reinforcing the idea of New England as the New Israel, and established Puritanism as the model theological tradition that reflected God's covenant with the elected community of believers. Consequently, Puritans believed that through divine election their community had been predestined by God to exemplify what constituted proper social, economic, political, and religious behavior in the eyes of God. American religious historian R. Marie Griffith notes Winthrop's warning that "as a city on a hill exposed to the eyes of all people, the community must not waver from the highest standards of Christian behavior and love ... lest they bring shame upon God and their faith."[14] Winthrop's sermon identified love as the foundation for the New England society that was established in response to the corruption of the Anglican Church and the social, political, and religious oppression the Puritans had experienced in English society. Ironically, New England Puritans became prominent examples of how the oppressed become oppressors, and the supposed love at the foundation of New England society was corrupted through the ideology of religious and racial superiority.

For the New England Puritans, being "a city on a hill" was the nucleus of their theology of white superiority. Kendi argues that Africans were stamped as inferior, racially distinct, and subhuman from the beginning of British colonial America.[15] The Puritan notion of inherited superiority, he asserts, was influenced by Aristotelian philosophy, which divided humanity into two classes—masters and slaves—and was designed to normalize the Greek practice of slavery.[16] Puritan enslavement of Africans and Native Americans, therefore, was foundational in building the "city on a hill," and the New England Puritans developed a theology to justify their role as slaveholders. Based on their belief in divine sovereignty, particularly through the

---

14. R. Marie Griffith, *American Religion: A Documentary History* (New York: Oxford University Press, 2007), 16.

15. Ibram X. Kendi, *Stamped from the Beginning: The Definitive History of Racist Ideas in America* (New York: Nation Books, 2016), 38.

16. Kendi, *Stamped from the Beginning*, 16–17.

Calvinist notions of providence and predestination, the New England Puritans rationalized the institution of slavery as a phenomenon that God had ordained for the "city on a hill."[17] Furthermore, they believed that slavery played a pivotal role in the work of God's redemption in that Native Americans and Africans were heathenistic savages in need of divine redemption.

While some people such as the New England Puritan cleric Jonathan Edwards identified race-based slavery as a moral disease,[18] slaveholders in New England believed that they would experience redemption if they treated their slaves with Christian benevolence.[19] Consequently, the New England Puritans viewed their mission work to enslaved persons as redemptive work necessary to deliver and redeem Native Americans and enslaved Africans of their supposed heathenistic savagery. While the New England Puritans believed that their mission work was for the spiritual benefit of the enslaved, the group known as Old Light Puritans failed not only to address their moral disease and their own need for spiritual transformation but to realize that enslaving others constituted evil.

Divine Election

At the heart of the Calvinist doctrine of divine election is the dichotomy of the elect (saved) and reprobate (damned). In his discussion on the Calvinist origins of New England Puritans, E. Brooks Holifield asserts that "the salvation of the elect and the reprobation of the damned resulted from an eternal decree of God, before time began, logically prior to any foresight of good or evil in the creature, prior to the decree to create a world, prior to the decree to permit the fall, prior to the decree to send the Son to redeem the world."[20] Therefore, strongly situated within the Calvinist tradition, the New England Puritans viewed salvation as a divine gift from God rather than a human achievement.[21]

The New England Puritans believed that there were various signs that verified and validated the election of visible saints. They believed that the Holy Spirit communicated directly with the elect, providing them with a supernatural sense of assurance.[22] American religious historian Peter J. Thuesen identifies visible saints as "people whose faith suggested that they were also

---

17. Bailey, *Race and Redemption*, 114.

18. Bailey, *Race and Redemption*, 119.

19. Bailey, *Race and Redemption*, 122.

20. Holifield, *Theology in America*, 38.

21. E. Brooks Holifield, *Era of Persuasion: American Thought and Culture, 1521–1680* (Lanham, MD: Rowman & Littlefield, 2004), 92–95.

22. Peter J. Thuesen, *Predestination: The American Career of a Contentious Doctrine* (New York: Oxford University Press, 2009), 71.

among the invisible saints of the elect, known only to God."[23] This idea of invisible saints correlates with the Calvinist predestinarian doctrine of God's divine secret plan on the chosen elect and damned reprobate, and Adam Smith's notion of the invisible hand of God, which was pivotal to the cultivation of the Protestant work ethic and global spirit of capitalism that pervaded the economic, social, political, and religious fabric of American society.

New England Puritans equated productivity and hard work with divine election; therefore, unwillingness to work signified being devoid of God's irresistible grace. Puritans believed that all work, both sacred and secular, was strictly for the glorification of God.[24] Puritan cleric William Perkins equated work with the notion of Christian vocation as a stipulation of the covenantal agreement between the Puritans and God. Perkins even viewed slavery as the calling of the master and the calling of the servant, asserting that, in each vocation, three things are required: "First, it must be done in obedience; secondly, in faith; and thirdly, it must be directed to the glory of God."[25] For the New England Puritans, an idle mind and idle hands were the work of the devil producing idleness and sloth, the antithesis to hard work. American literary critic Leland Ryken argued that the Puritan emphases on the doctrine of election and providence fostered the belief that God had called all persons to his or her vocation.[26] Ironically, the social and religious praxis of New England Puritans reflected a doctrine of divine election that was theoretically situated in irresistible grace but practically grounded in race. Therefore, New England Puritans, especially the antirevivalist Old Lights, would not affirm the productivity and hard work of enslaved persons as a sign of election. Divine election was reserved for visible saints, and visible sainthood was reserved for New England Puritans, who considered themselves religiously and racially superior.

Racist Ideologies

The migration of Puritans to the New World was embedded with racist ideologies. Historically, the negative view of physical and ontological blackness as a curse predated the institution of slavery. British colonists did not invent the supposed curse of blackness but transmitted and transformed the curse into the theological justification for the institution of slavery and other forms of racial discrimination. The racial views of the British colonists reflect Enlightenment theories of race, which dehumanized the

---

23. Thuesen, *Predestination*, 70.

24. Leland Ryken, *Worldly Saints: The Puritans as They Really Were* (Grand Rapids, MI: Zondervan, 1986), 26–27.

25. William Perkins, *A Treatise of the Vocations, Or, the Callings of Men with the Sorts and Kinds of Them and the Right Use Thereof* (Cambridge, 1605).

26. Ryken, *Worldly Saints*, 26.

racial other. Traditionally, evangelical Christian traditions, such as the New England Puritans, are characterized as rejecting Enlightenment thought. American religious historian Catherine A. Brekus challenges this traditional view, and, certainly, the racist ideologies perpetuated in Puritan theology vindicate her argument that evangelicals did adopt some of the ideas of the Enlightenment that aided them in excluding racial others (nonwhites) from the phenomenon of divine election. The Old Light Puritans also adopted the idea of the sovereign right of the individual white male from Enlightenment thinkers and integrated it into their theological beliefs regarding divine election.

Now, as Brekus argues, the Puritan evangelicals' adoption of Enlightenment ideas on the sovereign right of the individual shifted their emphasis from the welfare of the covenanted community of visible saints to the self-interest of the individual. Enlightenment thinkers imagined this individual as a white male. This idea of the white male being the sovereign individual with rights and the only form of human being with those sovereign rights, which constituted white male superiority, transformed into white supremacy and became the catalyst for the oppression of racialized others (nonwhites) in the United States.

The Puritan shift from community (New Israel) to the self-interest of the white male as influenced through Enlightenment ideology further fostered the exclusionary theology of Old Lights. They had settled and colonized the land of Native Americans and, through the Atlantic triangular slave trade, had participated in the enslavement and forced migration of African people to the New World yet considered Native Americans and enslaved Africans as "internal aliens."[27] Therefore, nonwhites were characterized as outsiders whom the Puritans attempted to eliminate from the body politic of Puritan society. However, their failure to eliminate nonwhites from the body politic of Puritan society necessitated racial negotiations about slavery and freedom and exposed the contradiction between the Enlightenment thinkers' racialization of the human nature of nonwhites and their supposed universalism that said all humans are created equal by nature. This reflects the racial and economic hypocrisy of the Declaration of Independence and the constitutional contradiction of the US Constitution, particularly the Bill of Rights.

Antiblackness and the Justification for Slavery

The Puritans' opposition to Africans and Native Americans as spiritual equals stemmed from the spirit of antiblackness within New England

---

27. Michael Hoberman, *New Israel/New England: Jews and Puritans in Early America* (Amherst, MA: University of Massachusetts Press, 2011), 22.

society.[28] This opposition is the forerunner of the modern White American evangelical ethos, which consists of moral codes, sexism, xenophobia, bigotry, homophobia, classicism, and racism.

Washington argued that antiblackness was opposed to all perceived black realities that are in opposition to all things white, and which, he contended, constituted the meaning of the Puritan notion of visible saints.[29] Kendi defines a racist idea as "any concept that regards one racial group as inferior or superior to another racial group in any way" and further defined anti-Black racist ideas as "any idea suggesting that black people, or any group of black people, are inferior in any way to another racial group."[30] The religion of antiblackness in New England Puritanism racialized the criteria for visible sainthood and further corrupted its theological presuppositions. This racialization is most evident in the Puritan spiritual division of Blacks and whites in New England. The New England Puritans believed that whites had been called by God to be masters and Blacks had been called by God to be slaves.[31] They believed that whites possessed saved souls (Puritans) and that Blacks possessed damned souls.[32]

One of the primary features here was the Puritan correlation of blackness with evil. While they considered Native Americans' and enslaved Africans' spiritualities equal as pagans, they were profoundly disturbed by the dark pigmentation of enslaved Africans.[33] The extremely negative characterizations and fetish of the Europeans with blackness led to them racializing sin and portraying people of African descent and Native Americans as "partners of the devil."[34] While New England Puritans believed that all non-believers (non-elected persons lacking visible sainthood) were children of the devil, they correlated blackness with all things evil.[35] Yet they believed that Native Americans and people of African descent could eradicate their demonic nature through the experience of regeneration.[36] This belief, however, contradicts the Puritan racialization of visible sainthood, which limited regeneration to those whom God had elected for regeneration. Despite this theological contradiction, the Puritans eventually affirmed catechesis for the enslaved Africans and Native Americans whom they had condemned as "pagans," "partners of the devil," and "children of the devil."

---

28. Bailey, *Race and Redemption*, 18.
29. Bailey, *Race and Redemption*, 284.
30. Kendi, *Stamped from the Beginning*, 5.
31. Kendi, *Stamped from the Beginning*, 5.
32. Kendi, *Stamped from the Beginning*, 200.
33. Bailey, *Race and Redemption*, 42.
34. Bailey, *Race and Redemption*, 46.
35. Bailey, *Race and Redemption*, 49.
36. Bailey, *Race and Redemption*, 49.

Cotton Mather

In 1706, New England Puritan cleric Cotton Mather published his essay "The Negro Christianized," becoming one of the first British colonists to promote the Christianization of Blacks through catechesis. Consequently, enslaved Africans were taught certain scriptural and foundational doctrines of the Christian faith such as the Lord's Prayer, the Ten Commandments, and the Apostles' Creed. Mather believed that Christianity was imperative for the salvation, civilization, and servitude of enslaved Africans. He also believed that the providence of God sent enslaved Africans to America to be Christianized.[37] However, despite this Christian catechesis of enslaved Africans, he still questioned their intellectual capacity. Mather's doubt resulted from his negative views of physical and ontological blackness, which promoted the notion of the inherent inferiority of enslaved Africans. In 1696, Mather published *A Good Master Well Served: A Brief Discourse on the Necessary Properties and Practices of a Good Servant*, through which he expressed the soteriological benefits for enslaved Africans of being washed in the white blood of Jesus, considering their presupposed mental and physical inferiority due to the darkness of their bodies. He exclaimed:

> So, though your Skins are of the colour of the Night, yet your Souls will be washed White in the Blood of the Lamb, and be Entitled unto an Inheritance in Light. Though you are in Slavery to men, yet you shall be the Free-men of the Lord, the Children of God. Though you are Fed among the Dogs, with the Orts [offal; scraps] of our Tables, yet you shall at length Lie down unto a Feast with Abraham himself in the Heaven of the Blessed. Been't you Discouraged; it will be but a Little, a Little, a Little While, and all your pains will End in Everlasting Joys.[38]

Mather correlates the plight of the enslaved African from the New England perspective with the plight of the woman with a demon-possessed daughter in Matthew 15 (the Canaanite woman) and Mark 7 (the Syrophoenician woman). In both instances, the Gospel writers present Jesus in an uncommon manner as Jesus utilizes the common Jewish nomenclature for gentiles. Jesus correlates the woman with dogs, and, in the biblical context, being characterized as a dog means being considered evil, wicked, and unclean. New England Puritans, such as Mather, built on the ethnic superiority of Jews to justify their dehumanization of people of color and legitimize their theological construction of white superiority.

---

37. Kendi, *Stamped from the Beginning*, 69.

38. Cotton Mather, *A Good Master Well Served: A Brief Discourse on the Necessary Properties and Practices of a Good Servant* (Boston: B. Green & J. Allen, 1696).

The New England Puritans utilized the dark color of the enslaved Africans' skin to justify their beliefs concerning slave inferiority and the notion that God created Africans inferior.[39] Mather instructed enslaved Africans to refrain from evil, insisting that evil would cause them to become blacker, and further insisted that their souls would be washed in the white blood of Jesus.[40] He warned enslaved Africans in his preaching against blackness, exhorting them to refrain from making themselves "infinitely Blacker than you already are."[41]

In his discussion on the type of ideal response to the question of the fundamental nature of the enslaved African, African American ethicist Riggins Earl argued that there was an "ideal Christian master type" slaveholder who believed that the slave had a soul, but his external physical color of blackness denoted evil and devalued the spiritual worth of the slave. Earl asserted:

> It was the theoretical, if not always the practical, belief of the Christian master that the slave of African origin was created in the image of God . . . but . . . it was the unchangeable blackness of the slave's body, which signified the demonic, that left the ideal Christian master type unwilling to assert theologically that the slave was made in the image of God. At best this type of master could only say theologically that the slave's soul was created in the image of God. In no way could this belief change the master's ethical understanding of the nature of the slave as body. A physical body was perceived as having only utility value for the master's economic end. This meant that the Christian master, in practice, could only accept the slave's soul as having sacred worth in the sight of God.[42]

Consequently, European enslavers believed that the spiritual level of enslaved Africans could be increased through the transformation of their souls despite the evilness of the blackness within their souls, and that this transformation occurred through the white blood of Jesus. Some slaveholders even believed that the conversion of the Black soul through the white blood of Jesus would not only increase the spiritual level of the enslaved but also increase their value on the slave market.[43] They believed that the blackness of the enslaved African's physical body and that of their soul was inherently evil, and therefore held an eschatological hope that their enslaved

39. Ibid, p. 13.

40. Washington, *Anti-Blackness*, 185.

41. Washington, *Anti-Blackness*, 277.

42. Riggins R. Earl, *Dark Symbols and Obscure Signs: God, Self, and Community in the Slave Mind* (Knoxville: University of Tennessee Press, 2003), 15–16.

43. Earl, *Dark Symbols and Obscure Signs*, 15–16.

Africans would not only experience the transformation of their soul in their earthly life as enslaved persons, but that God would also grant them eternal whiteness in their soul for the afterlife.[44] New England Puritans attempted to regenerate enslaved Africans into being theological "Oreos," having ontological blackness externally due to their black skin and spiritual whiteness internally after being washed in the white blood of Jesus. Puritans, such as Mather, believed that through this regeneration, divine election for enslaved Africans might be possible.

Mather epitomized the Puritans' theological contradictions and spiritual hypocrisy. He argued that the Puritans' "errand in the wilderness" was to serve God by saving the Black souls of enslaved Africans who suffered from inherent inferiority.[45] Furthermore, he exhibited the religion of antiblackness in his spiritual reconfiguration of the Black soul as white, making whiteness the prerequisite for Christian conversion. In other words, he intended to transform Black souls into white souls through Christian conversion.[46]

The Puritans' idea of antiblackness resulted in Native Americans being correlated with the white Puritan standard of beauty (whiteness) and characterized as "noble savages" and Blacks being rejected because of their blackness. Their theological presuppositions prohibited them from identifying Black Puritans as visible saints. Blacks could become Christians but not Black Puritans (visible saints). The Puritans' declaration of themselves as the people of the covenant and, therefore, the true church became the catalyst for the exclusion of others, including Jews, from the covenant.[47] New England Puritans viewed the spiritual cultivation of enslaved Africans as beneficial, believing that such would make enslaved Africans more dutiful and obedient.[48] Enslaved Africans participated in New England Puritan families and were permitted into their church fellowship but were prohibited admission into visible sainthood.[49] Bailey characterizes the Puritan phenomenon of social control as ventriloquism, the attempts of Puritan clergy to control their neighbors of color.[50] He argues that "the puritans demonstrated their ownership by using the whip, the church, and the court to discipline their red and black neighbors. In these various civil and uncivil attempts to control New Englanders of color, some white colonists began to express a sense of moral disease."[51]

44. Earl, *Dark Symbols and Obscure Signs*, 22.
45. Washington, *Anti-Blackness*, 183.
46. Washington, *Anti-Blackness*, 284.
47. Washington, *Anti-Blackness*, 212.
48. Washington, *Anti-Blackness*, 285.
49. Washington, *Anti-Blackness*, 252.
50. Bailey, *Race and Redemption*, 8.
51. Bailey, *Race and Redemption*, 8.

Nonwhites in New England suffered from a double consciousness of being characterized as property (chattel) and person (Christian).[52] New England Puritans situated the status of personhood in Christian conversion rather than divine creation. In other words, for an enslaved African to meet the criteria for being a Christian meant being transformed from blackness to whiteness, and therefore, becoming a person.

Finally, the New England Puritans believed that their doctrine of salvation provided enslaved Africans with spiritual freedoms and exonerated them from the sin and guilt of mistreating people of color.[53] In other words, they justified slavery through their spirituality. As God's elect, they believed that divine providence had spiritually destined them to function as stewards over the infidel Negroes through enslavement. They also believed that enslavement was the mechanism through which heathens, specifically enslaved Africans, were introduced to Christ.[54] Additionally, they believed that enslavement delivered Africans from idolatry and savagery, thus viewing slavery as an act of mercy that provided salvation for the souls of the enslaved.[55]

Old Light and New Light Theologies

As the architect of New Light theology, New England cleric Jonathan Edwards (1703–1758) developed a theological tradition within the Puritan heritage that fostered revivalism in New England and shifted from the self-interest of the enlightened individual to the true spirituality of the visible saints. The Old Light Calvinists rejected revivalism and condemned such "enthusiasm" as a threat to the old church order.[56] New Lights believed in the necessity of the work of God's Spirit in the preparation of the human heart for regeneration; and while the Old Lights conceded that the Spirit convinced the heart of the necessity for regenerating grace,[57] they considered the New Light revival theology of Edwards a source of religious heresy.

Disinterested Spirituality

Edwards's notion of disinterested spirituality became central to the New Light revival theological tradition and constituted Edwards's understanding of authentic Christian experience. His disinterested spirituality was God-centered and focused on the self-denial of the individual for the greater benefit of others through the affection of love. Edwards identified religious

---

52. Bailey, *Race and Redemption*, 8.
53. Bailey, *Race and Redemption*, 8.
54. Bailey, *Race and Redemption*, 257.
55. Bailey, *Race and Redemption*, 62.
56. Robert W. Caldwell, *Theologies of the American Revivalists from Whitefield to Finney* (Downers Grove, IL: InterVarsity Press, 2017), 18.
57. Holifield, *Theology in America*, 97–98.

affections as products of human volition and insisted that the chief affection and source of all other affections is love, which originated from the
heart. He believed that the affection of love is the hallmark of religious
affections. Edwards contended that true virtue fostered affection toward
Excellency, which for him was the first and main sign of authentic spirituality because it consisted of loving God for God's own sake.[58] The affection of
love for Edwards consisted of an inclination that transcended one's own self
and was opposed to a form of love for one's own self-interest.

Edwards defined Excellency as "the consent of being to being"[59] and consisted of loving God for God's own sake and not one's own sake. A person had
achieved Excellency if they were in harmony with God and God's creation.
Persons who possessed Excellency had a disinterested benevolence, which
meant loving others simply because they were a part of God's beauty, and
therefore possessing a love of impartiality. At the heart of Edwards's disinterested spirituality is the notion of benevolence.

The theological differences between the Old Lights and the New Lights
were essential to the success of revivalism in New England. Edwards characterized the affectivity of love toward God and one's neighbor as true virtue. However, his separation of beauty into general beauty and particular
beauty became problematic and contradictory to his notion of disinterested spirituality. Particular beauty was a theoretical notion of Enlightenment thinkers and Old Lights that influenced their participation in the slave
trade and the institution of slavery: the former viewed white males as the
reflection of particular beauty; and the latter viewed white Puritans, whom
they considered visible saints, also as the reflection of particular beauty.
Edwards argued that spiritual beauty and other forms of virtuous beauty
are secondary forms of beauty.[60] In agreement with the common opinion,
Edwards asserted that "beauty in the object is not always benevolence or
a disposition to the welfare of those that are not considered as beautiful;
unless mere existence is accounted as beauty."[61]

Historically, people of color, particularly people of African descent, were
not considered beautiful by European colonists. As noted above, Enlightenment thinkers and Old Lights considered people of color (non-Europeans)
heathens and savages possessing neither general beauty nor spiritual beauty.

Edwards considered his cultivated New Light theology as spiritual
beauty and believed that this theology was the most authentic expression

---

58. Jonathan Edwards, "The Nature of True Virtue," in John E. Smith, Harry S. Stout, and
Kenneth P. Minkema, eds., *A Jonathan Edwards Reader* (New Haven: Yale University Press,
1995), 249–50.

59. Edwards, "The Nature of True Virtue."

60. Edwards, "The Nature of True Virtue," 250–51.

61. Edwards, "The Nature of True Virtue," 247.

of Christian experience. Old Light theology was more reflective of the theology that was cultivated by John Calvin's followers in the Reformed tradition. The disinterested spirituality of Edwards shaped New Light theology, reflecting the true teleological objective of ontological existence and human actions simply for the glory of God. The disinterested spirituality of loving God and one's neighbor for God's own sake reflects the teleological objective of Calvin's theological thought. However, while Edwards and his New Light theology shifted evangelical Calvinism from being exclusive to inclusive, Blacks were excluded from this spiritual inclusivity, evident in Edwards's slaveholding practice.

Jonathan Edwards and Slavery

The revivalism of the Great Awakening caused Edwards to conclude that New England had become the redeemer nation by default, particularly for people of African descent.[62] Edwards believed that the revivalism foreshadowed the future glory of not just America but the world.[63] However, Edwards believed that the New England Puritans, as the New Israel and, therefore, people of the covenant, had brought shame upon this future glory because of their violation of the covenant. Edwards's belief stemmed from the plight of the Israelites in the aftermath of their disobedience and violation of the covenant causing "God to give the gospel to the Gentiles."[64] In the context of New England Puritanism, enslaved Africans were characterized in the same way that the Israelites had characterized the gentiles. Edwards believed that God delivered the gospel to enslaved Africans through the revivalism of the Great Awakenings. While there were many more conversions of enslaved Africans to evangelical Christianity during the Second Great Awakening, there were conversions during the First Great Awakening. In 1741, revivalists reported experiencing many Black conversions.[65] Antirevivalists complained about the success of Black exhorters, which implies that white evangelical revivalists were not the only spiritual conduits for conversion during the Great Awakenings, as there were Black exhorters. Enslaved Africans first gained admission into New England congregations during the First Great Awakening of 1730s and 1740s. Kenneth Minkema argues that the admission of Blacks into New England churches was "a trend that reflected their increasing numbers in New England as well

62. Gerald R. McDermott, "Jonathan Edwards, the City on a Hill, and the Redeemer Nation: A Reappraisal," *American Presbyterians* 69, no. 1 (Spring 1991): 42.

63. McDermott, "Jonathan Edwards, the City on a Hill," 42.

64. McDermott, "Jonathan Edwards, the City on a Hill," 42.

65. Kenneth P. Minkema, "Jonathan Edwards's Defense of Slavery," in *Massachusetts Historical Review* 4 [Race & Slavery] (2002): 34.

as growing concerns among colonists for the spiritual well-being of slaves and free blacks."[66]

Edwards gained a reputation for being a benevolent New England Puritan slaveholder. He viewed the proper treatment of slaves as a form of Christian benevolence. He was the first pastor in Northampton, Massachusetts, to baptize Blacks and admit them into the full membership of the congregation.[67] He rejected the Old Light definition of neighbor, which consisted solely of Puritans who racially identified themselves as the new children of Israel.[68] Furthermore, he correlated the New England enslavement of Africans with the Egyptian enslavement of the Israelites, using the image of the Exodus to reflect the plight of enslaved Africans whom he believed could not fully serve God while enslaved.[69] Puritans believed that slavery was a part of God's work of redemption and therefore concluded that slave masters experienced redemption for the moral disease of enslavement if they treated their slaves well. Like Mather, Edwards reflected the rhetoric of future abolitionists, accusing slaveholders of neglecting the spiritual welfare and agency of enslaved Africans.[70] However, the continuity between Mather and Edwards also reflects the social contradictions of their presuppositions concerning the benevolence of the slaveholder and the institution of slavery.

Social Contradictions

Edwards's contradiction is most evident in his view of the slave trade and the institution of slavery. He condemned the slave trade as an enterprise depriving enslaved Africans of their liberties enjoyed while on the continent of Africa.[71] He also viewed slavery as a sinful practice resulting from the fall of humanity.[72] Despite these views, his social contradictions regarding the morality of slavery can be found in his ontological view of enslaved Africans.

Edwards possessed a paternalistic view of enslaved Africans and Native Americans that caused him to conclude that they were less than whites, a position that was based on his understanding of social hierarchy. This paternalistic view is evident in a letter on slavery that he drafted in 1738 in which he defended the institution of slavery provided the practice of enslavement was legal, humane, and Christian. In the letter, Edwards criti-

---

66. Minkema, "Jonathan Edwards's Defense of Slavery," 34.

67. Bailey, *Race and Redemption*, 121.

68. Bailey, *Race and Redemption*, 38.

69. Bailey, *Race and Redemption*, 41.

70. Minkema, "Jonathan Edwards's Defense of Slavery", 42.

71. Kenneth P. Minkema, "Jonathan Edwards on Slavery and the Slave Trade," *The William and Mary Quarterly* 54, no. 4 (1997): 827.

72. Minkema, "Jonathan Edwards on Slavery," 828.

cized those who condemned slavery and yet benefited economically from the slave trade. He wholeheartedly believed that the practice of slavery was justified in the Scriptures, particularly based on his interpretation of the Mosaic Law, and further declared that Scriptures prohibiting the enslavement of one's neighbor were limited to the children of Israel as neighbors, not all of humankind.

The Old Calvinists had restricted the idea of neighbor to fellow New England Puritans, therefore only another New England Puritan was the neighbor of a New England Puritan. Theologically, it seems that only a visible saint constituted the neighbor of a visible saint in New England Puritanism. As with the religious and cultural practice of the Hebrews in the biblical text, foreigners or persons outside the Hebrew culture were not considered neighbors. The neighbor of the Hebrew person is another Hebrew. For example, Mosaic law stipulates, "You shall not covet your neighbor's house, you shall not covet your neighbor's wife" (Exod 20:17). The clear intent of the law is that a Hebrew should not covet the house of another Hebrew nor should he covet the wife of another Hebrew, because his fellow Hebrew is his neighbor. This did not include the houses and wives of persons of other racial, cultural, and ethnic backgrounds. New England Puritans as the New Israel adopted this model, and, therefore, the notion of who constitutes one's neighbor is at the heart of the theology of white superiority of the New England Puritans.

Edwards viewed whites and Blacks as being equal spiritually, yet he believed that Blacks lacked social and political equality with whites.[73] Despite his philosophical and theological notions of beauty about human nature in general, and his supposed notion of spiritual equality between whites and people of color, his views that enslaved Africans and Native Americans were heathens in need of conversion contradict these ideas.[74]

Edwards's role in the institution of slavery as a slaveholder and his ontological view of nonwhites is problematic specifically for his theological presuppositions related to disinterested spirituality. However, his followers, the Edwardsean Calvinists, attempted to offer a resolution to this problem through the development of the New Divinity theology.

The New Divinity Theology

The primary catalyst for the development of the New Divinity theology was Edwards's disinterested spirituality, through which he promoted true virtue, the theological root of Edwardsean revivalism. Edwards believed that true virtue resulted from the regeneration of the heart, which produced the

73. Minkema, "Jonathan Edwards's Defense of Slavery," 35.
74. Minkema, "Jonathan Edwards on Slavery," 828.

spirit of love or benevolence to Being in general.[75] The appeal of Edwards's disinterested spirituality for Edwardsean Calvinists was its supposed self-denial and detraction from self-love. However, one of Edwards's disciples, Samuel Hopkins, believed that the notion of true virtue was theologically deficient. American historian Joseph A. Conforti characterizes Hopkins as a neo-Edwardsean theologian and social reformer who became the leader of the New Divinity movement in the New England Congregational tradition. New Divinity theologians viewed themselves as the only authentic, "consistent Calvinists" in New England.[76] Hopkins's disenchantment with Edwards's attempt to correlate the natural theology of rationalists with the notion of self-love was the primary cause for the cultivation of Hopkins's theological notion of disinterested benevolence, which formed the heart of the New Divinity thought.

Hopkins's idea of disinterested benevolence was a theology of social reform. He integrated evangelical Calvinism with social activism. In 1773, Hopkins published *An Inquiry into the Nature of True Holiness*, in which he defined disinterested benevolence as possessing love of God and love of one's neighbor through the exaltation of God and serving one's neighbor. He characterized it as a form of universal love for humanity through disinterested goodwill (self-denial for the sake of God and humanity).[77] Hopkins's definition of disinterested benevolence corrected the theological deficiency of Edwards's disinterested spirituality by emphasizing love of God and love of one's neighbor. American historian David S. Lovejoy argues that Hopkins's notion of disinterested benevolence was the foundation for the abolitionist cause of the New Divinity movement. Hopkins believed that God was not a self-centered deity but a benevolent governor whose primary attribute was disinterested benevolence.

The Great Awakenings

The nineteenth century witnessed the shift from the individualism of the First Great Awakening (1730–1755) to an American society focused on social reform. The Second Great Awakening (1790–1840) advocated temperance, women's rights, and abolitionism, which consisted of freedom for the body and soul of enslaved persons. This new era also witnessed a shift in the theological construct of American society. American historian William McLoughlin argues that "the cultural consensus that emerged from the

---

75. Joseph A. Conforti, *Samuel Hopkins and the New Divinity Movement* (Grand Rapids, MI: Eerdmans, 1981), 111.

76. Conforti, *Samuel Hopkins*, 63.

77. David S. Lovejoy, "Samuel Hopkins: Religion, Slavery, and the Revolution," *The New England Quarterly* 40, no. 2 (1967): 233.

First Great Awakening was theologically Calvinistic, but it emphasized the willingness of God to save those who truly repented of their sins, and it stressed God's continued favor toward America as the potential sense of the millennium."[78] The spirit of revivalism and reform during the Second Great Awakening fostered the reconstruction of the new republic as a Christian nation and benevolent empire.[79]

The Second Great Awakening was apocalyptic and fostered the antislavery impulse. Revivalists of the Second Great Awakening believed that they were laying the groundwork for the coming of God's kingdom and believed that the revivalism of this awakening foreshadowed and reflected God's kingdom. American historian Barry Hankins argues that the revivalism of the Second Great Awakening was responsible for abolitionism becoming a national phenomenon.[80] The shift from the individualism of the First Great Awakening to the communalism of the Second Great Awakening was most apparent in the camp meetings, which were a distinctive feature of the Second Great Awakening. The significance of these camp meetings is that they transcended race, gender, and class. The camp meeting provided Blacks and whites of the early republic their first opportunity to come together in a socially inclusive and cohesive unit to worship. They also gave enslaved Africans the opportunity to practice their indigenous spirituality, which had been prohibited because of the fears of the slaveholders. They also gave women their first opportunity to preach on American soil through testimonials.

While the First Great Awakening brought about the initial spiritual transformation that was pivotal in attracting enslaved Africans in British colonial America to European American Christianity, the Second Great Awakening was much more appealing spiritually and resulted in many more conversions of enslaved Africans, despite the continuing fears and opposition of slaveholders.

In addition to the appeal of the phenomenon of spiritual ecstasy that pervaded the very fabric of the camp meetings, enslaved Africans could identify with the apparent theological shift between the awakenings. The theology of the First Great Awakening was not conducive to the spiritual, social, political, and economic equality of all persons, which is reflected in Hopkins's disenchantment with the social contradictions of Edwards's disinterested spirituality and lack of social activism. The revival theology of the Second Great Awakening, specifically the New Divinity notion of disinterested benevolence, affirmed and fostered the spiritual, social, and

---

78. William G. McLoughlin, *Revivals, Awakenings, and Reform: An Essay on Religion and Social Change in America, 1607–1977* (Chicago: University of Chicago Press, 1978), 98.

79. Conforti, *Samuel Hopkins*, 175.

80. Barry Hankins, *The Second Great Awakening and the Transcendentalists* (Westport, CT: Greenwood Press, 2004).

political equality of enslaved Africans and their liberation from enslavement.

Hopkins believed that the US Congress of the early republic had the responsibility to establish and ensure universal liberty for whites and Blacks.[81] He argued that if the purpose of the American Revolution was to establish rights for British colonists, those rights also belonged to Negroes.[82] Hopkins believed that the purpose of the American Revolution was the freedom and equality of enslaved persons with their white counterparts.[83] He viewed an antislavery stance as a form of disinterested benevolence and evidence of one's conversion. Hopkins argued that true Christians could not apply the notion of Black inferiority to justify enslavement and inequality. Hopkins believed that the injustice of enslavement was the cause of retributive justice on the empire of British colonial America and the early republic and argued that the British monarch's oppression of British colonists in North America was a divinely sanctioned providential punishment for American sins, specifically the sin of slavery. This affirms the fact that the enslavement of Africans constitutes America's original sin and that European colonists transgressed divine law with the heinous and repugnant institution of slavery.

Abolitionism

Three kinds of abolitionists developed during the era of the early American republic—humanitarians, paternalists, and racial purists. Humanitarian abolitionists affirmed the complete humanity of enslaved Africans and their equality with their white counterparts. In her critical description of humanitarianism and its influence on the evangelical movement, Catherine A. Brekus asserts:

> Humanitarians were a loose coalition of thinkers who were involved in many different causes—including prison reform, antislavery, and poor relief—but they were linked together by their faith that humans were essentially good and were called to alleviate suffering and create a better world. On one hand, evangelicals refused to see human happiness as the greatest good, and they defended doctrines that humanitarians found abhorrent, especially eternal punishment. Yet, on the other hand, evangelicals were fervent about creating a kinder, more compassionate world, and ultimately they forged an understanding of "benevolence" that was uniquely their own.[84]

---

81. Hankins, *The Second Great Awakening*, 235.
82. Hankins, *The Second Great Awakening*, 235.
83. Hankins, *The Second Great Awakening*, 242.
84. Catherine A. Brekus, "The Evangelical Encounter with the Enlightenment," 36.

Paternalist abolitionists affirmed the humanity of enslaved Africans but still prioritized whiteness over the racial other. The most prominent paternalist abolitionists were the Quakers, who initially embraced and practiced African enslavement but shifted to being antislavery. Though they became proponents of abolitionism, the Quakers prioritized whiteness over humanitarianism because they viewed Blacks as being second-class citizens.

Racial purist abolitionists did not affirm the humanity of enslaved Africans and sought to purify American society of blackness. They became abolitionists by default through advocating the importation of white male servants and the prohibition of African enslavement. In his discussion on social repercussions in colonial New England, African American historian Lorenzo Greene highlights the attempted influence of racial purists in the legislation of colonial assemblies, such as the Rhode Island Act of 1711 and the bill "An Act for Encouraging the Importation of White Male Servants and the Preventing of the Clandestine Bringing of Negroes and Mulattoes," which passed in the Massachusetts House of Representatives on June 7, 1718.[85] These colonial legislative bodies passed these legal mandates to purify the new British American society of nonwhites.

In addition to his belief that slavery was sinful and contrary to the will of God, Hopkins believed that enslaved Africans were the most oppressed people of British colonial America and the early republic. Therefore, he argued that they were in the most need of disinterested benevolence.[86] As disciples of Edwards, the New Divinity theologians offered resolutions to the problem of Edwards's social contradictions in his disinterested benevolence. One resolution was Hopkins's argument that Blacks and whites were equal members of humanity, which contrasted directly with Edwards's ontological view of nonwhites in New England. Hopkins's argument against slavery was based on the Protestant idea of sin and the notion of covenant. He viewed slavery as an open violation of God's law[87] and attempted to convince Puritans of its sinfulness.[88] He, along with other New Divinity theologians, defined slavery as a sexual sin—a lustful version of sinfulness that was evident in the generations of American mulattos.[89]

New Divinity theologian Jonathan Edwards the younger, like his father, the New Light leader Jonathan Edwards, condemned the slave trade as

85. Lorenzo Johnston Greene, *The Negro in Colonial New England* (New York: Columbia University Press, 1968), 51.

86. Lovejoy, "Samuel Hopkins," 234.

87. Samuel Hopkins, "A Dialogue Concerning the Slavery of the Africans," in Douglas A. Sweeney and Allen C. Guelzo, eds., *The New England Theology: From Jonathan Edwards to Edwards Amasa Park* (Grand Rapids, MI: Baker Academic, 2006), 152.

88. Lovejoy, "Samuel Hopkins," 242.

89. John Saillant, "Slavery and Divine Providence in New England Calvinism: The New Divinity and a Black Protest, 1775–1805," *The New England Quarterly* 68, no. 4 (1995): 593–93.

unjust, cruel, wicked, and an abomination. He concluded that the cruelties of the slave trade and slavery caused the moral deprivation of slaveholders. Edwards the younger offered theological justifications for his condemnation of the slave trade and the institution of slavery to combat proslavery theologies. He rejected the Hamitic theory of proslavery theology, asserting that "it is indeed generally thought that Ham peopled Africa, but that the curse on Canaan extended to all the posterity of Ham is a mere imagination."[90] Edwards the younger's theological explanation for his rejection demonstrates the biblical inaccuracy of the Hamitic curse theory and the theological irrationality of the proslavery argument. He also rejected the theological idea that divine providence functioned as the source for the inferiority and enslavement of Africans and identified the practice of enslaving others as a sin greater than theft and fornication.[91] He characterized the phenomenon of enslavement as a crime, contending that "to hold a slave, who has a right to his liberty, is not only a real crime, but a very great one."[92] Edwards the younger concluded that the defense of slavery by Puritan progenitors was immoral and unbiblical.[93]

Hopkins posed a rhetorical question about the participation of Christians in the slave trade asking, "Is it not impossible that a real Christian . . . should have any hand in this trade?"[94] In addition to invalidating the Christian status of slaveholders, Hopkins believed that white colonists were under divine judgment for the sin of enslaving Africans. The New Divinity movement laid the foundation for the abolitionist idea of sending freed Blacks in America back to Africa so that they could evangelize the continent. In addition to the evangelization, his idea of returning freed Blacks to Africa was his scheme for ensuring their freedom.[95] Abolitionism was the heart of the New Divinity movement's social activism.

Some historians have concluded, however, that Hopkins's immigration proposal, which propelled the abolitionist movement, was a colonization scheme. Washington accurately concluded that Hopkins's abolitionist views reflected the position and work of paternalist abolitionists, which, he argued, constituted "Christianizing-civilizing-colonizing evangelicalism." Hopkins viewed his schema of Christianization-civilization-colonization as the benevolence of virtuous whites.[96] Hopkins's schema became the

90. Saillant, "Slavery and Divine Providence," 15.

91. Saillant, "Slavery and Divine Providence," 26.

92. Saillant, "Slavery and Divine Providence," 25.

93. Joseph R. Washington, *Anti-Blackness in English Religion, 1500–1800* (New York: Edwin Mellen Press, 1984), 316.

94. Hopkins, "A Dialogue," 155.

95. Lovejoy, "Samuel Hopkins," 241.

96. Saillant, "Slavery and Divine Providence," 595.

model for abolitionist societies such as the American Colonization Society (ACS), which was founded in 1818 by Robert Finley. The purpose of the ACS was to promote the immigration of freed Blacks to the continent of Africa and reflected the theology of disinterested benevolence of the New Divinity theologians, who believed that God had designed the enslavement of Africans for the purpose of Christianizing Ethiopia.[97]

Hopkins concluded that slaveholders and slave traders had dehumanized and oppressed enslaved Africans, but God would vindicate and liberate them with Christianity.[98] The problem with this reasoning is that many of the slaveholders were Christian. The contradiction in Hopkins's Christianizing-civilizing-colonizing schema lies in the reality that it was not for the sake of God's glory but for the fulfillment of paternalistic benevolence, which became the ultimate purpose of the ACS. Washington asserted that "the ACS presented itself as a Society of men engaged in a purely benevolent Christian enterprise: as if Colonizationists were an altruistic general interest agency completely devoid of all public, private, and parochial as well as other special interests."[99]

Christian paternalism emanated from the religion of antiblackness, which permeated the very fabric of British colonial America and the early republic, originating with the evangelical piety of Puritanism and the establishment of white Christianity in New England committed to prioritizing and preserving the superiority of whiteness, which required antiblackness. John Saillant argues that the theology of the New Divinity theologians and their racism nourished each other.[100] The primary reason behind Saillant's argument was that even with their views on the sinfulness of slavery, the New Divinity theologians attempted to correlate slavery with divine providence, concluding that God had suffered some to be slaves.[101] Additionally, the New Divinity theologians decried the reality that slavery was the catalyst for miscegenation, which further validates the notion that racism corrupted their theology.[102]

97. Saillant, "Slavery and Divine Providence," 584.
98. Saillant, "Slavery and Divine Providence," 594.
99. Saillant, "Slavery and Divine Providence," 589.
100. Saillant, "Slavery and Divine Providence," 597.
101. Saillant, "Slavery and Divine Providence," 597.
102. Saillant, "Slavery and Divine Providence," 593.

3

Anglicanism and White Privilege

*He who drove out the Canaanites and gave their land to Israel for a pos-
session has been pleased to drive out the Indians from Virginia and
gave it to the white men and to the most amiable race of savages which I
believe exists upon the earth, and which is far more ready to receive the
Gospel than the ferocious Indian.*

—Joseph R. Washington,
Anti-Blackness in English Religion, 1500–1800

In his ecclesiastical history of colonial Virginia, evangelical Anglican and
bishop of the Protestant Episcopal Church Reverend William Meade (1789–
1862) described his religion of antiblackness in terms of antibrownness. For
the British colonists in the New World the initial purpose for colonizing the
New World was to convert brown people (Native Americans) to the true religion. This changed once Black people replaced brown people as the major
spiritual and economic objects of the British colonists.[1] Joseph Washington
offers a vivid depiction of this phenomenon:

> Priorities were reversed for Anglican laymen as their pecuniary inter-
> est mounted blacks over browns. The spiritual interest became both
> secondary and instrumental to primary economic and political inter-
> ests. And from blacks, unlike whites and brown, the latter two were
> completely withheld. Planters wished to withdraw the spiritual also.
> The Anglican establishment stepped in with a compromised sense
> of equality: profit for whites in the here and now and for whites and
> blacks in the hereafter.[2]

---

1. Joseph R. Washington, *Anti-Blackness in English Religion, 1500–1800* (New York: The
Edwin Mellen Press, 1984), 418–19.
2. Washington, *Anti-Blackness in English Religion*, 419.

Meade, a slaveholder in Virginia, correlated Native Americans with the Canaanites and the British colonists in Virginia with the Israelites and demonstrated his religion of antiblackness as the integration of Puritan and evangelical ideologies.

Like Calvinistic-based Puritanism, white people become God's chosen few, and Native Americans, due to their reprobation, become the damned in God's providential plan. Meade regarded Native Americans' rejection of Anglo-American Christian authority as evidence of their reprobation. In his ecclesiastical history, he identified enslaved Africans in Virginia as "the most amiable race of savages" and asserted that they were suitable for Christian conversion, thereby defining the relationship between evangelicalism and imperialism and giving whites privilege over nonwhites (savages). This chapter explores this theology of white privilege and its basis in providential ideology, hereditary heathenism, Protestant or white supremacy, and proslavery paternalism, all of which are factors that characterized the Anglican planter class in British colonial America and the early republic. Furthermore, we will demonstrate that, through an examination of Anglican missions and evangelicalism, the response to this theology of white privilege moved from propagation to resistance.

Providence, Promised Land, and Colonization

Many Anglicans of the eighteenth and nineteenth centuries, such as Meade, possessed a theology of white privilege. European colonists in British colonial America and the early republic believed that Christianity passed naturally through their bloodline and that Native Americans were heathens.[3] Consequently, Christianity was the inheritance of white people and, therefore, a part of white privilege; based on this belief, British colonists created a racialized society in the New World. Latin American anthropologist Johnny Ramirez-Johnson and New Testament scholar Love L. Sechrest assert that "a racialized society is one that uses race for maintaining the power and economic advantage for some while others are permanently disadvantaged and subjugated."[4] They view privilege as "the critical resource mediated in racist societies."[5] For European colonists, white privilege was the most robust resource in their development of imperial colonization and sup-

---

3. David J. Silverman, "Racial Walls: Race and the Emergence of American White Nationalism," in Ignacio Gallup-Diaz, Andrew Shankman, and David J. Silverman, eds., *Anglicizing America: Empire, Revolution, Republic* (Philadelphia: University of Pennsylvania Press, 2015), 184.

4. Love L. Sechrest and Johnny Ramirez-Johnson, "Introduction," in Love L. Sechrest, Johnny Ramirez-Johnson, and Amos Yong, eds., *Can "White" People Be Saved?: Triangulating Race, Theology, and Mission* (Downers Grove, IL: InterVarsity Press, 2018), 8.

5. Sechrest, Ramirez-Johnson, and Yong, eds., *Can "White" People Be Saved?*, 11.

posed civilization of the New World and epitomized racism. Race and racial hierarchies determined the physical, social, cultural, and socio-economic realities of colonial inhabitants. Asian American historian of American Christianity Peter Y. Choi argues that British subjects of the eighteenth century earnestly believed that their citizenship in the British Empire was indeed a privilege.[6]

British colonists regarded empire as the "protector and guarantor of liberty, property, and Protestantism."[7] Two-thirds of the trustees of colonial Georgia were members of the British Parliament.[8] Southern colonies in British colonial America functioned as oligarchies with wealthy white males owning an overwhelming majority of the property, including enslaved Africans.[9] American historian David J. Silverman notes that as the British colonies transitioned into the early American republic, the basic features of life within the new republic were white superiority, Black degradation, and dispossession of Native Americans.[10]

Whiteness and White Supremacy

Whiteness and white supremacy proved interdependent factors in British colonial America and the early republic and naturally generated white privilege and the dehumanization, desocialization, and depersonalization of blackness.[11] Eric Weed contends that, based on the dualism of Christian and heathen, the power of whiteness has been the ultimate concern of the American nation since its founding; he characterizes white supremacy as a religion in America, asserting, "white supremacy is not a system of ultimate concern that is constructed in an *ex nihilo* fashion in the United States. The very bedrock of white supremacy is constructed out of the symbols and traditions of Protestant Christianity as they developed over the past five centuries."[12] In fact, he concludes that the dualism of Christian and heathen evolved from the ethos and religious language of white supremacy.[13] Consequently, European colonists in colonial America and the early republic are

---

6. Peter Y. Choi, *George Whitefield: Evangelist for God and Empire* (Grand Rapids, MI: Eerdmans, 2018), 84.

7. Andrew Shankman, "A Synthesis Useful and Compelling: Anglicization and the Achievement of John M. Murrin," in Gallup-Diaz et al., *Anglicizing America*, 37.

8. Choi, *George Whitefield*, 21.

9. Shankman, "A Synthesis Useful," 36.

10. Silverman, "Racial Walls" 181.

11. Eric A. Weed, *The Religion of White Supremacy in the United States* (Lanham, MD: Lexington Books, 2017), 3. Weed argues that the epistemology of whiteness manifested the ontology of white supremacy through colonialism in America, resulting in the correlation of white superiority and black inferiority.

12. Weed, *The Religion of White Supremacy*, xix–xx.

13. Weed, *The Religion of White Supremacy*, 4.

Christians through the religion of white supremacy, and non-Europeans are heathens possessing pagan spirituality.

Whiteness is a robust form of idolatry that results from participation in the religion of white supremacy. Ramirez-Johnson and Sechrest state that "white supremacy can be defined as the ideology that centers whiteness . . . creates and sustains institutions and practices that promote the social, political, and economic dominance of whites and the oppression of people of color."[14] Weed argues that the ontology of white supremacy transforms the epistemology of whiteness from whites being superior and civilized to nonwhites being inferior and deficient.[15] Whiteness was the colonial identity of British colonialists, who were empowered to control and police enslaved Africans. As such, Silverman concludes, "whiteness became the basic quality of citizenship and blackness the basic symbol of subordination."[16] Furthermore, white superiority was the racial wall of the Constitution for the new American republic.[17] Silverman built his conclusions on the scholarship of American historian John Murrin about the subject of race in British colonial America. Murrin concluded that "American citizens had to perceive themselves as white before they could define themselves as a people."[18]

Now, Anglicization was the imperial process through which whiteness and white privilege developed and functioned in British colonial America and the early republic. Indeed, Murrin argues that Anglicization caused a crisis of identity and conflict in the British colonies between non-English ethnic groups and the Anglicizers.[19] According to American historian Nancy L. Rhoden, part of this process involved Anglicanization, which constituted the consolidation and expansion of the Church of England in British colonial America as the official religious counterpart of the British state.[20] In her discussion on the origins of Anglicization, she argues that "it resulted from the efforts of British leaders in church and state as well as colonial laity and clergymen."[21] The English colonists integrated Anglicization and racialization, which shaped the white ideology of the eighteenth century.[22]

Anglican spirituality fostered an Anglicization that promoted the rela-

---

14. Sechrest, *Can "White" People Be Saved*, 13.

15. Weed, *The Religion of White Supremacy*, 18.

16. Weed, *The Religion of White Supremacy*, 196.

17. Silverman, "Racial Walls," 182.

18. Silverman, "Racial Walls," 203.

19. John M. Murrin, "England and Colonial America: A Novel Theory of the American Revolution," in Gallup-Diaz et al., *Anglicizing America*, 14–18.

20. Nancy L. Rhoden, "Anglicanism, Dissent, and Toleration in the Eighteenth-Century British Colonies," in Gallup-Diaz et al., *Anglicizing America*, 125.

21. Rhoden, "Anglicanism," 126.

22. Silverman, "Racial Walls," 182.

tionship between church and state as normative for the British Empire during the eighteenth century. Rhoden contends that "theologically offering a middle path between Roman Catholicism and extreme versions of Calvinism, the Church of England prided itself on its moderation. The regularity of its liturgy, set out in the Book of Common Prayer, provided a fixed script for community prayer and an opportunity to promote unity in church and state as well as offering a source of private daily devotional readings."[23] The formation of the Society for the Propagation of Gospel in Foreign Parts (SPG) in 1701 was a robust resource for Anglican spirituality within British colonial America. Due to the limited number of Anglican clerics in British colonial America, Anglican cleric Thomas Bray founded the society to function as the missionary arm of the Church of England and promote Anglican spirituality in the British colonies. In 1698, Bray formed the Society for the Promotion of Christian Knowledge (SPCK) to promote Christian education through the publication of Christian literature that communicated the basic principles of the Christian faith. The ethos of the SPG promoted Anglicanism as the true church.

Based on the laws of the British colonies, the Church of England constituted the established church. Anglicization dominated the southern colonies and influenced the cultivation and perpetuation of racial slavery. In fact, due to the success of Anglicization in cultivating white privilege and based on its belief in white supremacy, Murrin concludes that "slavery rather than democracy may have been the most truly American creation of the colonial period."[24]

Hereditary Heathenism

American historian Rebecca Goetz developed the notion of hereditary heathenism based on her examination of the integration of superiority and universality by Anglo-Virginians in the seventeenth and eighteenth centuries. During that time, Goetz argues, Anglo-Virginians constructed the idea of race using Christianity. Anglicanism constituted the religious establishment and as the religious product of the British Empire exuded white privilege through the belief in white supremacy. She defines hereditary heathenism as "the notion that Indians and Africans could never become Christian."[25]

In 1705, the legislature of colonial Virginia passed and enacted slave codes, which included the prohibition of Christian conversion for enslaved

---

23. Rhoden, "Anglicanism," 133.

24. Murrin, "England and Colonial America," 12.

25. Rebecca Anne Goetz, *The Baptism of Early Virginia: How Christianity Created Race* (Baltimore, MD: Johns Hopkins University Press, 2012), 3.

Africans, and validated the Anglo-Virginian belief in hereditary heathenism. The English planter class in the New World believed that Native
Americans and enslaved Africans were inherently incapable of becoming
Christian, thus justifying their dehumanization of Native Americans and
enslavement of Africans.[26] Goetz asserts that "by questioning the ability
of Africans to become Christians, settlers defined both their own religious
and cultural identity and the identities of the Indians they lived beside and
the Africans they owned."[27]

Many Europeans viewed religion as hereditary. Therefore, the ideology
and praxis of hereditary heathenism were not difficult to impose on the
Native Americans and enslaved Africans in colonial Virginia. Furthermore,
this ideology stemmed from the religion of white supremacy, which promoted the dualism of Christian and heathen. In their quest for political,
social, cultural, and economic power, Anglo-Virginians created a world
that equated whiteness with Christianity.[28] Essentially, the English colonists cultivated Christianity as a racial identity; and as such, it was reserved
for whites only and was antithetical to nonwhite heathens. Goetz contends
that hereditary heathenism became the model used by other colonies in the
English Atlantic.[29]

White privilege was the culprit in establishing racial identities. In 1667,
the Virginia House of Burgesses passed a law stipulating that partaking in
the sacrament of baptism did not constitute the manumission of enslaved
persons. Goetz argued that "this law allowed Anglo-Virginians to create
a Christianity in which the traditional privileges of an Englishman, most
notably freedom, were denied to Africans and Indians."[30] Christianity,
therefore, became the vehicle through which Europeans defined human
difference and reinforced human unity.[31] This corruption of the Christian
faith—the notion of hereditary heathenism—was at the core of Anglicanism and its theology of white privilege. This created conflict between the
English planter class and Anglican missionaries, who challenged the notion
of hereditary heathenism through their advocacy for the Christian conversion of enslaved Africans. Some of the Anglo-Virginian enslavers viewed the
Christianity of enslaved Africans as vile hypocrisy.[32] Proslavery ideologies
corrupted biblical interpretation, such as the Hamitic curse theory, and the

---

26. Goetz, *The Baptism of Early Virginia*, 2.

27. Goetz, *The Baptism of Early Virginia*, 111.

28. Goetz, *The Baptism of Early Virginia*, 6.

29. Goetz, *The Baptism of Early Virginia*, 6. There was a "colonial link between being
Christian and being English, and being black and being heathen," therefore, Goetz concluded
that "Negro and Christian were opposing identities in Virginia," 4.

30. Goetz, *The Baptism of Early Virginia*, 86.

31. Goetz, *The Baptism of Early Virginia*, 4.

32. Goetz, *The Baptism of Early Virginia*, 160.

theology of the sacraments, all of which strengthened and perpetuated the concept of hereditary heathenism.

The Virginia law of 1667 was intended to encourage the baptism of enslaved Africans in colonial Virginia. Enslaved Africans there viewed partaking in the sacrament as their path to liberation. The 1667 law, however, had the opposite effect because it discouraged the Christian baptism of enslaved Africans. According to Goetz, the law was meant to combat "the heathenish behaviors and heretical racial ideas of Virginia's planters." However, "the very language of capability, which Virginia's burgesses perhaps thought would mitigate the issue of freedom by encouraging slaveholders to baptize at least children, paradoxically encouraged planters to think of their slaves as completely incapable of ever being Christian—as hereditary heathens."[33]

The exclusionary nature of hereditary heathenism weaponized Anglo-Virginians legally, theologically, and sacramentally against supposed non-white heathens. Lack of English baptism constituted exclusion from the Christian community, and especially the Anglican communion. Anglo-Virginians exploited the Anglican dependency on the sacrament of baptism, and Christianity became the vehicle of separation and oppression against nonwhites, with baptism as a tool of conquest, salvation, assimilation, and inclusion in religious and political contexts of the British Empire.[34]

Christian Conversion and Slavery

The corruption of the Christian faith is evident in the various views of Christian conversion for enslaved Africans among slaveholders. Anglican clerics in colonial Virginia attempted to devise a scheme for the Christian conversion of Native Americans and enslaved Africans by affirming the legal and moral status of slavery. Goetz postulates that Anglican clergy and missionaries made a deal with the devil in engaging the Anglo-Virginian planter class on the relationship between Christian conversion and slavery.[35] To reject the conversion of Native Americans and enslaved Africans, some Anglican clerics argued that hereditary heathens were incapable of giving an account of their Christian faith.[36] Some Anglican clerics even viewed the Christian conversion of supposed heathens as "a prostitution of a thing so sacred."[37] Secular colonial authorities even challenged the

---

33. Goetz, *The Baptism of Early Virginia*, 107. Goetz concluded that the passage of the 1667 law legalized the notion of hereditary heathenism in colonial Virginia upholding the enslavement of Africans and creating race.

34. Goetz, *The Baptism of Early Virginia*, 89–90.

35. Goetz, *The Baptism of Early Virginia*, 139–40.

36. Goetz, *The Baptism of Early Virginia*, 143.

37. Goetz, *The Baptism of Early Virginia*, 151.

Christian conversion of Native Americans and enslaved Africans based on white privilege. The Virginia colonial assembly questioned the intellectual capacity of enslaved persons to comprehend Christianity and therefore also questioned the authority of their conversion experiences.[38]

Nevertheless, some English slaveholders ignored the notion of hereditary heathenism and endorsed the Christian conversion of the nonwhite heathens. They believed that Native Americans and enslaved Africans suffered from savagery and that Christian conversion was the remedy as well as the catalyst for the development of civility.[39] Additionally, others believed that Christian conversion would make enslaved persons more docile.[40] Whether hereditary heathenism, conversion for civility, or conversion for docility, each of these views reflected the imperial nature of white privilege that shaped the racist ideologies of Anglo-Virginians.

The enslaved Africans in colonial Virginia rejected the notion of hereditary heathenism and challenged the Anglo-Virginian planter class and Anglican clerics on their espousal of such a dehumanizing ideology. Goetz argues that "the connection between hereditary enslavement and heathenism was a site for constant conflict and negotiation among planters, missionaries, and enslaved people."[41] Enslaved Africans challenged the institution of slavery and attempted to undermine hereditary heathenism, using Christianity to articulate their spirituality and rejection of slavery.[42] A common historical misnomer suggests that Africans were not introduced to the Christian faith until after enslavement and forced migration to the New World. While it is accurate that they were not introduced to European Christianity before enslavement in the New World, we must remember that European Christianity is only one form of Christianity. Enslaved Africans most likely possessed knowledge of the Christian faith, and, indeed, some were Christians before enslavement and employed their Creole indigenous spirituality and faith to resist and condemn the institution of slavery. There were enslaved Africans in Virginia who had been Catholics and, therefore, could identify with Anglicanism since both traditions were relatively similar. Enslaved Africans possessed a radically different view of Christianity from that of their slaveholders. The Christianity of enslaved Africans advocated for Christian abolitionism, which was based on "the idea that slavery and Christianity were fundamentally opposed for both slave owners and enslaved people alike."[43] While some of the Anglican clerics and mission-

38. Goetz, *The Baptism of Early Virginia*, 105.
39. Goetz, *The Baptism of Early Virginia*, 89.
40. Goetz, *The Baptism of Early Virginia*, 158.
41. Goetz, *The Baptism of Early Virginia*, 139.
42. Goetz, *The Baptism of Early Virginia*, 162.
43. Goetz, *The Baptism of Early Virginia*, 167.

aries in colonial Virginia rejected and challenged the notion of hereditary heathenism, their adherence to the theology and ideology of white privilege hindered them from rejecting and condemning slavery.

One of Goetz's primary arguments is that the English settlers in colonial Virginia invented race and used Christianity to foster human differentiation.[44] Her argument explains the shift from the universality of Christianity in the seventeenth century to its exclusivity in the eighteenth century. Religious diversity in colonial Virginia was pivotal to the construction of race, defying the Church of England's enforcement of Anglicanism as the established church.[45] Race, rather than religion, constituted the most important category of difference. Goetz concludes, therefore, that "Anglo-Virginians were more willing to accept dissenting white Christians, as long as the benefits of Christianity were not extended to enslaved people."[46]

While Goetz's argument concerning the invention of race is very compelling, the argument that Anglo-Virginians adopted Enlightenment theories of race is probably more accurate. The idea that the English constructed race has become a common scholastic argument in the field of American religious historiography and is often used to define modern racism. In the sixteenth century, many marriages in the English world were between African men and English women and were based on membership in the Church of England, suggesting that the African men were baptized members of the established church. As Goetz correctly argues, the sacrament of baptism solidified one's status in the Christian community. However, the Anglo-Virginians' notion of hereditary heathenism transformed English Christianity into a racial identity characterized solely by whiteness. By equating whiteness with Christianity, Anglo-Virginians viewed the baptism of nonwhites as not validating their membership in the Christianity community; it only made them honorary white persons. In other words, baptism did not change the status of nonwhites in Anglo-Virginian society.

Protestant Supremacy as White Supremacy

American historian Katharine Gerbner argues that the English colonists used Protestant supremacy to make Christianity a form of racial identity. She develops this idea by examining the anticonversion sentiment among Protestant traditions, which she concludes was "one of the defining features of Protestant slave societies in the seventeenth and eighteenth cen-

---

44. Goetz, *The Baptism of Early Virginia*, 170.

45. Goetz, *The Baptism of Early Virginia*, 7.

46. Goetz, *The Baptism of Early Virginia*, 7.

turies."[47] She claims that Protestant planters created Protestant supremacy to make Christian identity an exclusive ideal of religion based on ethnicity and incompatible with slavery.[48]

In the seventeenth century, Anglican slaveholders believed that being Protestant constituted freedom. Gerbner asserts that "the association between Protestantism and freedom was so strong that most slave owners came to dismiss the idea that their slaves were eligible for conversion."[49]

Protestant supremacy perpetuated the Christian and heathen dualism within Protestant traditions and also excluded enslaved people from established churches.[50] Protestant slaveholders correlated Protestant supremacy with Christian status and whiteness, thus replacing the religious language of the Protestant Christian faith with the language of race.[51] By 1700, whiteness had replaced Christianity as the primary indicator of freedom.[52] Protestant slaveholders used Christianity as an ethnic category, "white," in opposition to enslaved Africans.

The Protestant planter class begins to define slavery based on racial rather than religious terms, replacing Protestant supremacy with white supremacy.[53] Gerbner defines Protestant whiteness as the resistance of the Protestant planter class to slave conversion and the support of the established church in preserving the power of the planter class.[54] Despite efforts of the established church to empower the Protestant planter class and perpetuate Protestant supremacy and white supremacy through anticonversion sentiment, some Protestant missionaries, as we saw with the English slaveholders in the previous section, attempted to promote a Christian vision of slavery.

Protestant conversion for enslaved Africans was full of ambiguity. For example, some missionaries believed that true freedom constituted spiritual freedom that liberated the soul, and not manumission, which liberated the physical body. Others used conversion as a rhetorical weapon to manipulate enslaved Africans. Some promoted the idea that conversion would introduce these inferior heathens to the superior English civilization,[55]

---

47. Katharine Gerbner, *Christian Slavery: Conversion and Race in the Protestant Atlantic World* (Philadelphia: University of Pennsylvania Press, 2018), 2.

48. Gerbner, *Christian Slavery*, 2. Gerbner argues that Protestant Supremacy was most robust in the plantation colonies of the Atlantic world, especially where the enslaved population was in the majority

49. Gerbner, *Christian Slavery*, 2.

50. Gerbner, *Christian Slavery*, 31.

51. Gerbner, *Christian Slavery*, 30, 48.

52. Gerbner, *Christian Slavery*, 74–75.

53. Gerbner, *Christian Slavery*, 153.

54. Gerbner, *Christian Slavery*, 75.

55. Gerbner, *Christian Slavery*, 28.

while other Protestant missionaries viewed Christian conversion as a tool to make the heathen enslaved Africans more docile and subordinate.

Protestant missionaries envisioned converting enslaved Africans to a paternalistic form of Christianity with the hope of benevolent treatment. Evangelical Protestants attempted to convince the planter class of the need for a more inclusive and paternalistic Christianity.[56] In the nineteenth century, most white planters came to embrace this paternalistic vision that integrated human bondage with Christian duty and evangelization.[57] Before the evangelical awakenings of the eighteenth century, some enslaved and free Black Christians had undermined the ideology of Protestant supremacy through engagement in Protestant rituals and affiliation with Protestant churches.[58] The baptism of enslaved and free Blacks challenged the Protestant slaveholders' theological justifications for the institution of slavery. However, some reserved this white privilege of baptism for their most trusted enslaved Africans, a practice that was reflected mostly in their treatment of enslaved mulatto/a children.[59]

The enslaved mulatto/a—a person of mixed race—was generally the illegitimate offspring of the slaveholder. Mulatto theologian Brian Bantum identifies the mulatto/a vividly as "children of rape, illicit desire, and even possibly love. . . . Mixed-race children were in between the categories of colonizer and colonized, human and nonhuman, slave and free."[60] Some historians have claimed that the creation of enslaved mixed-race persons was intended by the slaveholder to form a schism within the enslaved population on the plantation. Generally, the mulatto/a functioned as a house slave and was treated with much more benevolence than the field slave, perpetuating the house slave/field slave distinction and fostering conflict within the enslaved community. In the British colonies, mulatto/a children were more likely to be baptized than Negro children.[61]

As we have noted, Protestantism was one of the foundational features in the development of Christian slavery and proslavery ideologies. Protestant planters, missionaries, and clerics perpetuated white privilege in the New World and justified religious exclusion based on race. Early Anglican Protestants viewed themselves as pure and free, and this purity was the product of their white privilege, and the freedom was a product of their Protestant Christianity. Nonwhite heathens did not possess this freedom

---

56. Gerbner, *Christian Slavery*, 195.
57. Gerbner, *Christian Slavery*, 190.
58. Gerbner, *Christian Slavery*, 11.
59. Gerbner, *Christian Slavery*, 80.
60. Brian Bantum, *Redeeming Mulatto: A Theology of Race and Christian Hybridity* (Waco, TX: Baylor University Press, 2010), 15.
61. Bantum, *Redeeming Mulatto*, 77.

and were, therefore, eligible for enslavement, even after Christian conversion, which constituted only spiritual freedom, not physical freedom. Furthermore, while the English Protestants initially viewed their freedom as a product of their emancipation from Catholicism, Christian slavery shifted their understanding of freedom to being white, and Anglicanism played a pivotal role in this shift and in perpetuating slavery.[62]

Proslavery Paternalism

American historian Charles Irons examines the biracial aspect of evangelicalism in colonial Virginia and situates the origins of proslavery Christianity within the relationship between Black and white evangelicals. His primary argument is that whites based their theological defense of slavery on the spiritual initiatives of enslaved Africans.[63] Contrary to traditional American historiography, there were enslaved Africans in colonial Virginia with knowledge of Christianity before their forced migration to the New World.[64] Despite Anglicanism's opposition to the enslavement of fellow baptized Christians, English colonists developed theological presuppositions based on Scripture in favor of such enslavement.

In the seventeenth century, some Anglican colonists adopted the curse of Ham theory as their primary scriptural justification for slavery. Based on their interpretation of Genesis 9, Anglo-Virginians believed that "English indentured servants, most of whom were baptized into the Anglican Church as infants, were the equivalent of the biblical *eved ivri* (Hebrew slaves), while men and women of African descent fit the description of *eved canaani* (non-Hebrew slaves).[65] Such scriptural interpretation automatically eliminated people of African descent from the divine covenant of promise, thereby validating their enslavement as providential.

Ironically, the evangelical community in colonial Virginia was biracial, consisting of Black and white evangelicals; but many Anglicans refused to accept this biracial nature of evangelical Christianity.[66] Various linguistic, cultural, and theological factors, including the curse-of-Ham ideology, created a dilemma for some Anglicans about including enslaved Africans in the body of Christ, and some English colonists were criticized for prohibiting enslaved Africans in Anglican churches.[67] Dissenting white evangelical

---

62. Michael Guasco, *Slaves and Englishmen: Human Bondage in the Early Modern Atlantic World* (Philadelphia: University of Pennsylvania Press, 2014), 32.

63. Charles F. Irons, *The Origins of Proslavery Christianity: White and Black Evangelicals* (Chapel Hill: University of North Carolina Press, 2008), 2.

64. Irons, *The Origins of Proslavery Christianity*, 24.

65. Irons, *The Origins of Proslavery Christianity*, 25.

66. Irons, *The Origins of Proslavery Christianity*, 33.

67. Irons, *The Origins of Proslavery Christianity*, 23–25.

preachers offered enslaved Africans in Virginia worship privileges, which some Anglican clerics viewed as a threat to their religious establishment and the racial hierarchy.[68]

Many Anglicans feared that converting enslaved Africans might cause them to assume that their conversion constituted emancipation.[69] In 1727, the bishop of London addressed this concern and assured English slaveholders that conversion would not change the civil status of enslaved persons.[70] Anglicans viewed the conversion of heathens as their Christian duty, but their economic benefit from slavery was a greater priority. Despite this fear, after conversion, enslaved Africans still equated Christian conversion with liberation from enslavement.

Black Evangelical Christianity

The Chesapeake Rebellion of 1730 reflected the spiritual independence of Black Virginians in the eighteenth century. Baptized enslaved Africans in Virginia revolted to achieve liberation. They regarded the institution of slavery and Christianity as incompatible and planned and executed the rebellion on a Sunday morning, while their white slaveholders were at worship.

In 1680, Anglican cleric Morgan Godwyn expressed his discontent with the failure of Anglo-Virginians to incorporate Native Americans and enslaved Africans in the Anglican communion.[71] Some Anglicans adhered to Godwyn's admonition and permitted enslaved Africans to participate in the sacraments, which they viewed as an act of benevolence.[72] Godwyn's advocacy for the conversion and catechetical teaching of enslaved Africans and his view of enslavement as a benevolent enterprise further developed and promoted proslavery theology. Anglo-Virginians of the religious establishment (Church of England) and colonial evangelicals perpetuated proslavery theology through their refusal to confront the problem of slavery either because of inaction or through intentional and complicit participation in the slave trade and institution of slavery.

At the heart of Black evangelical Christianity was resistance to the sinful act of enslavement. Black resistance caused problems for white evangelicals. Irons notes that evangelicalism in colonial Virginia had begun

68. Irons, *The Origins of Proslavery Christianity*, 36.

69. Irons, *The Origins of Proslavery Christianity*, 27.

70. Irons, *The Origins of Proslavery Christianity*, 30. At the time of this episcopal address from the bishop of London, Anglicans were still committed to the conversion of Native Americans. However, the campaign to convert Native Americans proved an exercise in futility for Anglicans. Therefore, the focus shifted to the enslaved Africans.

71. Irons, *The Origins of Proslavery Christianity*, 30.

72. Irons, *The Origins of Proslavery Christianity*, 28.

as biracial but unequal.[73] In eighteenth- and nineteenth-century Virginia, evangelicalism was biracial; white evangelicals demonized the skin color of Black evangelicals but affirmed their evangelical spirituality as evidence of their salvation.[74] What is problematic here is the universalization of Black evangelicals during this period. Just as there were theological differences among white evangelicals, as evident in the theological presuppositions of John Wesley and George Whitefield, there were theological differences among Black evangelicals. There were Black Calvinist evangelicals and Black radical evangelicals. The major theological differences between these two groups will be addressed in later chapters. However, due to their shared belief that conversion constituted liberation from slavery, Black evangelicals insisted that the institution of slavery and the Christian religion were incompatible.[75] Consequently, Black evangelicals aligned themselves with antislavery clerics and connected evangelicalism and liberation with a resistance to slavery.[76] Because of their white-privilege theology, white evangelicals promoted proslavery theology, espousing the belief that African enslavement was providentially part of God's divine plan.[77] Furthermore, the nature of the black and white binary that reinforced the heathen and Christian dualism undergirded the white evangelical defense of proslavery theology.

In the eighteenth and nineteenth centuries, white evangelical Christianity in British colonial America and the early republic functioned as white Christian proslavery paternalism, which espoused the belief that the conversion of enslaved Africans eradicated the notion of being heathen; and therefore, whites could not treat enslaved Africans as heathens.[78] White paternalism constituted the concerted effort of white evangelicals to civilize uncivilized enslaved Africans through Christianity.[79] White evangelicals regarded proslavery paternalism as a form of Christian virtue and ethics based on compassion and Christian duty. It became the vehicle through which Christian slaveholders justified the institution of slavery as righteous in that it constituted the spiritual and physical nurture that white men owed to enslaved Africans.[80] Irons notes that "in biracial evangelical churches, whites and blacks negotiated the set of reciprocal obligations that characterized paternalism."[81] He identifies benevolent paternalism as

73. Irons, *The Origins of Proslavery Christianity*, 18.
74. Irons, *The Origins of Proslavery Christianity*, 103.
75. Irons, *The Origins of Proslavery Christianity*, 31.
76. Irons, *The Origins of Proslavery Christianity*, 51.
77. Irons, *The Origins of Proslavery Christianity*, 43.
78. Irons, *The Origins of Proslavery Christianity*, 18.
79. Irons, *The Origins of Proslavery Christianity*, 12.
80. Irons, *The Origins of Proslavery Christianity*, 89.
81. Irons, *The Origins of Proslavery Christianity*, 88.

the paternalism of white evangelicals, which "with all of its assumptions of racial hierarchy was an adequate substitution for antislavery."[82]

Godwyn reflected this white Christian paternalism as one of the earliest Anglican missionaries promoting the catechization of enslaved Africans. Similarly, Bishop William Fleetwood, who did not view slavery as an "inhumane practice," affirmed the full humanity of enslaved Africans and simultaneously concluded that Christianity required the humanitarianism of slaveholders, not the freedom of the enslaved. Fleetwood believed that Christian slavery sealed enslaved Africans in Christ.

The ethic of benevolent paternalism proved an inefficient replacement for abolitionism and fostered the development of Black radical evangelicals. At the heart of Black radical evangelicalism was spiritual resistance, which we discuss in chap. 5. Black radical evangelicals such as David Walker and Nat Turner led the resistance of enslaved Africans against the white superiority, white supremacy, and white privilege of their white slaveholders.

Slaveholders believed that the catalyst for slave rebellions and insurrections was the catechetical teachings that fostered pedagogical methods giving enslaved Africans the ability to read and write. The slave-master class rejection of literacy for enslaved persons was most evident in the formation of plantation missions, which developed because of the critique and condemnation of slaveholders. Abolitionists accused slaveholders of neglecting the spiritual welfare of enslaved Africans with the prohibition of catechetical teaching enacted through antiliteracy legislation. Therefore, the religious establishment and evangelical denominations created plantation missions in collaboration with slaveholders to defend the institution of slavery against slave rebellions and insurrections; the missions were intentionally designed to foster docility, subordination, and assimilation by means of religion within the slave class. Love Henry Whelchel characterizes this phenomenon as "Religion without Letters."[83]

The white preachers of the plantation missions shifted from teaching the catechetical foundations of the Christian faith (such as the Apostles' Creed, Ten Commandments, and the Lord's Prayer) to teaching slaves orally about the imperative of honoring and obeying the slave master. For example, the slave was to

Count their masters "worthy of all honor," as those whom God has placed over them in this world: "with all fear," they are to be "subject to them," obey them in all things, possible and lawful, with good

---

82. Irons, *The Origins of Proslavery Christianity*, 88.
83. Love Henry Whelchel, *Hell without Fire: Conversion in Slave Religion* (Nashville, TN: Abingdon Press, 2002), 70.

will, and endeavor to please them well ... and let Servants serve their
masters as faithfully behind their backs as before their faces. God is
present to see, if their masters are not. Should they fall into the hands
of hard and unjust and unequal masters, and suffer wrongfully, their
course according to divine command is to take it patiently, referring
their case to God; looking to him for support in their trials, and for
rewards for their patience. And the Lord will surely remember them.[84]

Consequently, the work of the white preacher in the plantation mission
epitomized the nature and purpose of proslavery theology. Plantation missions functioned as a domesticated form of the missionary work reflected
in the efforts of the SPG, but with greater English planter class cooperation
and supervision.

George Whitefield's Revivalism

Evangelical Anglican George Whitefield was a product of John and Charles
Wesley's Holy Club at Oxford University. Whitefield popularized the evangelical emphasis on the necessity of new birth for Christian believers
through open-air preaching, which was an appealing feature of his revivalism in England and soon became a transatlantic phenomenon. Despite
this, Whitefield abandoned his Anglican identity. In her scholarship on
Whitefield, American historian Jessica M. Parr notes the conflict between
Anglican clerics and evangelical Anglicans and claims that "Whitefield
was, in some ways, a convenient target for Anglicans who saw revivalism as
a danger and hoped to establish Anglicanism as the true religion."[85] Many
Anglicans, except for the evangelical Anglicans of the Wesleyan Methodist
movement, rejected what they viewed as the dominance of religious enthusiasm within Whitefield's revivalism. In response to this rejection, revivalists spread the notion that the Anglican Church was spiritually dead.[86]
Rhoden concludes that revivalism during this period undermined clerical
authority and imperial bureaucracy, resulting in religious pluralism and
fragmentation.[87]

The effective and controversial nature of Whitefield's revivalism in the
British Empire proved the Great Awakening to be a social and political phenomenon as well as a religious one. In addition to his open-air preaching,

---

84. Mason Crum, *Gullah: Negro Life in Carolina Sea Islands* (New York: Negro Universities
Press, 1968), 205.

85. Jessica M. Parr, *Inventing George Whitefield: Race, Revivalism, and the Making of a
Religious Icon* (Jackson: University Press of Mississippi, 2015), 79.

86. Rhoden, "Anglicanism," 135.

87. Rhoden, "Anglicanism," 134.

itinerancy, and emphasis on regeneration, Whitefield also dominated the printing press of colonial America through which he promoted his revivalism and printed his sermons.[88] Whitefield initially emphasized evangelical heart religion and absolutized regeneration as the requirement of authentic Christianity.[89] However, because of his imperial leanings, Whitefield's revivalism shifted from an emphasis on evangelical conversion to the development and maintenance of religious and political bureaucracy. Choi concludes that just as Wesley declared "the world is my parish," Whitefield should have declared "the empire is my parish."[90]

Whitefield served as the theological agent of the British Empire, and his Calvinist inclinations became the theology of the new empire in British colonial America. The dissenting nature of Whitefield's message and his revivalism fueled the Anglican critique of his revivals as forms of religious hypocrisy.[91] Whitefield's Anglican critics condemned his revivalism as "imported divinity," asserting that his revivals were not indigenous to the colonies as were the Edwardsean revivals in Northampton, Massachusetts, and the Tennent revivals in New Jersey but were imported from England.[92] American historian Frank Lambert argues that Whitefield's revivalism reflected colonial culture because his sermons were rehearsed and revivals well publicized, and therefore, had been prepackaged.[93] In addition to the charge of "imported divinity," Whitefield's revivalism epitomized "imperial divinity." Empire shaped the Great Awakening as it occurred in the context of empire.[94]

Evangelical Calvinism

As a follower of the Wesleyan Methodists, Whitefield initially opposed slavery and vehemently condemned the practice as evil. However, his embrace and adoption of Reformed theology caused a shift in his beliefs that correlated with the political and economic priorities of the British Empire, which favored proslavery theology and advocacy. The British Empire influenced Whitefield's spirituality and his hermeneutical approach to Scripture.

While Whitefield was influenced by Puritan Calvinism, his revivalism and Methodist sensibilities fostered the shift from Puritanism to evangeli-

---

88. Frank Lambert, *Inventing the Great Awakening* (Princeton, NJ: Princeton University Press, 1999), 87–124.
89. Choi, *George Whitefield*, 30.
90. Choi, *George Whitefield*, 102.
91. Parr, *Inventing George Whitefield*, 61.
92. Lambert, *Inventing the Great Awakening*, 87–124.
93. Lambert, *Inventing the Great Awakening*, 87–124.
94. Choi, *George Whitefield*, 2.

cal Calvinism. The Puritan influence caused him to favor individual agency over institutional authority[95] and had a vast impact on Whitefield's evangelical preaching and revivalism through which he developed a grassroots folk religiosity that appealed to the masses in the southern colonies of British colonial America. Choi identifies Whitefield as a "Neo-Puritan" in that "the far-reaching aspirational quality of his ministry derived fuel from the Puritan vision of divine sovereignty but also, over time, cultural validation and empowerment on the broad canvas of a growing empire."[96] Whitefield's evangelical Calvinism fostered his justification for imperial slavery. Whitefield's paternalism predated his proslavery theology.[97] He believed that enslaved Africans were humans but subordinate creatures.[98]

Whitefield used Scripture to justify African enslavement and concluded that enslaving Africans was a part of God's providential plan; he became the most ardent advocate for the legalization of slavery in the colony of Georgia, citing the political, social, and economic benefits the colony would procure through the legalization of African enslavement.[99] He even suggested that the colony would have been more advanced and experienced more economic prosperity had slavery been legalized in the colony of Georgia prior to 1751.

In his defense of African enslavement, Whitefield adopted the view of Enlightenment thinkers such as Georges-Louis Leclerc, who, as we noted earlier, had argued that native people of cold climates were civilized, productive, and beautiful. Adopting this ideology as his own, which validated his view of enslaved Africans as "subordinate creatures," Whitefield believed that Blacks could develop only in hot climates, further justifying the legalization of slavery in Georgia. Whitefield also used Scripture to justify slavery, such as the biblical overture of Ethiopia from Psalm 68:31, which became the common nomenclature of self-identification for Black Calvinist evangelicals such as Phillis Wheatley, over whom he had direct theological influence. To advocate for the legalization of slavery, he further connected the potential plight of enslaved Africans in Georgia with the plight of perpetual slavery for the Gibeonites.

Whitefield's evangelistic revivalism had great appeal and influence on Black Calvinist evangelicals, such as Phillis Wheatley and Lemuel Haynes. Parr asserts that Whitefield's "revivalism had a remarkable impact on the conversion of African slaves to Christianity. It provided the means for a

---

95. Choi, *George Whitefield*, 30.
96. Choi, *George Whitefield*, 30.
97. Parr, *Inventing George Whitefield*, 65.
98. Parr, *Inventing George Whitefield*, 65.
99. Parr, *Inventing George Whitefield*, 76.

reconfiguration of their (religious) cultural heritage."[100] In addition to his revivalism, Whitefield emphasized the imperative of catechesis for enslaved Africans. True to his British ancestry, Whitefield believed that Christianity was the source of civilization for subordinate creatures (heathens). Whitefield fully endorsed and enacted the imperial scheme of Christianization, colonization, and civilization and viewed the indigenous spirituality of enslaved Africans as a threat to the new American empire. Parr contended that "slaves who practiced traditional religious rituals were undermining not only civil control but also an important nonsecular control. One of Whitefield's justifications for owning slaves was to catechize them, bringing them under legal, social, and moral control."[101]

In 1762, the trustees of colonial Georgia enacted a slave code that forbade slave labor on Sundays and required slaveholders to catechize enslaved Africans.[102] Whitefield's instruction of enslaved Africans led some to embrace abolitionism. Due to the influence of Whitefield's catechism, Wheatley viewed Christianity as an equalizer for the enslaved African. In her poetic prose to William, Earl of Dartmouth, Wheatley exclaimed:

> *HAIL, happy day, when smiling like the morn,*
> *Fair Freedom rose New-England to adorn:*
> *The northern clime beneath her genial ray,*
> *Dartmouth, congratulates thy blissful sway;*
> *Elate with hope her race no longer mourns,*
> *Each soul expands, each grateful bosom burns,*
> *While in thine hand with pleasure we behold*
> *The silken reins, and Freedom's charm unfold.*[103]

Haynes embraced Whitefield's notion of universal spiritual equality. He condemned slavery, believing that it was "morally and politically incompatible with American values."[104] Selina Hastings (Countess of Huntingdon) financially championed the cause of Methodist Calvinism; and, in addition to her consummate support for the revivalism of Whitefield, she was also a benefactor of Black Calvinist evangelicals. However, she did not embrace the cause of abolitionism, believing that such matters were in God's hands.[105]

Imperial motivations propelled Whitefield's imperial project in the

---

100. Parr, *Inventing George Whitefield*, 79.

101. Parr, *Inventing George Whitefield*, 74.

102. Parr, *Inventing George Whitefield*, 76.

103. Phillis Wheatley, "To the Right Honorable William Legge, Earl of Dartmouth," in *Phillis Wheatley: Complete Writings* (New York: Penguin Books, 2001), 128.

104. Parr, *Inventing George Whitefield*, 152.

105. Parr, *Inventing George Whitefield*, 148.

southern colonies through his unique British Protestant preaching.[106] Before Whitefield's missionary enterprise in the American colonies, the New England colonies were the most Anglicized of British colonial America.[107] The southern colonies were the most Americanized and driven most by African enslavement. As a penal colony designed for British debtors, Georgia was fertile ground for Whitefield's vision of benevolent Christianity. Therefore, Whitefield avoided the New England colonies and focused his efforts on the southern colonies, particularly Georgia and South Carolina.[108] However, the economic plight of poor British subjects not only was connected to the spiritual objectives of Whitefield's revivalism but, as Parr contends, was also a way of "simultaneously fulfilling religious duty and investing in the cause of a Protestant empire."[109]

In addition to Whitefield's Calvinist shift and imperial motivations, there were personal interests behind his advocacy for the legalization of slavery. Due to his pursuit of the orphanage project, he became derelict in his parish duties in Savannah. Choi suggests that in addition to the possible philanthropic work and religious motivations, Whitefield was recruiting orphans already in decent homes for his economic benefit.[110] If Choi is correct, it would nullify Whitefield's supposed vision of benevolent Christianity and strongly situate him in the commercial revolution of the British Empire, which was driven by capitalistic greed through the exploitation of human bodies and was the primary interest of the trustees of Georgia in their cultivation of the colony.

Benevolent Christianity

Whitefield's evangelical preaching and teaching cultivated docility within enslaved Africans on the South Carolina and Georgia plantations. Whitefield believed that the institution of slavery reflected his vision of benevolent Christianity through which enslaved Africans would receive adequate catechetical teaching. As such, he epitomized Christian proslavery paternalism, a view that he possessed before his embrace of African enslavement.[111] Parr maintains that "when Whitefield embraced slavery, he did so on both paternalistic and economic grounds."[112]

Despite being a slave apologist and proslavery theologian, Whitefield's paternalism eventually led him supposedly to abhor the horrors of slavery.

---

106. Parr, *Inventing George Whitefield*, 15.
107. Shankman, "A Synthesis Useful," 34.
108. Shankman, "A Synthesis Useful," 31.
109. Choi, *George Whitefield*, 26.
110. Choi, *George Whitefield*, 151.
111. Choi, *George Whitefield*, 64–66.
112. Choi, *George Whitefield*, 64.

In 1740, Whitefield avoided theologizing about the practice of slavery but theologized instead about the treatment of enslaved Africans at the hands of their slaveholders. He urged slaveholders to treat enslaved Africans with at least the same level of care that they bestowed upon their animals. In the same letter, Whitefield warned against the cruel and heinous treatment of enslaved Africans and cited some divinely imposed consequences for such treatment.

Whitefield undoubtedly referred to the Stono Rebellion of 1739 in Charleston, South Carolina, and warned that in addition to the divinely imposed diseases and plagues, slave revolts were justified consequences for the ill treatment of enslaved Africans. Nevertheless, because of Whitefield's failure to affirm the full humanity of enslaved Africans, his outcry against the slaveholders' deplorable and inhumane treatment of enslaved Africans should be interpreted with suspicion. Furthermore, his instruction to slaveholders to treat enslaved Africans with the same care as they gave their animals was inhumane, and his blatant reluctance to condemn the practice of slavery as sinful demonstrated his religion of antiblackness whether he was yet at the point of embracing slavery or not.

An essential part of Whitefield's vision of benevolent Christianity was the religious instruction of enslaved Africans, which consisted of Christian slaveholders being responsible for the catechizing of their enslaved Africans.[113] Parr maintains that Whitefield promoted Protestant Christianity for enslaved Africans as a form of social control.[114] Choi, however, argues that in the colony of Georgia, Whitefield was more concerned with cementing his legacy through the cultivation of educational institutions than religious institutions, a feature of his imperial strategy.[115] In addition to catechesis, "legal, social, and moral control" constituted the imperial rationale for Whitefield's ownership of enslaved Africans.[116] The Calvinist evangelical ministry of George Whitefield reinforced the Anglican theology of white privilege as is evident in his religion of antiblackness through which he shifted from abolitionism to proslavery theology.

---

113. Parr, *Inventing George Whitefield*, 76–77.
114. Parr, *Inventing George Whitefield*, 71.
115. Choi, *George Whitefield*, 55–66.
116. Parr, *Inventing George Whitefield*, 74.

Part II

THE RESISTANCE

4

Black Calvinist Evangelicals

Remember, Christians, Negros, black as Cain,
May be refin'd and join th' angelic train.
                                        —Phillis Wheatley

In 1773, twenty years after she was abducted and enslaved, Phillis Wheatley wrote her poem "On Being Brought from Africa to America." Her poem reflects her theological affinity with Calvinism and her belief that African enslavement was the providential will of God. Additionally, Wheatley adopted the oppressive proslavery theology in which, to justify the enslavement of Africans, Blacks were regarded as the offspring of Cain. Ironically, she regarded enslavement as evil but saw the providential will of God in such evil.[1] This chapter explores Black Calvinist evangelicals such as Wheatley, Jupiter Hammon, Lemuel Haynes, and John Marrant, all of whom embrace and adopt the empire theology that hindered their spiritual resistance to African enslavement.

Phillis Wheatley

Phillis Wheatley's Calvinism stemmed from the appeal of the supposed benevolence of New England slaveholders. She was treated as a family member, which was a common practice within New England slavery, as most enslaved Africans in the region functioned as house slaves rather than field slaves on the plantation—a major distinction between enslaved Africans in New England and enslaved Africans in the South. This treatment came with privileges not extended to the enslaved Africans in the South, such as the legal right to be baptized, to marry, and to learn to read.[2] Wheatley was

---

1. Vincent Carretta, *Phillis Wheatley: Biography of a Genius in Bondage* (Athens, GA: University of Georgia Press, 2011), 60.
2. Carretta, *Phillis Wheatley*, 15.

at the mercy of her white enslavers, who had no tolerance for her African heritage, convincing her that her African indigenous spirituality was erroneous and false.[3]

American literary critic John C. Shields, however, maintains that Wheatley's elegies were rooted in political astuteness and the correctness of her African tradition.[4] Historically, Wheatley's intellectual and poetic gifts seem to have been cultivated through the same source as her Puritan spirituality—her enslavement. Even in her poetry, Wheatley attributes her academic enrichment and certainly her Christian spirituality and salvation to the supposed Christian paternalistic nurture of her New England enslavers. Nevertheless, Shields's compelling argument regarding her spirituality affirms the richness of indigenous African spirituality. Unfortunately, as a result of her New England Puritanism, Wheatley adopted the imperial theology of Calvinism through spiritual acculturation and indoctrination, resulting in her condemnation of her native land of Africa as a pagan land.

Wheatley has been characterized as "the most prominent African American writer of the Revolutionary period."[5] Much of her acclaim comes from the theological implications of her poetry as well as her intellect and literary artistry. Wheatley developed an affinity with Calvinism within the context of New England Puritanism. Therefore, the religious piety evident in her poems was shaped by the tenets of the Reformed tradition and from the Puritan perspective of the empire.

Wheatley's affinity with Calvinism and her religious piety were shaped by the evangelical and social conditioning of the New England Puritan family that had purchased and enslaved her. She was from the Senegambia region of Senegal whence she was abducted by slave catchers.[6] Thomas Fitch, a wealthy merchant from the colony of Massachusetts, was responsible for Wheatley's forced migration to British colonial America and her eventual enslavement.[7] Boston merchant John Wheatley purchased her as a gift for his wife, Susanna. When purchased, Wheatley "had been stripped

---

3. Shields, *Phillis Wheatley's Poetics of Liberation* (Knoxville, TN: University of Tennessee Press, 2008), 15.

4. Shields, *Phillis Wheatley's Poetics of Liberation*, 113. Her famous elegy of George Whitefield captivated the attention of Selina Hastings, Countess of Huntingdon, who would become the primary financial benefactor to Wheatley and other Black Calvinist evangelicals who fulfilled her agenda of spreading and expanding the Calvinistic Methodist tradition.

5. Mark A. Noll, *In the Beginning was the Word: The Bible in American Public Life, 1492–1783* (New York: Oxford University Press, 2016), 215.

6. Carretta, *Phillis Wheatley*, 5. The Senegambia region was the primary source for the British transatlantic slave trade during the seventeenth and early eighteenth centuries because of its geographic proximity to Europe and the British American colonies.

7. Carretta, *Phillis Wheatley*, 4. Fitch profited from trade in goods as well as human beings from Philadelphia to New England and across the Atlantic to the west coast of Africa.

of her African identity and made a commodity on the eighteenth-century global market."[8]

The Seasoning Process

Wheatley survived the Middle Passage and the seasoning process, both designed to divest enslaved Africans of their indigenous African heritage, culture, religion, and humanity. American historians James H. Dorman and Robert R. Jones describe the elements of this process:

> The seasoning process, which many slaves did not survive, provided a period of enculturation during which the slave came to experience and sometimes to accept the realities of his new condition. He came to know new work techniques, repressive discipline, new values, new life priorities, new imperatives for subsistence and survival, a new religion, a new language, a new kinship system, and new modes and styles of day to day living. The new slaves were taught these things in the huts and provisioning areas of the older, more established bondsmen in whose midst they were placed precisely for this purpose. Their psychic survival (as opposed to their physical survival) depended on their ability to make necessary cultural adjustments.[9]

The goal of the seasoning process was to divest the African of his or her cultural heritage by those who had been acculturated to the plantation life of colonial America.[10] European enslavers believed that Africans suffered from primitive savagery and therefore were barbaric and uncivilized. Additionally, they believed that the Africans suffered from pagan influence and attempted to suppress such practices as ancestor veneration, drumming, dancing, shouting, and spirit possession.[11]

American historian William D. Piersen notes that seasoning in New England was harsher than any other region in British colonial America.[12] In fact, in order to control them, New England slaveholders punished, disciplined, and even renamed their enslaved Africans.[13] The renaming, which

8. Carretta, *Phillis Wheatley*, 1.

9. James Dormon and Robert R. Jones, *The Afro-American Experience: A Cultural History through Emancipation* (New York: John Wiley & Sons, 1974), 82.

10. Albert Raboteau, *Slave Religion: The Invisible Institution in the Antebellum South* (New York: Oxford University Press, 2004), 53.

11. Love Henry Whelchel, "My Chains Fell Off: Heart Religion in the African American Methodist Tradition," in Alton Pollard and Love Henry Whelchel, eds., *How Long This Road: Race, Religion, and the Legacy of C. Eric Lincoln* (New York: Palgrave Macmillan, 2003), 203.

12. William D. Piersen, *Black Yankees: The Development of an Afro-American Subculture in Eighteenth-Century New England* (Amherst, MA: University of Massachusetts Press, 1988), 21.

13. Bailey, *Race and Redemption*, 94.

generally occurred at either the purchase or birth of an enslaved African, emphasized Puritan dominance and inherent inferiority. John Wheatley renamed his purchased slave "Phillis," after the ship that transported her across the Atlantic. Richard Bailey notes that "being renamed was one of many acts of deracination suffered by enslaved people of African descent as whites sought to erase their African personal identities and redefine them as property" and "offers a window into the conscious and unconscious racial ideologies of the eighteenth-century slave trade"—the slaveholder as a Puritan and the enslaved as an inferior being.[14] For John and Susanna Wheatley, therefore, Phillis Wheatley was a reflection of their status, piety, charity, and commitment to evangelical Christianity.

Piety and Intellect

Wheatley is an excellent example of how enslaved Africans in New England were treated more humanely than enslaved Africans in the South; the former had to endure forced labor inside the house as opposed to the latter's forced labor outside on the plantation. New England slaveholders also provided their enslaved Africans with sufficient clothing, housing, and food because of the cold climate.[15]

Historically, an intelligent slave was the most valuable asset to New England colonists.[16] However, Enlightenment thinkers, such as David Hume, had questioned whether people of African descent possessed the intellectual capacity to write as brilliantly as Wheatley, and Thomas Jefferson affirmed Wheatley's piety but rejected her poetry, believing that "Africans have souls; they merely lack the intellectual endowments of other races."[17] African American historian Henry Louis Gates argues that Jefferson's harsh literary criticism of Wheatley was directed at antislavery writers who used her work to justify abolition.[18] There could be some validity to Gates's argument, yet Jefferson's criticism of Wheatley was probably not merely for the sake of his anti-abolitionist sentiments but rather a blatant attack on her intellect solely because of the color of her skin. Despite his supposed acceptance of the soul and humanity of the enslaved African, Jefferson's dehumanizing belief in Black inferiority per-

---

14. Bailey, *Race and Redemption*, 94–96.

15. Lorenzo Johnston Greene, *The Negro in Colonial New England* (New York: Columbia University Press, 1968), 225.

16. Greene, *The Negro in Colonial New England*, 237.

17. Henry Louis Gates Jr., *The Trials of Phillis Wheatley* (New York: Basic Books, 2003), 26, 42–44. Jefferson's suspicion of Wheatley's literary abilities was based solely on his conclusion of black mental inferiority. He argued that blacks were equal to whites regarding memory but inferior regarding reason.

18. Gates Jr., *The Trials of Phillis Wheatley*, 44.

petuated the racial subjugation of Native Americans and people of African descent.

Evangelical Calvinism

Wheatley was brought to British colonial America during the era of the First Great Awakening. Her New England enslavers were faithful Congregationalists, and therefore connected to the racism, sexism, classicism, and capitalism of Calvinism, the theology of the new American empire and the foundation of the New England Puritans.

In 1771, Wheatley was baptized a Congregationalist.[19] Her evangelical sentiments were strongly influenced by George Whitefield and Selina Hastings, the Countess of Huntingdon. This influence is most evident in a poem she wrote following the death of Whitefield where she writes:

> *Hail happy Saint on thy immortal throne! . . .*
> *He leaves this earth for Heaven's unmeasur'd height:*
> *And worlds unknown, receive him from our sight;*
> *There WHITEFIELD wings, with rapid course his way,*
> *And sails to Zion, through vast seas of day...*
>
> *Great COUNTESS! We Americans revere*
> *Thy name, and thus condole thy grief sincere:*
> *We mourn with thee, that TOMB obscurely plac'd,*
> *In which thy Chaplain undisturb'd doth rest. . . .*
> *No more to brighten these distressful days!*
> *His lonely Tabernacle, sees no more*
> *A WHITEFIELD landing on the British shore.*[20]

It is through Whitefield, who had served as the chaplain to the Countess of Huntingdon, that enslaved Black intellectuals such as Wheatley, to whom Whitefield's evangelical message appealed, were connected to the countess. The Countess of Huntingdon, a Calvinistic Methodist, was the wealthy benefactor of Whitefield's evangelical Calvinist cause, which was concerned with the paganism of African souls.

As we noted in the previous chapters, some evangelicals, such as Whitefield and the Countess of Huntingdon, believed that the enslavement of Africans was the mechanism through which pagan Africans were introduced to Christ; therefore, they not only justified slavery but did not view slavery as being incompatible with Christianity.[21] Indeed, Calvinist evangelicals

---

19. Carretta, *Phillis Wheatley*, 34.
20. Phillis Wheatley, "An Elegiac Poem on the Death of George Whitefield," in *Phillis Wheatley: Complete Writings*, 113–14.
21. Carretta, *Phillis Wheatley*, 30.

advocated for enslaved Africans to serve as missionaries to fellow enslaved persons.[22] Consequently, Wheatley advocated for the evangelization of her homeland of Africa, which she declared as a heathen land, through the return of freed Blacks.

Vincent Carretta argues that Wheatley neither accepted nor endorsed slavery, suggesting that she believed in an omniscient and benevolent deity and that "physical slavery paradoxically leads to the spiritual freedom offered to servants, or slaves of Christ," further arguing that, far from being an accommodationist, that her value and embrace of Christianity were due to her enslavement.[23] Wheatley may not have accepted slavery and condemned such as evil; however, her belief in slavery as a part of God's providential plan is certainly an endorsement of slavery. Despite her abolitionism, which was the point of departure from her New England slaveholders, Wheatley's affirmation of colonization through the return of freed Blacks to Africa to evangelize supposed African heathens demonstrates her accommodation to the values and ideologies of her slaveholders.

Wheatley's theology and ideology reflect the dichotomy between blackness and whiteness and her embrace of the proslavery theology that relates to the supposed blackness of Cain and his offspring. In her "Address to the Deists," Wheatley identified herself as an "Ethiopian" rather than an "African," asserting, "Must Ethiopians be imploy'd for you, greatly rejoice if any good I do."[24] Carretta argues that "appropriating the term 'Ethiopians' does much more than simply reveal Wheatley's complexion, ethnicity, and probable status to her readers. By calling herself an Ethiopian rather than an African or a Black in a religious poem, she claims an identity that grants her biblical authority to speak to her readers."[25] Wheatley uses this term specifically to address the Deists who were products of Enlightenment thought and who had been corrupted by those theories of race that we discussed earlier: the terms "African" and "Black" relate to racial or ethnic identity and connote evil, sin, and inferiority, whereas "Ethiopian" relates to a biblical religious identity and connotes goodness and affirms religious equality.

New Divinity Calvinism

The theology of the New Divinity also appealed to Wheatley and influenced and informed her support of abolitionism. Her emphasis on the benevolent love of God reflects the New Divinity theology of disinterested benevolence and was a major point of departure from the emphasis on divine wrath in

22. Carretta. *Phillis Wheatley*, 60.

23. Carretta. *Phillis Wheatley*, 60–61.

24. Phillis Wheatley, "An Address to the Deist," in *Phillis Wheatley: Complete Writings* (New York: Penguin Books, 2001), 72.

25. Carretta, *Phillis Wheatley*, 57.

other forms of Calvinism.[26] Wheatley fully embraced the evangelization scheme of Samuel Hopkins, which consisted of Christianization, colonization, and civilization, and formed the foundation for her advocacy for returning freed Blacks to the homeland of Africa to evangelize and convert Africans to Christianity.

Wheatley's integration of Old Light and New Divinity Calvinism reflects her new empire and Puritan theological perspective. Consequently, Wheatley sacrificed the spiritual and ontological values of African people to accommodate the religious project of the white Puritans, who—as the presupposed superior race (visible saints) chosen by God to rule—believed they had been called to Christianize, colonize, and civilize their enslaved and inferior Native Americans and Africans.

Despite her view of slavery as the providential will of God, Wheatley embraced some of the tenets of New Divinity Calvinism, which condemned slavery as sinful. She adopted the Puritan ideology of British colonial America and the early republic as the New Israel. Certainly, she believed that the Puritans were God's chosen people (the elect), and the new republic in North America—specifically the New England region—was God's chosen nation. However, she concluded that even God's elect were sinful and had committed the sin of enslavement. She further argued that those elected who had committed the sin of enslavement would suffer divine consequences.[27]

Interestingly, it was the characterization of slavery as sinful by Black Calvinist evangelicals that fueled their views of abolition and emancipation. For example, Shields argues that Wheatley's literary work is permeated by the dialectic of slavery and freedom, defining her liberation as "her struggle to achieve freedom through her poetry, which she freely offered to public scrutiny and/or vicarious participation."[28] He concludes that her poetry challenged the injustice of the status quo, which, for Wheatley, was New England white religiosity.[29]

Abolition

In addition to challenging slavery, Shields's view of Wheatley as possibly the most revolutionary writer of her day is related to her race and gender. Certainly, Wheatley strongly advocated for the emancipation of enslaved Africans and for the abolition of slavery, but her literary work does not reflect liberation. The problem with Shields's argument is his assertion that Wheatley employed moderate, Enlightenment ideas to confront the inad-

---

26. Carretta, *Phillis Wheatley*, 59.

27. Carretta, *Phillis Wheatley*, 57–58. Based on the book of Isaiah, Wheatley maintained that war with other nations was God's justice against the elect for their sinfulness.

28. Shields, *Phillis Wheatley's*, 17, 41.

29. Shields, *Phillis Wheatley's*, 108.

equacy of her New England white religiosity. Even a moderate understanding of the Enlightenment indicates that the intent of thinkers consisted of making white males superior to all other forms of humanity. For example, consider Thomas Jefferson, a pioneer of the American Enlightenment, who dismissed as a farce the intellectually astute literary work of Wheatley, a brilliant rational thinking Black woman.

Wheatley's literary work integrated Enlightenment philosophy and revolutionary theology, both of which served the purposes of the new American empire. Her theology and spirituality were influenced by her New England white religiosity worldview, reflected primarily in her condemnation of her native Africa as pagan. Despite Shields's assertion that Wheatley's condemnation was based on the geographical difference between rural and urban land and the Latin derivative of the term pagan as non-Christian, it cannot be disputed that the Calvinist theology she acquired from her New England slaveholders convinced her that she had been transplanted from a land of heathenism. Hence, her advocacy for the return of freed Black Christians for the evangelization of the supposed heathens in Africa.

Jupiter Hammon

Jupiter Hammon and Wheatley are considered the father and mother of African American literature.[30] Cedrick May argues that the major themes of Hammon's Calvinism were fear and labor, which reflected his temporal condition as an enslaved African.[31] Influenced by the Old Light Calvinists, Hammon believed that the elect always demonstrated outward signs of their election and that their labor in the Christian life was evidence of their election.[32]

"A Winter Piece"

Fear is the most prevalent theme in "A Winter Piece," his exhortation to unconverted sinners. Hammon believed that a doctrine of salvation was impossible without a doctrine of damnation. He stated:

> Let me, my brethren, persuade you to a serious consideration of your danger while you continue in an unconverted state. Did you feel the operations of God's holy spirit, you then would leave all for an interest in the merits of Christ; "For the kingdom of heaven is like a treasure

---

30. Thabiti M. Anyabwile, *The Decline of African American Theology: From Biblical Faith to Cultural Captivity* (Downers Grove, IL: InterVarsity Press, 2007), 139.

31. Cedrick May, *Evangelism and Resistance in the Black Atlantic, 1760–1835* (Athens, GA: University of Georgia Press, 2008), 31.

32. May, *Evangelism and Resistance*, 30–31.

hid in a field; for which a man will sell all that he hath to purchase, Matt.x.44. So will every true penitent part with all for the sake of Christ. I shall not attempt to drive you to Christ by the terrors of the law, but I shall endeavor to allure you by the invitation of the gospel, to come laboring and heavy laden.[33]

Hammon's writings reflect the Old Lights' Calvinist tradition, which affirmed that enslavement of Africans constituted the will of God.[34] Wheatley also believed that African enslavement was the divine will of God, but her emphasis on the divine love of God and the sinfulness of slavery reflected how her Calvinism differed drastically from that of Hammon.

Another major theme in Hammon's exhortation is the spiritual equality between Blacks and whites that resulted from the condition of original sin. He writes:

My Brethren, it is not we servants only that are unworthy, but all mankind by the fall of Adam, became guilty in the sight of God. Gen. ii. 17. Surely then we are sinners by nature, and are daily adding thereto by evil practices, and it is only by the merits of Jesus Christ we can be saved, we are told that he is a Jew that is a Jew in his heart, so he is a Christian that is a Christian in his heart, and it is not everyone that says Lord, Lord shall enter into the Kingdom of God, but he that doth the will of God. Let our superiors act as they shall think it best, we must resolve to walk in steps our Saviour hath set before us, which was a holy life, a humble submission to the will of God.[35]

In classical Christian doctrine, original sin is the condition that causes actual sins. Since Hammon believed that all humans suffered from original sin, he concluded that Blacks and whites are equal not only as natural sinners but also as active sinners.[36] This view reflects the influence of his Reformed soteriology and the empire theology of Calvinism. The problem is that he completely disregards human equality, even at the expense of his own liberation. Hammon offers a romantic view of salvation through which enslaved Africans have spiritual equality with their slaveholders that is based primarily on sinfulness rather than salvation. Another fun-

---

33. Jupiter Hammon, "A Winter Piece: Being A Serious Exhortation, with a Call to the Unconverted: and a Short Contemplation on the Death of Jesus Christ" in Cedrick May, ed., *The Collected Works of Jupiter Hammon: Poems and Essays* (Knoxville: University of Tennessee Press, 2017), 26.

34. May, *Evangelism and Resistance*, 36.

35. Hammon, "A Winter Piece," 25.

36. Anyabwile, *The Decline of African American Theology*, 104.

damental problem with Calvinist soteriology is the belief in salvation for
God's elect and damnation for the divinely predetermined reprobate, which
essentially eradicated the possibility of spiritual equality since not all persons have been elected for salvation. Puritans in the New World believed
and functioned as if they were the only elect, and all others—even those
in other Christian traditions, specifically Native Americans and enslaved
Africans—constituted those whom God had damned.

Reformed Theology

Calvinism, the theology of the American empire, influenced Hammon's view
that enslaved Africans, the subordinates of American society, were just as
sinful as the slaveholders. However, this view prioritizes the dehumanizing
empire agenda of imperialism and colonialism. In other Christian traditions, such as Roman Catholicism, there are different levels of sinfulness.
In addition to original sin, Roman Catholics distinguish between mortal
(grave) sins and venial (minor) sins. Mortal sins result in separation from
God. Venial sins weaken the soul, and sins committed through ignorance
do not result in eternal damnation. The dehumanization and oppression
of slavery constitute mortal sin, and any sinfulness that enslaved persons
exhibit, especially under the horrific conditions of enslavement, constitutes a venial sin. As an adherent of Reformed theology, Hammon rejected
the distinction between mortal and venial sins; however, this distinction
was more applicable to the spiritual differences between slaveholders and
the enslaved. Hammon based his notion of the spiritual equality between
Blacks and whites on his view of sinfulness and therefore participated in
his own dehumanization.

Thabiti Anyabwile validates and celebrates Black Calvinist evangelicals
such as Hammon for possessing a theological appropriation that reflected
his view of true African American Christian theology. Anyabwile argues
that the earliest generation of African American writers, such as Jupiter
Hammon, Phillis Wheatley, Lemuel Haynes, and John Marrant, was shaped
by the Reformed theology of the New England Puritans. Characterizing
Reformed theology as "orthodox Christian theology," he argues that it was
the accurate reflection of biblical faith.[37] He criticizes and rejects theologies
such as Black liberation theology, which correlates the biblical text with
the Black experience of oppression at the hands of white supremacists to
achieve liberation.

The celebrated father of Black liberation theology, James Cone, identified

---

37. Anyabwile, *The Decline of African American Theology*, 20. Anyabwile suggests that
African American Christian theology has become captive to culture and shifted from the
biblical faithfulness of Reformed theology.

the sources and norms of this theology as Black experience, Black history, Black culture, revelation, Scripture, and tradition.[38] He writes:

> Black theology is biblical theology. That is, it is theology which takes seriously the importance of scripture in theological discourse. There can be no theology of the Christian gospel which does not take into account the biblical witness. It is true that the Bible is not the revelation of God, only Jesus is. But it is an indispensable witness to God's revelation and is thus a primary source for Christian thinking about God.[39]

In the development of proslavery theologies, Reformed theology was primary in that it promoted biblical justifications for the institution of slavery and was complicit in cultivating the American empire that was built economically on the institution of slavery. Anyabwile even identified the early rationalizations of proslavery theologians for the institution of slavery, which included the erroneous notion that Africans were subhuman and had no soul and lacked intellectual capacity and moral virtue.[40] Yet, rather than condemn Reformed theology for its theological role in the dehumanization and enslavement of Africans, Anyabwile condemns the African American church for rejecting Reformed theology in its quest for liberation from the oppression, enslavement, and suffering imposed on people of color through the efforts of white supremacists and especially white Christian supremacists.

Hammon's writing reveals the negative effects of Reformed theology on the early American empire. Being theologically situated in the Reformed tradition, he emphasized the central concept of God's sovereignty, which was at work in the institution of slavery.[41] Believing that God permitted slavery, Hammon encouraged enslaved Africans to be obedient to their slave masters, which he exclaimed was sanctioned in Scripture. Consequently, Anyabwile explains that for Hammon, "the sovereignty of God extended to the daily treatment that Africans received at the hands of both righteous and unrighteous slave owners and was the only basis upon which the command to obey could be trusted and hope for peace and comfort could be expected."[42] This is the scandal of Reformed theology, for the critical questions are: What is a righteous slave owner? How can one who holds another

---

38. James H. Cone, *A Black Theology of Liberation*, Fortieth Anniversary Edition (Maryknoll, NY: Orbis Books, 2010), 24–37.

39. Cone, *A Black Theology of Liberation*, 32.

40. Anyabwile, *The Decline of African American Theology*, 103.

41. Anyabwile, *The Decline of African American Theology*, 66.

42. Anyabwile, *The Decline of African American Theology*, 67.

in bondage against his or her own will, particularly without a debt, be considered righteous? The scandal is applying God's sovereignty to justify the evil of slavery. This makes God complicit in the evil of slavery and confirms God as the author of evil. There was nothing righteous about the practice of chattel slavery in America. Unfortunately, Reformed theology prevented Hammon from condemning his very own enslavement and seeking his own liberation.

Slavery

The major difference between Wheatley and Hammon was her denunciation of slavery and his accommodation of it. In his poem "An Address to Miss Phillis Wheatley," Hammon discourages Wheatley's denunciations of slavery and her engagement in abolitionist politics.[43]

Building on his Calvinist presuppositions, Hammon reminds Wheatley that (1) her enslavement was an act of divine benevolence; (2) her enslavement liberated her soul from the paganism of her homeland; and (3) real freedom from oppression occurred only after the achievement of eternal life through death.

Hammon adopted the notion of disinterested benevolence from New Light and New Divinity theologians that slaveholders would eventually emancipate their enslaved Africans. He concluded that Christ would provide this freedom for enslaved Africans and that enslaved Africans would rejoice when slavery has ended but that such may not occur until Christ's return.[44] Hammon viewed the emancipation of enslaved Africans as spiritual freedom more so than physical freedom:

> *Salvation be thy leading Staff,*
> *To set the Sinner free.*
> *Dear Jesus unto thee we fly;*
> *Depart, depart from Sin*
> *Salvation doth a length supply,*
> *The glory of our King.*[45]

---

43. Jupiter Hammon, "An Address to Miss Phillis Wheatley, Ethiopian Poetess, in Boston, who came from Africa at eight years of age, and soon became acquainted with the Gospel of Jesus Christ," in Wheatley, *Phillis Wheatley*, 204–7.

44. Jupiter Hammon, "An Essay on Slavery, with Submission to Divine Providence, Knowing that God Rules Over All Things," in Cedrick May, ed., *The Collected Works of Jupiter Hammon: Poems and Essays* (Knoxville: University of Tennessee Press, 2017), 79–82.

45. Jupiter Hammon, "An Evening Thought: Salvation by Christ, with Penitential Cries," in Stanley Austin Ransom Jr., ed., *America's First Negro Poet: The Complete Works of Jupiter Hammon of Long Island* (Port Washington, NY: Kennikat Press, 1970), 46.

Ultimately, Hammon equated the liberation of enslaved Africans with the phenomenon of rapture, implying that they would not experience freedom from earthly oppression, bondage, and enslavement until they were raptured into the heavenly realm.

Like Wheatley, he characterized people of African descent as pagans and believed that the remedy for the paganism of enslaved Africans was Christian catechism.[46] Consequently, he was not concerned with slavery but the conversion of enslaved Africans through a Calvinist understanding of the Scriptures.[47] Hammon's literary work reflects the message of an enslaved African who accommodated his oppression and views that the institution of slavery was benevolent. He did not advocate for radical resistance to enslavement and other forms of oppression leveled against people of African descent by European colonists corrupted by white supremacy.[48] Hammon was not concerned with resistance and did not foster a revolutionary message.[49] He correlated slavery with the will of God and urged enslaved Africans based on God's will to give full submission to the civil order and civil authorities. Hammon concluded that God had empowered white enslavers with civil authority and permitted slavery.[50]

Based on his interpretation of Pauline texts, Hammon attempted to convince enslaved Africans that obeying their white masters was the divine will of God, even if the system of slavery was sinful.[51] Thus emerged the theological contradiction between Calvinism, the theology of the empire, and that of Black Calvinist evangelicals. On the one hand, Hammon believed that slavery was the divine will of God and exhorted enslaved Africans to obey their masters. On the other hand, he struggled with the sinfulness of slavery. Most forms of New England Calvinism—whether Old Calvinist, New Light, or New Divinity—affirmed the theological presupposition that God is the author of sin, and as such, could divinely will the enslavement of Africans and supposedly use the institution of slavery as a form of divine benevolence for predestined enslaved persons.

Lemuel Haynes

Like Wheatley, Haynes affirmed the sinfulness of slavery, but he viewed the sin of slavery from the perspective of New Divinity theodicy. John Saillant asserts that "New Divinity ministers emphasized that God used sinners and their evil deeds as instruments in a plan to glorify himself and to gather the

46. May, *Evangelism and Resistance*, 29.
47. May, *Evangelism and Resistance*, 29.
48. May, *Evangelism and Resistance*, 39.
49. May, *Evangelism and Resistance*, 24–25.
50. May, *Evangelism and Resistance*, 34.
51. May, *Evangelism and Resistance*, 44.

saints around him in heaven."[52] New Divinity theologians essentially made
God the author of sin and believed that God used the evil of sin for good
and that sin was a providential means of revealing divine providence.[53] As
an adherent to this doctrine, Haynes embraced the understanding that
God caused sinful actions rather than the view of moderate Calvinists, who
argued that God merely tolerated them.[54] For Haynes, the sin of slavery had
been divinely designed for the Christianization of Africa, yet he argued that
God would overrule the evil of slavery, which would result in the eventual
emancipation of enslaved Africans.[55]

God, Evil, and Slavery

Haynes's understanding of evil through the sinfulness of the slave trade and
the institution of slavery demonstrates the scandalous nature of Reformed
theology of the American empire. He argued that God was not only the cause
of all things but also the sustainer of all things and, therefore, that even evil
constituted the providential will of God, thus rejecting the notion of God
merely tolerating evil. In assessing Haynes's treatment of the relationship
between God and evil, Anyabwile suggests that he distinguished between
the nature of something and its cause—a distinction that resulted in him
characterizing moral evil as an aspect of divine providence and concluding
that moral good resulted from moral evil.[56] Therefore, Haynes rejected any
theology that permitted sin, believing that such theologies failed to be vindicated in the face of evil.[57]

Basing himself on the covenant theology of Calvinism, Haynes believed
that God intended enslaved Africans to be beneficiaries of the Abrahamic
covenant and advocated for the emancipation of enslaved Africans.[58] Furthermore, he viewed the slave trade and the institution of slavery as violations of this covenant.[59] In challenging the idea that desires are selfish, he
encouraged enslaved Africans to desire freedom, which would foster their
knowledge and worship of God. Haynes argued that the sinfulness of the
slave trade and slavery violated the natural right of liberty and produced
the ignorance of Christianity and republicanism.[60] Through the covenant of

---

52. John Saillant, *Black Puritan, Black Republican: The Life and Thought of Lemuel Haynes,
1753–1833* (New York: Oxford University Press, 2003), 84.
53. Saillant, *Black Puritan, Black Republican*, 87.
54. Saillant, *Black Puritan, Black Republican*, 89–90.
55. Saillant, *Black Puritan, Black Republican*, 99.
56. Anyabwile, *The Decline of African American Theology*, 69–70.
57. Anyabwile, *The Decline of African American Theology*, 71.
58. Saillant, *Black Puritan, Black Republican*, 116.
59. Saillant, *Black Puritan, Black Republican*, 116.
60. Saillant, *Black Puritan, Black Republican*, 104.

grace and disinterested benevolence, Haynes believed that the egalitarianism of races was the solution to the problem of slavery and would result in the emancipation of enslaved Africans.[61]

Liberty and Enlightenment

By integrating republican ideology with his New Divinity Calvinist theology, Haynes viewed the slave trade and slavery as divine instruments for the greater good. Saillant asserts that "Haynes put the sufferings of slaves on par with the Revolution as a means to further liberty and accord between the races. God was using the evil of the slave trade and slavery to emphasize the goodness and beauty of a free and benevolent society."[62] In short, Haynes presented the argument that God had sanctioned slavery to foster liberty and enlightenment.

Unlike Hammon, who found the equality of the races in human sinfulness, Haynes situated this equality in liberty. In other words, humans are equal in their universal quest for freedom as an innate desire in human nature regardless of race. This argument for the universality of liberty was his attempt to combat the racial superiority of whites and to argue for the full inclusion and full humanity of Africans in the early American republic.[63]

Consequently, Haynes rejected the proslavery theological theory of the Hamitic curse, condemned European enslavers for their erroneous claim of Christianizing Africans through the slave trade, and criticized their failure to spread the gospel to all Africans.[64] However, his critique is problematic in that his very criticism of the European enslavers suggests they possessed a superior Christianity to the religion of the Africans whom they were seeking to enslave, even the African Christians. The critical question and contradiction that emerges here is: How could the European enslavers spread the Christian gospel while evidently violating that same gospel in their slave trafficking?

Therefore, Haynes's spiritual resistance to the evil of slavery and dehumanization did address the anthropological ideas of European enslavers but failed to correct the empire theology that justified both slavery and dehumanization. By denouncing the slave trade as evil, Haynes affirmed an anthropology that made the African equal to other humans.[65] Anyabwile contends that Haynes saw the error in the anthropological claims of European enslavers and the effect of slavery on enslaved Africans and

---

61. Saillant, *Black Puritan, Black Republican*, 101.
62. Saillant, *Black Puritan, Black Republican*, 103.
63. Anyabwile, *The Decline of African American Theology*, 106–7.
64. Anyabwile, *The Decline of African American Theology*, 109–10.
65. Anyabwile, *The Decline of African American Theology*, 109.

believed, therefore, that freedom for Africans followed naturally from correct anthropology.[66] But what about the correct theology? If freedom is the
criterion for correct theology, Reformed theology fails miserably.

Reformed Theology

After the death of Calvin, the primary tenet of Reformed theology became
the notion of predestination, particularly through the efforts of Calvin's followers at the Synod of Dort in 1618. The Reformed doctrine of divine election eradicated the natural freedom of Africans and any other persons not
considered part of the elect. Consequently, those divinely elected have natural freedom, and the damned or nonelected are naturally enslaved to the
bondage of the human will. In the mind of the European enslavers, people
of African descent had been divinely elected for enslavement rather than
Christian salvation. Reformed theology was the theology of the American
empire. This reality reveals the scandal of Reformed theology, which is
incompatible with liberty and enlightenment, especially, as Haynes presupposed, with regard to enslaved Africans.

New Divinity theologians believed that God's benevolent design
redeemed sin from absolute evil, and that the Christianization of supposed
heathen Africa would occur through the return of Blacks to Africa.[67] Haynes
attacked the plan of Samuel Hopkins and the New Divinity regarding their
providential view of the slave trade and slavery. His weakness was evident
in that he had adopted their empire theology as his own. By proposing the
cultivation of an egalitarian American society rather than the expatriation
of Blacks, he provided robust support for the American republic, regardless
of his opposition to slavery and the American republic's religious and political hypocrisy concerning the institution of slavery.[68] Furthermore, despite
the fact that Haynes advocated for the full citizenship of Africans in the
American republic, by adopting their empire theology, he was unable to
affirm the full humanity of Africans.

Calvinist theologies eradicate the possibility of egalitarianism in any
shape or form because the doctrine of divine predestinarian and divine
election make one individual superior to another individual by divine
design. In the American empire of the eighteenth and nineteenth centuries,
Calvinism, combined with Enlightenment ideology, prioritized one race
over another, resulting in the dominance of white supremacy, white superiority, and white privilege.

---

66. Anyabwile, *The Decline of African American Theology*, 107–8.
67. Anyabwile, *The Decline of African American Theology*, 98–102.
68. Anyabwile, *The Decline of African American Theology*, 72.

John Marrant

John Marrant, a Calvinist Methodist and a member of the Countess of Huntingdon's Connexion, made slavery compatible with the doctrines of divine predestination and divine election. Wesleyan Methodists had asserted that, because enslavement eradicated a person's volition, the institution of slavery infringed upon the soteriological rights and benefits of enslaved Africans, prohibiting them from having access to salvation. The founder and financier of the Huntingdon connection, Selina Hastings (Countess of Huntingdon), believed that the Arminian theology of Wesleyan Methodists undermined the Methodist movement within the Anglican Church.[69]

As noted earlier, George Whitefield, who was also Marrant's spiritual mentor, defected to Calvinist Methodism through his association with the Countess of Huntingdon, whom he served as chaplain. May asserts that "Whitefield deferred to the pressure he received from members of his colonial congregations as well as the countess's priorities on the matter. Slavery was acceptable as long as it was nonbrutal and paternalistic."[70] While Whitefield's theological influence on Marrant is evident in his spiritual autobiography, Marrant departed from Whitefield on the issue of slavery.

Marrant appealed to the Christianity of white enslavers to advocate for the Christian conversion of enslaved Africans, emphasizing their duty to save the souls of enslaved Africans.[71] Like Hammon, he seemed more interested in converting the souls of enslaved Africans than emancipating their bodies. In the closing paragraph of his spiritual autobiography, Marrant writes:

> I have now only to intreat the earnest prayers of all my kind Christian friends, that I may be carried safe there; kept humble, made faithful and successful; that strangers may hear of and run to Christ; that Indian tribes may stretch out their hands to God; that the black nations may be made white in the blood of the Lamb; that vast multitude of hard tongues, and of a strange speech, may learn the language of Canaan, and sing the song of Moses, and of the Lamb; and, anticipating the glorious prospect, may we all with fervent hearts, and will-

---

69. May, *Evangelism and Resistance*, 74–75. John Wesley and Charles Wesley both condemned the practice of slavery as repugnant to the Christian faith and deemed it anti-Christian.

70. May, *Evangelism and Resistance*, 75.

71. May, *Evangelism and Resistance*, 73.

ing tongues, sing hallelujah; the kingdoms of the world are become the kingdoms of our God, and of his Christ.

The empire theology of Calvinism also influenced Marrant, and these concluding words demonstrate the possibility that he adopted some of the dehumanizing theology of white enslavers. For example, his words "that the black nations may be made white in the blood of the Lamb" validate the belief of white enslavers that the souls of enslaved Africans are saved by being washed in the white blood of Jesus. Another aspect of these dehumanizing theologies is the belief that being washed in the white blood of Jesus would ensure that the supposed evil black soul of the enslaved African would become a redeemed and clean white soul—a theology that connects white slaveholders to their condemnation of external blackness. Therefore, the critical question is: Did Marrant internalize the theology of white enslavers to the point of self-condemnation of external and internal blackness?

Conclusion

Despite their efforts to abolish slavery and achieve emancipation for enslaved Africans, Black Calvinist evangelicals theologized from the perspective of the empire rather than from their own experience of oppression. May argues that Hammon's work constituted the beginnings of Black theology, Wheatley's work constituted the charge toward progressive Black theologies, and Marrant's work developed a Black theology rooted in progressive social action.[72] However, Black theology has been understood as a form of liberation theology, and while the Black Calvinist evangelicals advocated for the emancipation of enslaved Africans through the abolition of slavery—either through immediate or gradual means—their embrace of empire theology hindered their capacity to address the theological motivations for African enslavement and marred their spiritual resistance against the dehumanization of European slaveholders evident in the slave trade and the institution of slavery.

Another major theological deficiency of the Black Calvinist evangelicals was the lack of a liberative pneumatology. If the Black Calvinist evangelicals possessed a pneumatology, it was defective in that it promoted the presence of the Holy Spirit yet void of true liberty. Furthermore, their embrace of empire theology hindered their advocacy for true liberty and true equality because the theology they espoused was complicit in the dehumanization and oppression of people of African descent.

---

72. May, *Evangelism and Resistance*, 24–82.

Black Calvinist evangelicals were also heavily influenced by New Divinity theology, which emphasized the notion of disinterested benevolence. While this theological notion originated with Jonathan Edwards, Samuel Hopkins became its theological architect, and through his theological construction, disinterested benevolence stipulated loving God and loving one's neighbor for the sake of God's glory. The theology of disinterested benevolence proved imperative to the abolitionist cause in the early republic. However, the problem here was that disinterested benevolence does not require sanctification. Christian love is a matter of the heart, and for its theological authenticity and actualization, the human heart must possess sanctification. A person cannot authentically love God even for God's own sake and glory without being sanctified. The theology of disinterested benevolence needed a robust liberative pneumatology. However, a liberative pneumatology would not fit within the theological constructs of the Reformed tradition, primarily because of its doctrine of divine election. The Reformed doctrine of election sanctions exclusion and therefore constitutes exclusionary theology, which disqualifies the entire Reformed theological system from holding a liberative pneumatology. Therefore, the cultivation and activation of liberative pneumatology proved impossible for Black Calvinist evangelicals.

5

Black Radical Evangelicals

He gave them a plenty of everything calculated to do them good—not satisfied with this, however, they wanted slaves, and wanted us for their slaves, who belong to the Holy Ghost, and no other, who we shall have to serve instead of tyrants.

—David Walker

In 1829, David Walker published *Walker's Appeal... to the Coloured Citizens of the World*,[1] which he addressed to afflicted Blacks and white American Christians. He declared that enslaved Africans were the property of the Holy Ghost. This declaration was imperative to his rejection of chattel slavery as practiced by white Christians in British colonial America and the early republic. Walker was appealing to the supposed Christianity of white American slaveholders, urging them to heed the guidance of the Holy Spirit to liberate enslaved Africans. Ultimately, Walker's *Appeal* foreshadowed the Black revolution and spiritual resistance to the evil of their enslavement and oppression.

American pastoral theologian James Newton Poling defines evil as an abuse of power, and religious evil as the most dangerous in that it results from the cultivation of theology designed to eradicate humanity and spirituality.[2] He defines religious evil as organized opposition to God's love and power and as the most difficult form of evil to detect.[3] This chapter explores

---

1. His appeal to African Americans entitled *Walker's Appeal, in Four Articles; Together with a Preamble, to the Coloured Citizens of the World, but in Particular, and Very Expressly, to Those of the United States of America, Written in Boston, State of Massachusetts, September 28, 1829.* The purpose of the document was to encourage readers to take an active role in fighting their oppression, regardless of the risk, and to press white Americans to realize the moral and religious failure of slavery.

2. James Newton Poling, *Deliver Us from Evil: Resisting Racial and Gender Oppression* (Minneapolis: Fortress Press, 1996), xv.

3. Poling, *Deliver Us from Evil*, 132–33.

the theology of spiritual resistance grounded in liberative pneumatology in response to the oppressive empire theology of white slaveholders and analyzes the acculturation of some enslaved Africans to the culture of their white enslavers as a form of spiritual resistance.

Theology of Spiritual Resistance

White supremacy was the driving force behind religious evil in British colonial America and the early republic. As we noted earlier, the natural hierarchy of white supremacy and white male dominance stemmed from Enlightenment ideology, the Puritan theology of superiority, and the Anglican theology of privilege, making race and gender factors in this evil.[4] Poling argues that evil was "sanctioned by religion and theology, but masked by abstract claims to virtue, love, and justice."[5]

The ideology of Black inferiority was connected primarily to black skin. White supremacist theologians emphasized black skin as the source of Black inferiority, which became the catalyst for their construction of racial oppression.[6] Riggins J. Earl identifies this emphasis in the "ideal Christian-type master," who reflects the theological roots of white supremacy:

Ideal Christian-type masters believed that the souls of slaves satisfied the norm of biblical anthropology, but at the same time had ambiguous concerns about whether the slave's body, because of its blackness, met these same norms. . . . Whites readily concluded that the dilemma of the external blackness of slaves' bodies gave them the right to be God's viceroys of slave's souls and ultimately the rulers of their bodies on earth. It was conceded that while the blood of Jesus could not change the blackness of the slave's body, it would transform the status of the slave's soul.[7]

White theologians with white supremacist worldviews and tendencies developed a Christology validating the slave trade and slavery as benevolent enterprises.[8] Poling asserts that "under the assumptions of white supremacy, white preachers could interpret their oppression of African

---

4. Poling, *Deliver Us from Evil*, 62.

5. Poling, *Deliver Us from Evil*, 132.

6. Poling, *Deliver Us from Evil*, 115. The varied forms of oppression in the African diaspora consisted of capture, murder, enslavement, torture, rape, lynching, massive poverty, and forced labor.

7. Riggins J. Earl Jr., *Dark Symbols, Obscure Signs: God, Self, and Community in the Slave Mind* (Maryknoll, NY: Orbis Books, 1993), 16.

8. Poling, *Deliver Us from Evil*, 141.

Americans as benevolent and paternalistic for their own good."[9] The religion of the white Christ fostered the oppression of enslaved Africans. Womanist theologian Kelly Brown Douglas declares that "this Christ allowed for white enslavers to be Christians, and for black Christians to be slaves."[10]

Part of the scandal of white supremacist theologians was the cultivation of a corrupted Christian theology based on the salvation of an individual and the promotion of a white Christ, which proved irrelevant and insufficient for the survival and liberation of oppressed people.[11] Furthermore, this corrupted Christian theology contributed to the theological justification for the oppression of enslaved Africans. Therefore, Black liberation theologians developed a suspicion of Christology inherited from white supremacist theology.

Jesus, the Model of Spiritual Resistance

Enslaved Africans cultivated a spirituality of resistance to the oppression that was based on the religion of the white Christ. Womanist theologians, such as Kelly Brown Douglas, Jacquelyn Grant, and Delores Williams, emphasize the liberative nature of Jesus as an alternative and argue that, in addition to resisting evil, Jesus promoted survival and liberation.[12] Therefore, Jesus becomes the spiritual model for communities of resistance that view Jesus as their co-sufferer.[13] Religion was the first institution that provided enslaved Africans with the tools needed for resistance.[14] Enslaved Africans were a historical community of resistance against all forms of evil, specifically religious evil, and they appealed to religion in their struggle, since resistance to evil is an element of God's creation being both divine and human.[15]

Jesus resisted evil, validating the divine imperative of spiritual resistance. In his life and ministry, Jesus symbolized resistance and revolution. Poling argues that "in spite of the established churches' abuse and misuse of Jesus Christ as a religious symbol, resistance communities draw on a liberated and critical consciousness to reject lies about Jesus and to find in Jesus a friend who empowers them for liberation."[16] The essence of Jesus's resistance is embodied in the words "deliver us from evil" from the Lord's

9. Poling, *Deliver Us from Evil*, 152.

10. Kelly Brown Douglas, *The Black Christ* (Maryknoll, NY: Orbis Books, 1994), 17.

11. Douglas, *The Black Christ*, 139.

12. Douglas, *The Black Christ*, 146.

13. Douglas, *The Black Christ*, 152.

14. Cedrick May, *Evangelism and Resistance in the Black Atlantic, 1760–1835* (Athens, GA: University of Georgia Press, 2008), 3.

15. Poling, *Deliver Us from Evil*, xv.

16. Poling, *Deliver Us from Evil*, 156.

Prayer, which became a prayer of resistance.[17] Jesus is the model of spiritual resistance for enslaved Africans both practically and theologically.

The Holy Spirit and Community

Pneumatology is fundamental to the theology of spiritual resistance for the Holy Spirit is the primary source of liberation from oppression. African American Christian ethicist Leonard Lovett argues that the Holy Spirit empowers believers to respond authentically in community and witness against the dehumanization through the Spirit of the Liberator (Jesus Christ). Lovett characterizes this phenomenon as "pneumatological liberation."[18] As the liberator, Jesus is the Spirit who resides within the oppressed and empowers them to resist evil. The Spirit lives in true obedience to Jesus by imitating his actions.[19] The presence of God's Spirit constitutes the church, and the Spirit proceeds from the love of God.[20]

The day of Pentecost following Jesus's ascension into heaven celebrates the official birth of the Christian Church. Pentecost reflects the community in which the Spirit brings together the oppressed and marginalized and liberates them without "coercion, pressure, or persuasion."[21]

The Spirit of God led to the phenomenon of spiritual ecstasy in the community of enslaved Africans, which some of their slaveholders condemned as religious enthusiasm and regarded as false claims of divine inspiration. Anglicans possessed a robust fear of religious enthusiasm, which was evident in the 1740 publication of the lord bishop of London tract *Observations upon the Conduct and Behaviour of a Certain Sect, Usually Distinguished by the Name of Methodists.* Cedrick May argues that the Anglican authorities considered religious enthusiasm as a threat to the established church and state (civil authorities).[22] In fact, one of the most prominent charges leveled against John Wesley and evangelical Anglicans in their cultivation of Methodism was the charge of religious enthusiasm.[23]

Religious enthusiasm reflected the unique nature of the Christianity practiced by enslaved Africans and functioned as a robust form of spiritual resistance. In his analysis of enslaved African spirituality and resistance, May shifts religious enthusiasm's negative connotations and redefines it

---

17. Poling, *Deliver Us from Evil*, xiii.

18. Leonard Lovett, "Black Holiness-Pentecostalism: Implications for Ethics and Social Transformation" (PhD diss., Emory University, 1979).

19. José Comblin, *The Holy Spirit and Liberation* (Maryknoll, NY: Orbis Books, 1989), 156.

20. Comblin, *The Holy Spirit and Liberation*, 36–39.

21. Comblin, *The Holy Spirit and Liberation*, 95–96.

22. May, *Evangelism and Resistance*, 19.

23. David Hempton, *Methodism: Empire of the Spirit* (New Haven: Yale University Press, 2005), 13. Hempton characterizes Methodism as an "empire of the Spirit."

as "the outward bodily and verbal expression of a real or imagined connection with a divine being."[24] May's definition accurately reflects the spiritual phenomenon of enslaved Africans as mediated through the work of the Holy Spirit. He argues that "these enthusiastic practices were popular impulses that appealed to blacks as activities predicated on resistance compatible with the inherently populist, revolutionary nature of Protestant Christianity."[25] In other words, the religious enthusiasm of enslaved Africans provided outward expression of their spiritual resistance against oppression and solidified their relationship with God evident in the inward witness of their sanctification.

The theology of the Spirit is antithetical to the theology of empire, which perpetuated conquest, colonization, and enslavement.[26] Theological traditions such as Puritanism and Anglicanism were based on white supremacy, white superiority, and white privilege and proved antithetical to the work of God's Spirit. The Spirit, however, fosters a diversity of race, language, culture, gender, age, geography, history, and spiritual gifts.[27] Through this diversity, the Spirit becomes the primary resource for the spiritual resistance against oppressive theological forces.

David Walker

As we noted at the opening of this chapter, David Walker was an African American abolitionist who wrote the *Appeal* to encourage the spiritual resistance of enslaved Africans against their white slaveholders and to warn white Americans of the dangers of their false Christianity. Walker was most disturbed by notions of Black inferiority perpetrated by whites and their refusal to consider Blacks as members of the human race.[28] Walker concluded that white Americans possessed a false Christianity because of their erroneous theology, which scandalized the Christian faith. Stefan M. Wheelock argues that Walker's *Appeal* exposed "the perverse undertones of American republican freedom based on errant theology" and concludes that the errant theology of white Christian Americans was a theology of racial inheritance.[29]

24. May, *Evangelism and Resistance*, 17.

25. May, *Evangelism and Resistance*, 20. This spiritual phenomenon, such as ecstatic dancing and spirit possession, were condemned as an alien practice of enslaved Africans.

26. May, *Evangelism and Resistance*, 54.

27. Comblin, *The Holy Spirit and Liberation*, 96.

28. Sterling Stuckey, *Slave Culture: Nationalist Theory and the Foundations of Black America* (New York: Oxford University Press, 1987), 123.

29. Stefan M. Wheelock, *Barbaric Culture and Black Critique: Black Antislavery Writers, Religion, and the Slaveholding Atlantic* (Charlottesville, VA: University of Virginia Press, 2016), 103.

Racial Inheritance

The theology of racial inheritance reinforced brutality through language and was a key factor within an American covenant ideology that perpetuated the subjugation of Blacks to whites.[30] In his *Appeal*, Walker notes how white Christians in the early American republic viewed themselves as superior to what they characterized as heathen nations. Jonathan Edwards identified these nations as heathen because they were not considered a part of the covenant and were nations of nonwhites.[31]

American whites possessed an erroneous theological belief that God had created Blacks as an inheritance for whites, which shaped the early understandings of American exceptionalism.[32] Therefore, Walker argued that Blacks needed to overcome a false theology.[33] In reflecting the theology of racial inheritance, whites authenticated and preserved white supremacy as a religious and cultural norm in the American context.[34] This reality was most evident in the attempt of white American Christians to convince enslaved Africans that their enslavement resulted from God's divine providence.

In his *Appeal*, Walker explained, "it is a notorious fact, that the major part of the white Americans, have, ever since we have been among them, tried to keep us ignorant, and make us believe that God made us and our children to be slaves to them and theirs."[35] He concludes that white supremacy and the practice of African enslavement solidified white Christian slaveholders as tyrants not stewards of divine providence.[36] They even used Scripture to rationalize and justify their enslavement of Africans. Consequently, those erroneous proslavery scriptural ideologies that we have already noted were promoted and developed, such as the idea that Blacks, being the offspring of Cain or as the descendants of Ham, were cursed with enslavement.

Walker accused white Christian Americans of apostasy and contended that they violated the Holy Scriptures. He wrote:

Have not Americans the Bible in their hands? Do they believe it? Surely they do not. See how they treat us in open violation of the Bible? They no doubt will be greatly offended with me, but if God does not awaken

30. Wheelock, *Barbaric Culture and Black Critique*, 107.
31. Wheelock, *Barbaric Culture and Black Critique*, 107.
32. Wheelock, *Barbaric Culture and Black Critique*, 101.
33. Wheelock, *Barbaric Culture and Black Critique*, 102.
34. Wheelock, *Barbaric Culture and Black Critique*, 102.
35. David Walker, *Walker's Appeal, in Four Articles Together with a Preamble to the Coloured Citizens of the World* (Mansfield, CT: Martino Publishing, 2015), 33.
36. Wheelock, *Barbaric Culture and Black Critique*, 121.

them, it will be, because they are superior to other men, as they have represented themselves to be.[37]

In his *Appeal*, Walker argued that white Christians in America were suffering from barbarism, which he attributed to their practice of African enslavement. He further contended that these white Christians possessed depraved hearts, asserting that "we see the depravity of men's hearts when in pursuit only of gain, particularly when they oppress their fellow creatures to obtain that gain, God suffers some to go on until they are lost forever."[38] For Walker, the practice of African enslavement, and particularly chattel slavery, reflected the actions of a reprobated heart and mind. He believed that the practice of slavery had transformed white Christian America into a modern Sodom and Gomorrah[39] and suggested that white repentance for this sinfulness of African enslavement was impossible. Walker writes:

> To be plain and candid with you, Americans! I say that the day is fast approaching, when there will be a greater time on the continent of America, than ever was witnessed upon this earth, since it came from the hand of its Creator. Some of you have done us so much injury, that you will never be able to repent. Your cup must be filled. You want us for your slaves and shall have enough of us. God is just, who will give you your fill of us.[40]

He concluded that universal repentance for the sinfulness of slavery was imperative. Yet, the sin of slavery had transformed slaveholders into reprobates; and, being beyond the hope of redemption, slaveholders could expect the day of reckoning for the punishment of their sin.

Black Citizenship

Walker offered a robust argument for Black citizenship in America, which challenged the motivations of the American Colonization Society (ACS). He condemned efforts to colonize Liberia for the emigration of freed Blacks and declared that American land was just as much the land of enslaved Africans as it was the land of their white enslavers. Walker exclaimed:

> Why should they send us into a far country to die? See the thousands of foreigners emigrating to America every year: and if there be ground sufficient for them to cultivate, and bread for them to eat, why would

---

37. Walker, *Walker's Appeal*, 38.
38. Walker, *Walker's Appeal*, 51.
39. Wheelock, *Barbaric Culture and Black Critique*, 138.
40. Walker, *Walker's Appeal*, 49.

they wish to send the first tillers of the land away? Africans have made fortunes for thousands, who are yet unwilling to part with their services; but the free must be sent away, and those who remain, must be slaves. I have no doubt that there are many good men who do not see as I do, and who are for sending us to Liberia; but they have not duly considered the subject—they are not men of colour. This land which we have watered with our tears and our blood, is now our mother country, and we are well satisfied to stay where wisdom abounds and the gospel is free.[41]

Walker accused the ACS of hypocrisy and concluded that America was a land of contradictions with a system of oppression.[42] He believed that colonizationists such as Thomas Jefferson had been corrupted by the errant theology of racial inheritance, which fostered the cultivation of proslavery catechesis.[43] Ironically, the seeds for the ACS were planted through the Christianization, civilization, and colonization scheme of Samuel Hopkins and New Divinity antislavery theology. However, some historians, such as Saillant, conclude that the New Divinity theologians designed colonization for the creation of a permanently white society through Black emigration.[44] He argues that the New Divinity theologians viewed blackness as repugnant and were disgusted by the prospect of a future mixed-race society in America. If Saillant's presuppositions are accurate, such would robustly situate New Divinity adherents in the category of racial purist abolitionists rather than paternalist abolitionists.

Walker's *Appeal* was as an indictment of the Christianity of white Americans, which he identified as hypocritical, false, and barbaric. He offered major differences between Black and white Christianity in America and questioned the nature of the latter:

Have you not brought us among you, in chains and hand-cuffs, like brutes, and treated us with all the cruelties and rigour your ingenuity could invent, consistent with the laws of your country, which (for the blacks) are tyrannical enough? Can the American preachers appeal unto God, the Maker and Searcher of the hearts, and tell him, with the Bible in their hands, that they make no distinction on account of men's colour?[45]

---

41. Walker, *Walker's Appeal*, 57–58.
42. Walker, *Walker's Appeal*, 127.
43. Wheelock, *Barbaric Culture and Black Critique*, 123.
44. Saillant, *Black Puritan*, 101.
45. Walker, *Walker's Appeal*, 42.

Black Christian Faith

Walker urged white American Christians to listen to the voice of the Holy Ghost to avoid the vengeance of God for the crime and injustice of slavery.[46] He viewed the Holy Ghost as the source of true Christianity.

Based on his pneumatic view of Black Christianity, Walker identified enslaved Africans as the property of the Holy Ghost, believing that the Holy Ghost was the heart of Black Christian faith in America and that the spiritual ecstasy of enslaved Africans fueled through the Holy Ghost brought their deliverance and justice against the oppression and injustice of slavery. Walker exclaimed that "the Lord has a suffering people, whose moans and groans at his feet for deliverance from oppression and wretchedness, pierce the very throne of Heaven, and call loudly on the God of Justice, to be revenged."[47] He believed that the cries and moans of the oppressed were consequences of their oppression and that slavery was the principal cause of the enslaved Africans' oppression, but that God is the God of justice for them.[48] He asserted:

> They [whites] are so happy to keep ignorance and degradation, and to receive the homage and the labour of the slaves, they forget that God rules in the armies of heaven and among the inhabitants of the earth, having his ears continually open to the cries, tears, and groans of his oppressed people; and being a just and holy Being will at one day appear fully in behalf of the oppressed, and arrest the progress of the avaricious oppressors.[49]

Walker believed that people of color possessed a moral superiority to whites and concluded that because of the authenticity of their brand of Christianity, Blacks possessed a messianic role in the salvation history of America.[50]

Black Nationalism

In response to the racial nationalism that had been constructed by the founding fathers, which made the white race superior to other races of people in America, Walker cultivated a Black nationalism designed to encourage racial pride among enslaved Africans. At the heart of his Black nationalist agenda were the themes of redemption and destiny, which were

---

46. Walker, *Walker's Appeal*, 47.
47. Walker, *Walker's Appeal*, 48–49.
48. Walker, *Walker's Appeal*, 5.
49. Walker, *Walker's Appeal*, 3.
50. Stuckey, *Slave Culture*, 132.

based on the biblical imagery of Ethiopianism.[51] African American historian Sterling Stuckey argues that "Walker's pride in blackness, his respect for the achievements of blacks in the ancient world, and his belief in African moral character and the need for African autonomy provided elements of cultural nationalism."[52] Walker believed that Blacks were more humane than the enlightened whites of America.[53] He also believed that Blacks transformed Christianity in America with their spirituality.[54] Ultimately, he concluded that the world would only become truly Christianized through Blacks.[55]

Walker's *Appeal* called on enslaved Africans to revolt through armed resistance mediated through spiritual resistance. He believed that Blacks had more reason to revolt against whites than white Americans had to revolt against Britain.[56] Eddie Glaude argues that "Walker believed it was the duty of every black Christian to fight (even if it meant death) against the scourge of slavery and racial discrimination because submission to such evils was tantamount to a sin against God."[57] For Walker, true Christianity is a living religion that takes action in word and deed.[58] His objective was to awaken Blacks and equip them to respond with armed resistance to white supremacy. According to Glaude, "Walker hoped through his demonization of white slaveholders and racists to provoke blacks to think of freedom apart from white people and to define themselves not by their standards

---

51. African American church historian Love Henry Whelchel Jr. used Scripture to justify his argument that Africa is the birthplace of the three Abrahamic religions: Judaism, Christianity, and Islam. He asserted that "Africans are mentioned throughout the Bible. The Hebrew Bible alone cites Ethiopia over forty times and Egypt over one hundred times . . . the fact of Africa's prominent role in the Bible comes into play later in the sixteenth century as Europeans initiated their massive enslavement of African people. They wished to rationalize their behavior, and it was the Portuguese, the first Europeans involved in the enslavement of Africans, who coined the term Negroes, or the Blacks. Prior to this time, Europeans mostly referred to Africans as Moors or Ethiopians. The Moors were despised as they had just been overthrown after ruling over most of Hispania (the Iberian Peninsula) for the preceding seven hundred years. For the Portuguese, using the term Negro helped to obscure the fact that Africans, via the terms Ethiopia or Egypt, were repeatedly mentioned throughout the Bible." See Love Henry Whelchel, *The History and Heritage of African American Churches: A Way Out of No Way* (St. Paul, MN: Paragon House, 2010), 8.

52. Stuckey, *Slave Culture*, 135.

53. Walker, *Walker's Appeal*, 24.

54. Stuckey, *Slave Culture*, 132.

55. Walker, *Walker's Appeal*, 18.

56. Stuckey, *Slave Culture*, 130.

57. Eddie S. Glaude Jr., "Of the Black Church and the Making of a Black Public," in Cornel West and Eddie S. Glaude Jr., eds, *African American Religious Thought: An Anthology* (Louisville, KY: Westminster John Knox Press, 2003), 360.

58. Stuckey, *Slave Culture*, 135.

but by the laws of God."[59] Wheelock argues that Walker's *Appeal* articulated "the violent potential in a redeemed black liberation."[60] Slave revolt was the medium through which this redemption from slavery for enslaved Africans could be achieved.

Walker's *Appeal* cultivated a spirituality of armed resistance for enslaved Africans against the oppression of their enslavers and the scheme for colonization. Walker argued that whites know that Blacks are equally human but realize that they have committed so much injustice that Blacks may retaliate. He wrote:

> Man, in all ages and all nations of the earth, is the same. Man is a peculiar creature—he is the image of his God, though he may be subjected to the most wretched condition upon earth, yet the spirit and feeling which constitute the creature, man, can never be entirely erased from his breast, because the God who made him after his own image, planted it in his heart; he cannot get rid of it. The whites knowing this, they do not know what to do; they know that they have done us so much injury, they are afraid that we, being men, and not brutes, will retaliate, and woe will be to them; therefore, that dreadful fear, together with an avaricious spirit, and the natural love in them, to be called masters (which term will yet honour them with to their sorrow) bring them to the resolve that they keep us in ignorance and wretchedness, as long as they possibly can, and make the best of their time, while it lasts.[61]

Walker believed that the God of justice would impose retributive justice against whites in America for their injustices against Blacks. He argued that white Christians had chosen to preserve Blacks' savage and apostate cultural contexts, and therefore, slave insurrection was an ethical possibility to achieve liberation.[62] He predicted a second American revolution if whites refused to repent and end their oppression of Blacks.[63] Walker's *Appeal* reflected his apocalyptic vision of the destruction of whites for the sinfulness and injustice of African enslavement through the spirituality of armed resistance. It also reflected his liberative pneumatology through his exhortation to enslaved Africans to listen to the Holy Spirit and his conclusion that enslaved Africans were the property of the Holy Spirit.

---

59. Glaude, "Of the Black Church," 358.
60. Wheelock, *Barbaric Culture and Black Critique*, 111.
61. Walker, *Walker's Appeal*, 61–62.
62. Walker, *Walker's Appeal*, 61–62.
63. Walker, *Walker's Appeal*, 139.

Nat Turner

In 1831, African American prophet and slave preacher Nat Turner led a successful slave insurrection in Southampton County, Virginia, under the guidance of the Holy Spirit. Turner's pneumatic life experiences and gifts, particularly the gift of prophecy, fueled his spiritual resistance against the oppression of white enslavers.

Spiritual Gifts

There were signs of Turner's prophetic gift from his childhood, which included physical evidence. Biographer Stephen B. Oates explained that "Nat had congenital bumps and scars on his head and chest. African tradition held that a male with markings like these was destined to become a leader."[64] In African spirituality and culture, certain markings on the human body such as birthmarks indicated supernatural powers and spiritual gifts. Turner believed that God had called him to be a prophet before his birth. In his *Confessions*, which were reported by his white attorney, Thomas R. Gray, following his slave insurrection and capture, Turner wrote:

> I surely would be a prophet, as the Lord had shewn me things that had happened before my birth. And my father and mother strengthened me in this my first impression, saying in my presence, I was intended for some great purpose, which they had always thought from certain marks on my head and breast. . . . To a mind like mine, restless, inquisitive and observant of every thing that was passing, it is easy to suppose that religion was the subject [that] principally occupied my thoughts—there was nothing that I saw or heard of to which my attention was not directed.[65]

Turner's mother convinced him as a child that he had special powers of divination.[66] He began preaching on the Turner plantation and evolved into an itinerant Baptist preacher. Oates asserts that "inevitably, Nat began exhorting Turner's slaves in the cabins and out in the fields. The man was spellbinding. He cried out what the slaves felt inside. He now told them about his communion with the Spirit, a miracle that awed them and enhanced his

---

64. Stephen B. Oates, *The Fires of Jubilee: Nat Turner's Fierce Rebellion* (New York: HarperCollins, 1975), 12.

65. Thomas R. Gray, *The Confessions of Nat Turner* (Baltimore: Lucas & Deaver, 1831), in Herbert Aptheker, *Nat Turner's Slave Rebellion: Including the 1831 Confessions* (Mineola, NY: Dover Publications, 2006), 133–34.

66. Walter C. Rucker, *The River Flows On: Black Resistance, Culture, and Identity Formation in Early America* (Baton Rouge: Louisiana State University Press, 2006), 190.

reputation as a young holy man."[67] Turner's preaching reflected his pneumatic, revolutionary theology.

Theology

Turner's theology foreshadowed future liberation theologies that portray a
divine partiality to the plight of oppressed people. African American theologian Karl W. Lampley argues that Turner was not a systematic theologian
but offered a theology that was "fragmented, mystical, and guided by his
understanding of his personal relationship with and experience of the Holy
Spirit."[68] Therefore, in the same vein as David Walker, Turner promoted a
God of justice and revolution who eradicated white oppression and liberated black people.[69] Lampley concludes that Turner's view of God combined
the Christ of the Gospels and the God of the Old Testament and demonstrated his belief in the compatibility of the love and the wrath of God.[70]
Consequently, Turner believed that the righteousness of God would dis-
rupt the institution of slavery and impose judgment on white enslavers. He
emphasized that divine justice, through the work of the Holy Spirit, was
integral to understanding the difference between the theology of Black
evangelical Christianity and theology of white evangelical Christianity.

Turner cultivated a Black liberation theology that was antithetical to the
theology of white Christian slaveholders. Furthermore, his theology radi-
calized Black Christianity, affirming the freedom, equality, and humanity
of Blacks.[71]

Revolutionary Violence for Liberation

In addition to making the Christ of the Gospels compatible with the God
of the Old Testament, Turner correlated the God of the Exodus and the
liberating Christ, which exposed a God who liberated the enslaved and
oppressed.[72] He thereby demonstrated the trajectory of divine liberation
from the Hebrew Scriptures to the New Testament, which in some instances
sanctioned divine violence. Turner's biblical hermeneutics, coupled with
his theological compatibility between the love of God and the wrath of God,
produced his theory of revolutionary violence for liberation.

Turner viewed the revolutionary violence of enslaved Africans against
their white enslavers through insurrections as the counterviolence of God

---

67. Oates, *The Fires of Jubilee*, 27.

68. Karl W. Lampley, *A Theological Account of Nat Turner: Christianity, Violence, and
Theology* (New York: Palgrave Macmillan, 2013), 40.

69. Lampley, *A Theological Account of Nat Turner*, 68.

70. Lampley, *A Theological Account of Nat Turner*, 16.

71. Lampley, *A Theological Account of Nat Turner*, 19.

72. Lampley, *A Theological Account of Nat Turner*, 68.

for the sinfulness of slavery and dehumanization. His theology demonstrated the compatibility of violence and Christianity.[73] Violence divinely inspired was a necessity for enslaved Africans, who were forced to theologize from a context in which they were oppressed and persecuted because of the violence of their white enslavers. Turner's social context, which consisted of dehumanization, poverty, and slavery, formed his theological inclination toward violence.[74] Essentially, Turner's theology promoted divine violence as the resolution of human injustice. He was determined to combat the demonically induced slaveholding Christianity of whites in America.[75] Turner believed that God was on the side of enslaved Africans, prophetically guiding them to divine violence, and that slave insurrection against the oppression of white slaveholders was the will of God.[76]

The revolutionary nature of Turner's theology was the catalyst for his insurrection. Like David Walker, Turner envisioned a living religion, a religion of action. His revolutionary spirit was influenced by his spirituality and theology.[77] Jesus indeed suffered and liberated sinful humanity and rebelled against the injustices of the Roman Empire and the religious legalism of the Jewish law, which fostered human bondage rather than liberation. Biblical scholar Obery Hendricks identifies Jesus as a political revolutionary and argues that as a political revolutionary, Jesus exemplified "liberation of mind, body, and soul from the tranny of principalities and powers and unjust rulers in high places."[78] Like Jesus, Turner's revolutionary theology of violent resistance and action was the product of his inner piety and spiritual discipline based on the evangelical Black slave religion.[79] Consequently, he developed a Black radical evangelical Christianity that sanctioned divine violence when necessary, as prompted by the Holy Spirit.

Turner's revolutionary theology demonstrates the spiritual resistance of enslaved Black radical evangelical Christians to enslavement and oppression. Rebellion, as prompted by the Holy Spirit, constituted the proper response of enslaved Africans to the institution of slavery. Enslaved Africans were victimized and terrorized by the institution of slavery. Institutional and structural violence as practiced through chattel slavery in British colonial America and the early republic was the catalyst for the resistance of those victimized by such violence. Lampley asserts that "Turner's violence

---

73. Lampley, *A Theological Account of Nat Turner*, 32.

74. Lampley, *A Theological Account of Nat Turner*, 36.

75. Lampley, *A Theological Account of Nat Turner*, 124.

76. Lampley, *A Theological Account of Nat Turner*, 60–64.

77. Aptheker, *Nat Turner's Slave Rebellion*, 36.

78. Obery M. Hendricks, *The Politics of Jesus: Rediscovering the True Revolutionary Nature of Jesus' Teachings and How They Have Been Corrupted* (New York: Doubleday, 2006), 10.

79. Aptheker, *Nat Turner's Slave Rebellion*, 15.

was the liberating violence of revolt against the fundamentally violent system of slavery and white supremacy."[80] American historian Joseph Drexler-Dreis argues that Turner's rebellion was not separate from the Christian faith of the slave community but rather "a radicalization of the Christianity lived out by enslaved Africans."[81]

Spirituality

Indigenous African spirituality was complicit in the radicalization of the Christianity of enslaved Africans. Drexler-Dreis maintains that the white evangelical Baptist tradition and the "invisible institution" where Blacks assembled to worship in secrecy are the two factors that shaped Turner's spirituality.[82]

In addition to his prophetic gift, Turner was a conjurer and preacher on the slave plantation, which reflected the most prominent influence of indigenous African spirituality. Whites accused Turner of engaging in the practice of conjuration, which he denied.[83] Rucker argues that Turner behaved like a typical conjurer on the slave plantation, yet Turner robustly denied possessing such power and even claimed to view such practices as profane. In his *Confessions,* he exclaimed:

> Knowing the influence I had obtained over the minds of my fellow servants (not by the means of conjuring and such like tricks—for to them I always spoke of such things with contempt) but by the communion of the Spirit whose revelations I often communicated to them, and they believed and said my wisdom came from God.[84]

Considering Turner's own words and despite evidence of conjuration, some historians such as U. B. Philips, Kenneth Stampp, and Herbert Aptheker conclude that Turner's spiritual inspiration had purely Christian roots.[85] Rucker traced this conclusion to the scholarship of William Drewry, who limits the scope of Turner's spirituality to that of the Baptist tradition of nineteenth-century America.[86]

The controversy over Turner's conjuration reflects the dichotomy between Black radical evangelical Christianity and the pervasiveness of

---

80. Lampley, *A Theological Account of Nat Turner*, 10.

81. Joseph Drexler-Dreis, "Nat Turner's Rebellion as a Process of Conversion," *Black Theology: An International Journal* 12, no. 3 (2014): 240–48.

82. Drexler-Dreis, "Nat Turner's Rebellion as a Process of Conversion," 233.

83. Oates, *The Fires of Jubilee*, 38.

84. Rucker, *The River Flows On*, 187.

85. Rucker, *The River Flows On*, 187.

86. Rucker, *The River Flows On*, 187.

religious respectability on the slave plantations based on the norms of white evangelical Christianity. Rucker's analysis of Turner's spirituality offers a counter-argument to the notion that the conjurer and slave preachers were archenemies on the slave plantation. He contends that there was a middle ground between conjuration and Christianity consisting of the slave exhorter, preacher, and prophet, whom Rucker suggested "bridged the two spiritual worldviews while not completely belonging to either."[87] W. E. B. Dubois had argued that identifying Turner as either a Christian preacher or a conjurer abandoned the understanding of Turner as a transnational figure.[88] Certainly, Turner had to deny and condemn acts of conjuration to preserve religious respectability with his white masters, a situation that reflects his struggle with the reality of enslaved Africans having to develop a dialectical double consciousness to survive the terror of enslavement. Nevertheless, conjuration was the natural product of indigenous African spirituality, particularly among those with supernatural gifts as empowered by the Spirit of God. Furthermore, the demonization of indigenous African spirituality by white evangelical Christianity has contributed to the development of Christian worldviews that delegitimize and eradicate the work of God's Spirit in indigenous African spirituality. The pneumatic experiences and actions of Turner—whether as acts of conjuration or the evangelical work of the slave preacher—reflect the relationship between the sacred and the secular in Turner's communion with the Spirit of God. On the one hand, this proves Dubois's contention about characterizations of Turner being erroneous; yet, on the other hand, we can concur with Rucker that Turner could have interpreted Christianity through the lens of conjuration.[89]

Rebellion or Revolution

The complicity of indigenous African spirituality through the lens of conjuration contributed to the construction of an African American consciousness within Black radical Christian evangelicals that necessitated spiritual resistance through violence to achieve liberation.

Before Turner's 1831 insurrection, whites in British colonial America and the early republic had reduced slave revolts to some form of illness that had been transported from Santo Domingo of the West Indies on slave ships and infected American slaves with the illicit mentality to run away or murder white people.[90] White slave owners in Southampton County, Virginia, viewed Turner's rebellion as an act of terrorism, which resulted in the

87. Rucker, *The River Flows On*, 188.
88. Rucker, *The River Flows On*, 188.
89. Rucker, *The River Flows On*, 188.
90. Oates, *The Fires of Jubilee*, 16.

execution of approximately 120 enslaved and free blacks, including Turner. Now Lampley argues that Turner's rebellion was not a form of terrorism but a legitimate revolution for liberation. He notes:

> Terrorism is the violence of the desperate and cruel. It utilizes brutality and horror to manipulate, threaten, and coerce submission through fear and distress. By contrast, Nat Turner was fighting a legitimate war and revolution for his freedom and that of other black slaves. His acts were viewed as terrorism at the time because his white slave masters were shocked by his open defiance. They expected blacks to accept their fate passively and submissively. The real terrorists were the slaveholding perpetrators of forced labor, broken families, rape, surrogacy, intimidation, coercion, and violence. Turner, however, was a freedom fighter whose liberating and revolutionary violence against slavery was also prophetic Christian violence condemning and judging the peculiar institution in America.[91]

Turner and his revolutionary disciples engaged in prophetic violence against white Christian slave masters. Lampley notes that "prophetic violence is God's violence through the prophets against the enemies of Israel and against Israel for sins and transgressions."[92] Like the Hebrew prophets to the Israelites, Turner was divinely called and appointed as God's prophet to enslaved Africans in Southampton County, Virginia, with the divine burden of prophecy as God's oracle to the people and God's executor of justice against their enemies, the whites who had enslaved and oppressed them in the name of Christ. As a Black radical evangelical Christian, Turner viewed his insurrection as a Christian experience. Proslavery Christian theologians had convinced white Christian slaveholders that the institution of slavery was a means of grace; therefore, of necessity Turner viewed his spiritual resistance through violent rebellion as a participation in God's grace.[93] Hence, Turner's rebellion constituted a Christian means of grace through which God would grant liberation to enslaved Africans.

At the heart of Black radical evangelical Christianity is an affinity with pneumatic experiences, which is evident in Turner's visions from the Spirit of God. The Holy Spirit had an essential role in Turner's theology.[94] Without a robust emphasis on the work and imperative of the Holy Spirit, Turner's theology would collapse into the same abyss of theological mediocrity and hypocrisy as the theology of white Christian enslavers. By demonstrating

---

91. Lampley, *A Theological Account of Nat Turner*, 11.
92. Lampley, *A Theological Account of Nat Turner*, 10.
93. Drexler-Dreis, "Nat Turner's Rebellion as a Process of Conversion," 230.
94. Lampley, *A Theological Account of Nat Turner*, 131.

the parallels between the conjurer on the slave plantation and the supernatural phenomena of Turner, as evident in his visions, Rucker argues that both the conjurer and slave preacher lived as ascetics.[95] Turner's life and spirituality reflected the same asceticism, for he would separate from other enslaved Africans to have communion with the Holy Spirit.[96] In his *Confessions,* Turner declared:

> I now withdrew myself as my situation would permit, from the intercourse of my fellow servants, for the avowed purpose of serving the Spirit more fully—and it appeared to me, and reminded me of the things it had already shown me, and that it would then reveal to me the knowledge of the elements, the revolution of the planets, the operation of tides, and changes of the seasons.[97]

He claimed to receive revelation from God in the form of visions mediated through the Holy Spirit. White Christian evangelicals viewed Turner's experience of supernatural phenomena as a form of religious fanaticism and a source of entertainment. Enslaved Africans were attracted to his supernatural phenomena, as they viewed his religious enthusiasm in the manner that Cedric May described the nature of religious enthusiasm within the community of enslaved Africans—as an outward physical expression of inner spirituality mediated through the Holy Spirit and an outward manifestation of spiritual resistance against the oppression of African enslavement.

The climax of Turner's spiritual phenomena was his pneumatic experience of visions. In the second vision, Turner reported experiencing an apocalyptic vision of war between black and white spirits. He exclaimed, "I had a vision and I saw white spirits and black spirits engaged in battle, and the sun was darkened—the thunder rolled in the Heavens, and blood flowed in streams—and I heard a voice saying, 'Such is your luck, such you are called to see, and let it come rough or smooth, you must surely bare it.'"[98] In addition to warfare between black and white spirits, Turner envisioned deadly warfare between freedom and slavery and a struggle between good and evil, all of which were situated in expectations of future social and political equality for enslaved Africans through justice achieved as a result of racial warfare. Lampley concludes that Turner's vision of apocalyptic justice "leads to active opposition of evil and

---

95. Rucker, *The River Flows On*, 194.
96. Rucker, *The River Flows On*, 194–95.
97. Gray, *The Confessions of Nat Turner*, 136.
98. Gray, *The Confessions of Nat Turner*, 136.

dehumanizing conditions."[99] Turner's ultimate vision occurred when he received a divine sign from God in February of 1831 in the form of a solar eclipse.[100] The eclipse of the sun caused many in Southampton County, Virginia, to question if the eclipse signified the end of the world. However, for Turner, the eclipse signified the divine sign that he had been patiently awaiting as the clearance for him and his chosen associates to engage in warfare through divine violence. Turner had initially declared July 4, 1830, as the day of reckoning, the day of judgment, and the day of death for white enslavers for the sinfulness of slavery. However, Turner became ill on Independence Day, which prevented warfare from commencing on that date.[101] Nevertheless, the date exposed the hypocrisy of the notion of American independence, which had secured the political, social, religious, and civil liberties of whites in British colonial America and the early republic while refusing to affirm the full humanity of enslaved Africans and denying them the same rights, privileges, and liberties of whites.

Turner believed that divinely sanctioned warfare through violence not only constituted the day of reckoning and judgment for the sinfulness of slavery, it also constituted the inauguration of the Jubilee that emanated from the spirit of liberation. Drexler-Dreis argues that this spirit of liberation had been concealed by the institution of slavery and had been obscured by the religious norms of white evangelical Christianity.[102] Turner viewed the Holy Spirit as radical and revolutionary, believing that the Holy Spirit commanded and encouraged his insurrection. The Holy Spirit breaks the power of racism and injustice, an extension of the work of the liberating Christ.[103]

Conclusion

Ultimately, Turner's theology was parallel to the theological presuppositions within David Walker's *Appeal*; both Black radical evangelicals fostered the radicalization of Black evangelical Christianity mediated through a liberative pneumatology which they believed would achieve liberation for enslaved Africans through spiritual resistance.

The characteristics and function of liberative pneumatology include (1) fostering community; (2) liberating the oppressed; (3) fostering the phenomenon of spiritual ecstasy that, through physical and verbal expression and the empowerment of the Holy Spirit, challenges oppression; (4) oppos-

---

99. Gray, *The Confessions of Nat Turner*, 58.
100. Aptheker, *Nat Turner's Slave Rebellion*, 44.
101. Aptheker, *Nat Turner's Slave Rebellion*, 44.
102. Drexler-Dreis, "Nat Turner's Rebellion as a Process of Conversion," 240.
103. Lampley, *A Theological Account of Nat Turner*, 64.

ing and challenging empire theology; (5) empowering cultural resistance through the spiritual tools of the culture of oppressed persons; (6) affirming the oppressed as the property of the Holy Spirit evident in their spiritual ecstasy; (7) empowering revolutionary action of the oppressed against oppression; (8) activating divine justice against oppression; (9) cultivating humanitarianism; and (10) promoting egalitarianism.

Enslaved Africans developed their own brand of Christianity by necessity. They constructed their liberative pneumatology as persons enslaved by white Christians. Consequently, enslaved Africans rejected the spiritual hypocrisy and false Christianity of their white Christian enslavers.

The spiritual resistance of enslaved Africans, particularly Black radical evangelicals, demonstrates how Black Christianity became divorced from oppressive classical white Christianities because when these oppressive forms of Christianity were laced with ideologies and theologies of white supremacy, white superiority, and white privilege, they lacked the spiritual capacity to address the ultimate concerns and needs of the Black soul. The complicity of these white Christianities in the oppression of supposed racial others validates their being classified as false Christianities.

In the nineteenth century, Frederick Douglass distinguished between the hypocritical slaveholding religion of American Christianity and the Christianity of Christ of enslaved Africans. He characterized the former as corrupt and fraudulent. Based on Douglass's characterization, we begin to see that the Christianity of enslaved Africans actually Christianized American Christianity and functioned as the supernatural medium through which America received the Holy Spirit.

Part III

THE IMPACT

6

Antebellum Evangelicalism

The black millennial dream of freedom and equality ran counter to the narrowing definition of what it meant to be an American that emerged from the awakening. Black Evangelical prophets saw more realistically than the white prophets of revitalization that a long hard road lay ahead.
—William G. McLoughlin

In 1978, William G. McLoughlin published his seminal work *Revivals, Awakenings, and Reform*,[1] in which he identifies the evangelical hope of Blacks during the Second Great Awakening and explains how the hopes of Black evangelicals, who possessed an earthly hope for abolition and equality, differed from the hopes of white evangelicals. As we discovered in the last chapter, the prophetic visions of Nat Turner reveal that his successful insurrection to combat the evil atrocities of African enslavement was situated in Christian spirituality. Turner's insurrection in 1831 occurred almost a decade before the end of the Second Great Awakening, which provided the spiritual foundation for social reform in American society.

The Second Great Awakening

The revivalism of the first camp meeting organized by the Presbyterian revivalist James McGready on the frontier of Cane Ridge, Kentucky, in 1801, became a fixture of American religion. These camp meetings became popularized through the revivalism of American Methodists.[2] The revivalism of the Second Great Awakening appealed to common people in American

1. William G. McLoughlin, *Revivals, Awakenings, and Reform: An Essay on Religion and Social Change in America, 1607–1977* (Chicago: University of Chicago Press, 1978).

2. See Roger Finke and Rodney Stark, *The Church of America, 1776–2005: Winners and Losers of Our Religious Economy* (Rutgers, NJ: Rutgers University Press, 2005), who conclude that the Baptists and Methodists were the winners of the American religious economy from the inception of the American republic through the nineteenth century.

society, particularly those on the Western frontier and rural areas of the South.

The theology and polity of the Baptists and Methodists were effective in attracting common people, especially enslaved Africans. The spiritual ecstasy of the Second Great Awakening revivalism was reminiscent of indigenous African spirituality and consisted of falling or being slain in the Spirit, holy dancing, jerking, barking, shouting, rolling, running, holy laughter, speaking in tongues, and singing in the Spirit. Winthrop Hudson and Ann Taves indicate that both Blacks and whites in the Methodist camp meetings experienced spiritual ecstasy and were known as "shouting Methodists."[3] Love Henry Whelchel Jr. has argued that this spiritual ecstasy originated with people of African descent:

> Our African American ancestors were brought to the United States with the Holy Ghost fire shut up in their bones. They arrived on this continent with an insatiable hunger for the spiritual world. From West and Central Africa, they brought a strong belief that the personal and communal had a continuous involvement in the spirit-world in the practical affairs of daily life.[4]

In support of this claim, Eugene Genevose suggests that whites who engaged in ecstatic behavior were imitating the ecstatic behavior of Blacks and even maintains that "the blacks did not hide their disdain for white shouters, whom they regarded as a plain copy of themselves . . . even in the early camp meetings the blacks notoriously outshouted the whites and stayed up singing and praying long after the whites had retired."[5] Consequently, it is reasonable that white Christians would not have had knowledge of the spiritual ecstasy of the Holy Ghost nor possessed or experienced this phenomenon without the Christianity of enslaved Africans.

During the Second Great Awakening, the camp meetings were most prominent on the frontier of American society, where sexual promiscuity and alcohol abuse were rampant. Therefore, in addition to advocacy for abolitionism, social reform included advocacy for temperance and women's rights.

The driving force for social reform was the theology of the revivalists, which shifted with the Second Great Awakening from Calvinism to Armin-

---

3. See Winthrop S. Hudson, "Shouting Methodists," *Encounter* 29 (Winter 1968): 73–84; and Ann Taves, *Fits, Trances, and Visions: Experiencing Religion and Explaining Experience from Wesley to James* (Princeton, NJ: Princeton University Press, 1999), 76–117.

4. Love Henry Whelchel Jr., "How America Got the Holy Ghost: The Uniqueness of the African American Experience of Holiness," *Quarterly Review* 25, no. 2 (2005): 158.

5. Eugene D. Genovese, *Roll Jordan Roll: The World the Slaves Made* (New York: Vintage Books, 1974), 240.

ianism, the belief that God created humans with free will to choose eternal salvation or damnation. Calvinists, however, believed that God chose some people for divine election or eternal life and others for damnation or eternal reprobation. As we discovered in our study of Puritanism and white superiority, theologies of election are dangerous. Biblical scholar Michael Coogan notes the dangers of theologies of election in his analysis of the myth of divine chosenness:

> From antiquity to the present, the idea of being divinely chosen has had powerful and often pernicious effects. If only one group has been divinely chosen then others have not been, and that justifies subjugating them and taking their land. Such rationalization has been used repeatedly, in the most virulent forms of anti-Semitism, in the enslavement and even extermination of aboriginal peoples, and in the confiscation of land by force from those not chosen—be they Canaanites, Jews, Muslims, Africans, Native Americans, Palestinians, and too many others.[6]

Tribalism, whether ethnic/racial, religious, or both, naturally evolves from theologies of election. Mark Lindsay asserts that "humans are tribal creatures."[7] He identifies the therapeutic nature of being tribal—belonging—but warns that tribalism generally consists of prioritizing the group to which you belong over another group. This chapter examines the tribalism of white Christian supremacists who integrate ethnic/racial and religious tribalism with racial othering, dehumanization, oppression, exploitation, and exclusion of any particular religious or cultural group.

Charles Finney

The most prominent revivalist and theologian of the Second Great Awakening was Charles Finney. Finney was born in Connecticut and reared in the Presbyterian tradition. In 1821, he had a spiritual awakening and, in 1824, was ordained a Presbyterian cleric. In the same year of his ordination, Finney, as a benefactor of the Female Missionary Society of the Western District, began preaching in upstate New York,[8] an area that was very significant to his success as a revivalist, which began in the Burned-Over

---

6. Michael Coogan, *God's Favorites: Judaism, Christianity, and the Myth of Divine Chosenness* (Boston: Beacon Press, 2019), 2.

7. Mark R. Lindsay, *God Has Chosen: The Doctrine of Election through Christian History* (Downers Grove, IL: InterVarsity Press, 2020), 214.

8. Randall Balmer, *The Making of Evangelicalism: From Revivalism to Politics and Beyond* (Waco, TX: Baylor University Press, 2010), 20.

district, a seedbed for religious revivalism, apocalyptic visions, communal living, and social reform.[9]

Revivalism

Finney was a trained attorney who employed the tactics of a trial lawyer in his revivalism. In his seminal work *Lectures on Revival and Religion,* Finney introduced "new measures," which are still used in modern revivalism. These new measures consisted of using "you" rather than "they" in his references to the wicked. Those convicted of their sins were brought to what Finney called the "anxious bench," which was equivalent to being brought to the witness stand. John Wesley, the father of the Methodist and Holiness movements and the grandfather of the Pentecostal movement, had employed similar tactics in his revivalism in which sinners would come to the mercy seat or "mourner's bench" to confess their sins, repent, and experience regeneration and sanctification. Generally, the front pew of the church served as the anxious or mourner's bench.[10] Historically, the mourner's bench has been pivotal to the conversion experience in the African American Christian tradition. In his revivalism, Finney employed other new measures, such as delivering revival messages spontaneously, preaching with a theatrical delivery, encouraging women to testify and pray in public, and the use of advertising.[11] Because of these effective new measures, Finney is considered the "Father of Modern Revivalism."

As a Presbyterian, Finney's initial theological orientation was Calvinism. However, he viewed Calvinism as impractical for revivalism. As we noted earlier, as a Calvinist, the New England revivalist Jonathan Edwards characterized revivalism as "the surprising work of God," reflecting the

---

9. In 1828, Joseph Smith received his revelation from the Angel Moroni for the Book of Mormon resulting in the formation of Mormonism; in 1831, William Miller experienced his apocalyptic vision announcing the Second Coming of Christ in 1844 resulting in the formation of Seventh-Day Adventism; in 1837, the settled community of the Shakers experienced major revivalism through the spiritual direction of their founder, Mother Ann Lee; and in 1848, John Humphrey Noyes founded the Oneida Society, a utopian community that believed that Christ had returned in AD 70 and practiced communal living. Furthermore, the pioneer of the Social Gospel, Washington Gladden, spent his formative years being influenced by the preaching and revivalism of the Burned-Over District. See Whitney R. Cross, *The Burned-Over District: The Social and Intellectual History of Enthusiastic Religion in Western New York, 1800–1850* (Ithaca, NY: Cornell University Press, 1950).

10. In the modern context, many Methodist churches have utilized the chancel rail as the mourner's bench. In Holiness and Pentecostal traditions, the mourner's bench is equivalent to the altar, where the work of the Spirit occurs and converted sinners are to travail until sanctification and Spirit baptism has been achieved. For Pentecostals, this is generally evidenced by the initial physical evidence of *glossolalia* (speaking in unknown tongues) or *xenolalia* (speaking in missionary tongues).

11. Balmer, *The Making of Evangelicalism,* 20.

central theme of Calvinism that all things, even damnation, are for the glory of God.

Due to his theological shift, Finney characterized revivalism as "the work of man."[12] The different approaches to revivalism reflect Edwards's Calvinist soteriology, which viewed revivalism as the work of God alone (monergism), and Finney's Arminian soteriology, which viewed revivalism as the cooperative work of God and humans (synergism) and the integration of regeneration and social reform as evidence of sanctification. In fact, Finney viewed regeneration—the transformation of the heart—as the catalyst to social reform.

Oberlinism

Oberlinism originated in the founding of Oberlin College, which was established as an institution of Christian radicalism[13] and was the center of Finney revivalism, perfectionist theology, and social holiness. Oberlinism provided the theological foundation for the doctrine of civil disobedience, and the feminist, peace, and temperance movements, but had the greatest theological influence on the abolitionist movement.[14]

The founding of Oberlin College in 1833 was directly related to the issue of abolitionism. Students at Lane Theological Seminary in Cincinnati, Ohio, led by student Theodore Weld, rebelled against the administration and board of trustees because they felt that the institution did not possess a robust position on abolition. While Lane was one of the first institutions to admit Black students, the position of the college on slavery under the leadership of the president, Lyman Beecher, was colonization and gradual emancipation. Students demanded that the institution adopt the position of immediate abolitionism and insisted on Blacks being treated as social equals. As a result, the members of the board of trustees for Lane forbade faculty and students from even discussing the issue of slavery.[15] Therefore, many of the students and some of the faculty abandoned Lane and founded Oberlin, where Finney became the premier professor of theology and served as the second president of the institution.

At the heart of Oberlinism was the integration of the Wesleyan doctrine of Christian perfection and the New Divinity doctrine of disinterested benevolence. Wesley believed that possessing perfect love of God and perfect love of one's neighbor was evidence that one had achieved Christian

12. Balmer, *The Making of Evangelicalism*, 21.
13. Donald W. Dayton and Douglas M. Strong, *Rediscovering an Evangelical Heritage: A Tradition and Trajectory of Integrating Piety and Justice*, 2nd ed. (Grand Rapids, MI: Baker Academic, 2014), 39.
14. Dayton and Strong, *Rediscovering an Evangelical Heritage*, 85.
15. Dayton and Strong, *Rediscovering an Evangelical Heritage*, 85–87.

perfection or entire sanctification. The New Divinity theologian Samuel Hopkins believed, as noted earlier, that loving God and loving one's neighbor through the exaltation of God and service to one's neighbor constituted disinterested benevolence. Both doctrines fueled Oberlinism as a theology of social holiness through which one's salvation and sanctification are determined by the transformation of one's heart and one's advocacy for social change. Therefore, Oberlin would not affirm any claim of Christian faith without social reform.

Abolitionism

Oberlin students founded the Oberlin Antislavery Society, which was committed to immediate abolitionism, and engaged in antislavery missions. In fact, they refused to associate themselves with any entity that did not prioritize immediate abolitionism and refused communion with any Christian body that practiced slavery.[16]

Weld and the Grimke Sisters

The leader of the rebellion at Lane Theological Seminary, Theodore Weld, was pivotal to the immediate abolitionism campaign. He was converted under the revival ministry of Finney and has been characterized as the greatest of abolitionists for devoting his life to the struggle. He influenced Arthur and Lewis Tappan, wealthy New York businessmen, to join the antislavery efforts and was the driving force behind Finney implementing his own new measure of allowing women to speak in mixed assemblies of men and women.[17] Eventually, Weld married one the most prominent abolitionists and feminists, Angelina Grimke.

Grimke's father was a medical doctor and slaveholder; therefore she and her sister Sarah were raised on their father's plantation in Charleston, South Carolina. Witnessing the atrocities of slavery firsthand, the Grimke sisters became disenchanted with the institution of slavery. Both migrated to Philadelphia and became Quakers, which eradicated any sense of southern respectability in their favor. Nevertheless, in 1836, Angelina appealed to the supposed Christian conscience of southern white woman to support the antislavery cause, citing the Declaration of Independence and the teachings of Christ.[18] That same year, Sarah appealed to the supposed Christian conscience of southern white clergyman in favor of the abolitionist cause.[19]

---

16. Dayton and Strong, *Rediscovering an Evangelical Heritage*, 91.

17. Dayton and Strong, *Rediscovering an Evangelical Heritage*, 75–84.

18. See Angelina Grimke, *Appeal to the Christian Women of the South* (New York: American Anti-Slavery Society, 1836).

19. See Sarah Grimke, *Epistle to the Clergy of the Southern States* (New York, 1836).

In 1839, Weld, as a trained journalist, and the Grimke sisters published *American Slavery as It Is: Testimony of a Thousand Witnesses*, which was a collection of testimonies from the experiences of enslaved Africans that had appeared in southern newspapers.[20] The significance of the Grimke sisters is that not only were they fierce crusaders for immediate abolitionism, they also believed in racial equality. While the Quakers were indeed abolitionists and committed to the cause of freedom for enslaved persons, being paternalist abolitionists, they still viewed people of African descent as second-class citizens. However, the Grimke sisters were humanitarian abolitionists because they not only opposed slavery but they also opposed racial inequality.

The Tappan Brothers

The Tappan brothers, Arthur and Lewis, were born in Northampton, Massachusetts, the town in which the First Great Awakening had been ignited through the revivalism of Jonathan Edwards. Their mother, Sarah Tappan, instilled in them the piety of Edwardsean Calvinism. However, while living in Boston, they became enamored with the preaching of Unitarian cleric William Ellery Channing. In 1825, Lewis became the treasurer of the American Unitarian Association. In 1828, the Tappan brothers decided to rediscover their evangelical heritage and in the process were attracted to the evangelical revivalism of Charles Finney. As wealthy New York businessmen who considered themselves stewards of God's money, they became major benefactors of Finney's revivalism and social reform, leading them to adhere to a practical theology of piety and good works, which was evident in their financial efforts to end prostitution.[21]

Another major feature of their practical evangelical theology was their commitment to supporting Christian missions financially and advocating for racial equality.[22] They abandoned their financial support for colonization because Arthur disagreed with the rum trade, which was driving the economy of Liberia, and Lewis was troubled by the issue of racial equality, which colonization failed to address. With the development of the idea of immediate abolitionism through the journalism of William Lloyd Garrison in the abolitionist newspaper *The Liberator*, the Tappan brothers withdrew their financial support from the American Bible Society and the American

---

20. See Theodore Weld, ed., *American Slavery as It Is: Testimony of a Thousand Witnesses* (Mineola, NY: Dover Publications, 2017).

21. Dayton and Strong, *Rediscovering an Evangelical Heritage*, 107–17.

22. The Tappan brothers were major financial supporters of the American Bible Society and American Tract Society. They initially provided financial backing to the American Colonization Society which was primarily due to their economic interests of investing in the creation of Liberia for freed Africans.

Tract Society because both failed to prioritize the cause of abolitionism in
their publications.

In 1833, the Tappan brothers founded the New York Anti-Slavery Society and, in 1846, were among the founders of the American Missionary
Association, whose goals included the abolition of slavery, racial equality,
and the education of Blacks. Arthur Tappan was elected the president of
the American Missionary Society. Lewis Tappan financially supported the
return of enslaved Africans on the *Amistad* to their home in Africa, with
some missionaries from Oberlin accompanying them.[23] Like Weld and the
Grimke sisters, the Tappan brothers were humanitarian abolitionists who
advocated for the abolition of slavery and racial equality.

Many evangelical abolitionists struggled with their white privilege,
which—consciously or unconsciously—caused them to view people of African descent as inferior. Charles Finney laid the theological foundation for
the abolitionist movement. Yet even Finney struggled with his own white
privilege and religion of antiblackness. Arthur and Lewis Tappan were
major supporters of the "free church" movement in New York City, which
advocated for the eradication of the common nineteenth-century practice
of churches selling and renting church pews to finance the maintenance
of church buildings. Egalitarianism was at the heart of the "free church"
movement, which was opposed to certain people being excluded based on
their economic class. Another common practice was racially segregated
seating, a practice that is challenged in a letter Lewis Tappan wrote regarding segregated seating at the Chatham Street Chapel in New York City,
which was pastored by Finney:

> Some of us thought that the "negro Pew" should be done away for
> although people were invited to sit where they pleased, it was under-
> stood, by whites and blacks, that the colored people should sit by
> themselves in a certain place in the galleries. . . . In the Chatham St.
> Chapel we succeeded in bringing the colored part of the congrega-
> tion downstairs to occupy a range of slips on one side of the church,
> but were never able, though Mr. Finney was the pastor, to abolish the
> distinction altogether, in seats and allow the people to sit, in fact as
> they were invited to, wherever they chose. . . . Finding nothing could be
> done in a matter so near to my heart I left the church.[24]

These words from Lewis Tappan's letter exposes the paternalist abolitionism of Finney and epitomizes the reality that some evangelical

---

23. Dayton and Strong, *Rediscovering an Evangelical Heritage*, 107–17. *Amistad* was a ship
of the Atlantic triangular slave trade that came to Long Island, New York.

24. Dayton and Strong, *Rediscovering an Evangelical Heritage*, 110–11.

abolitionists viewed slavery as evil and sinful but failed to condemn racial inequality.

The Wesleyan Methodists

The hallmarks of abolition, social holiness, and social justice are rooted in regeneration, sanctification, and Christian perfection—the DNA of the Wesleyan tradition. John Wesley believed that his Methodist movement represented the restoration of primitive Christianity, focusing on this early standard for liturgical purity and holy living.[25] Wesley's doctrine of holiness has been characterized as "social holiness" because of its social justice agenda. As such, Wesley advocated for the physical, social, and spiritual welfare of the poor, oppressed, and marginalized, especially enslaved Africans, all of which represented an imitation of Christ's ministry and primitive Christianity.

In 1774, John Wesley published his pamphlet *Thoughts upon Slavery*, through which he vehemently condemned the institution of slavery and offered a scathing critique of slaveholders. Wesley believed that the institution of slavery violated natural justice; therefore, he was most troubled by the involvement of his native land in the slave trade. He concluded that the slave trade was the greatest evil in England.[26] Appealing to natural justice rather than human laws, Wesley challenged the Christianity of slaveholders, using moral reasoning against their evil motivations and racist stereotypes.

Wesley rejected the stereotype that Negroes were culturally destitute. In fact, David Scott concludes that Wesley attributed "Africans' lack of education to a cultural deficiency rather than an innate mental deficiency."[27] Wesley argued that it was a mistake to misrepresent Africa as a horrid, dreary, and barren country to justify slavery, as though slaveholders were practicing kindness in delivering the African slaves out of Africa, and concluded that Negroes had been corrupted through interaction with Europeans.[28]

Another negative stereotype was the identification of Africans as heathens and pagans, which Wesley rejected but not completely. He asserted:

All natives of this coast, though heathens, believe there is one GOD, the author of them and all things. They appear likewise to have a con-

25. Geordan Hammond, *John Wesley in America: Restoring Primitive Christianity* (New York: Oxford University Press, 2014), 5–13. Wesley viewed the early church as a community possessing holiness of heart.

26. Irv Brendlinger, "John Wesley and Slavery: Myth and Reality," *Wesleyan Theological Journal* 41, no. 1 (2006): 227.

27. David Scott, "Racial Images in John Wesley's Thoughts upon Slavery," *Wesleyan Theological Journal* 43, no. 2 (2008): 91–93.

28. John Wesley, *Thoughts upon Slavery* (Gloucestershire, UK: Dodo Press, 1644/2009), 3–9.

fused apprehension of a future state. And accordingly, every town and village has a place of public worship.[29]

Wesley's affirmation of indigenous African beliefs demonstrated his desire to find the spirituality of Africans and Christianity compatible. However, characterizing enslaved Africans as heathens—a reflection of his European Christian context—proved problematic in his attempts to eradicate the negative stereotypes. Through his interactions with enslaved Africans, Wesley was assured of their religious ability to achieve the spirituality of European Christianity.

Wesley had been a high church Anglican until, in 1738, his heart was strangely warmed during his Aldersgate experience, from which emerged Wesleyan revivalism and the development of evangelical Anglicanism. As we noted earlier, Anglicans possessed a theology of white privilege, undergirded by the religion of antiblackness. Wesley's Anglican heritage, the source of his white privilege and antiblackness, situates him firmly as a paternalist abolitionist. However, through his Methodist movement, Wesley became the progenitor of evangelical Anglicanism and transformed his religion of antiblackness. Therefore, a critical question develops regarding Wesley as an abolitionist: Was Wesley truly transformed from paternalist abolitionism to humanitarian abolitionism? If so, such transformation and the eradication of antiblackness could have been achieved only through his emphasis on social holiness and social justice, which led to his advocacy for the liberation of the oppressed.

American Methodists were engaged in holy conferencing during the war for American Independence, which definitely influenced their proceedings. Ironically, while clerics of British colonial America believed that the American Revolutionary War was divinely ordained and sanctioned, John Wesley believed that the war was unjustified. While there are several reasons for Wesley's opposition to the war, the primary reason for his opposition was American slavery.[30] In addition to Wesley's vehement opposition to slavery, his motivations for opposing the American Revolution might explain the actions of early American Methodists.[31] Unfortunately, during the forma-

---

29. Wesley, *Thoughts*, 6.

30. John Fea, *Was America Founded as a Christian Nation: A Historical Introduction* (Louisville, KY: Westminster John Knox Press, 2011), 120. British colonists in America were seeking freedom from what they characterized as British tyranny while they still enslaved Africans.

31. In the same year of the founding of the Methodist Episcopal Church (MEC) but prior to the organizing conference in 1784, American Methodist circuit riders had "voted to expel members who sold slaves or bought them for nonhumanitarian reasons" and voted "to warn and then suspend local preachers who would not emancipate their slaves in states where the laws admit it." See Donald G. Matthews, *Slavery and Methodism: A Chapter in American Morality, 1780–1845* (Princeton, NJ: Princeton University Press, 1965), 9.

tive years of the Methodist Episcopal Church (MEC), Methodist clerics were faced with the spiritual and moral dilemma of accommodating slavery, specifically in the southern region of the United States. By 1820, following the General Conference of 1816, American Methodists concluded that there was not much left that they could do to abolish slavery and that they lacked the authority to change the civil laws that legalized it.[32]

In 1841, after separating from the MEC, the Wesleyan Methodist Connection was formed. The Wesleyan Methodists separated because of the MEC's accommodation to slavery in American society; therefore, they had the distinction of being founded solely based on their belief in abolitionism. Like the Finneyites, the Wesleyan Methodists integrated piety with radical social reform. In addition to their opposition to slavery, they opposed racial prejudice and racial exclusion. They condemned slavery as sinful and evil.

Orange Scott was a presiding elder in the New England Conference of the MEC who engaged his district in abolitionist teachings. As a result of his teachings and the district's subscription to William Lloyd Garrison's newspaper, *The Liberator*, the New England Conference delegation to the 1836 General Conference of the MEC was abolitionist. The delegation proposed a resolution that would have added language to the Methodist Book of Discipline with a robust rebuke and condemnation of slavery as evil. The resolution failed; and after the General Conference, the bishop supervising the New England Conference threatened to demote Scott if he refused to stop the abolitionist teaching in his district. Scott defied the bishop's command and was demoted.

Throughout the MEC, bishops prohibited the submission of antislavery resolutions at annual conferences and would bring Methodist clerics to trial for attending abolitionist meetings or even for reading abolitionist literature. Standing strong on his conviction for abolitionism, Scott abandoned his membership in the MEC and became the leading cleric in the formation of the Wesleyan Methodist Connection.[33]

Another evangelical abolitionist and leading cleric in the founding of the Wesleyan Methodist Connection was Luther Lee, who presided over three of its first six general conferences and edited the *True Wesleyan*, a weekly newsletter that was created by Orange Scott with an emphasis on reporting about antislavery causes; it eventually became the official organ of the Wesleyan Methodist Connection.[34]

The Wesleyan Methodists sanctified suffrage, concluding that voting against slavery constituted one's obedience to God. For the Wesleyan Meth-

---

32. Matthews, *Slavery and Methodism*, 18–29.

33. Dayton and Strong, *Rediscovering an Evangelical Heritage*, 119–25.

34. In 1840, Lee played a pivotal role in the formation of the Liberty Party, a political organization that functioned more as an evangelical institution committed to sanctified living.

odists, engagement in the political abolitionist movement constituted complete conversion. Their opposition to racial inequality and racial exclusion is evident in that there were several African Americans who served in the leadership of the Wesleyan Methodist Church during the antebellum era.[35]

Denominational Schisms and
African American Christian Independence

The showdown of denominational schisms in the 1840s over the issue of slavery foreshadowed the Civil War. Clarence Goen argues that the denominational schisms of the Methodists, Baptists, and Presbyterians were an antebellum disruption to national unity:

> It seems plausible to hypothesize that when Presbyterian, Methodist, and Baptist churches divided along North–South lines, they severed an important bond of national unity; that the forebodings of their leaders and of contemporary observers regarding the probability of disastrous political consequences were well founded; and that the denominational schisms, as irreversible steps along the nation's tortuous course to violence, were both portent and catalyst of the imminent national tragedy.[36]

The Methodist Episcopal Church

While the MEC had accommodated itself to the legalization of slavery in the United States, particularly in the southern states, the issue of slavery was still very controversial, especially in a denomination that had officially opposed slavery from its inception. The language concerning slavery in the Book of Discipline was a significant point of contention. Central to the debate during the 1844 General Conference was the outrage of northern Methodists related to Bishop James O. Andrew's ownership of two slaves. Bishop Andrew was from the Georgia Conference and at the convening of the 1844 General Conference presided over his home conference. Anticipating the issue with Bishop Andrew's ownership of slaves, an influential Georgia delegate, Lovick Pierce, proposed what would be acceptable to the southern delegates regarding a discussion on slavery. Pierce stipulated that language in the new Discipline only allow legislation for the general conference to address the slave trade, separation of families, and treatment of slaves.[37] The southern delegates were even willing to accept the limitation

---

35. Dayton and Strong, *Rediscovering an Evangelical Heritage*, 126–33.

36. Clarence C. Goen, *Broken Churches, Broken Nation: Denominational Schisms and the Coming of the Civil War* (Macon, GA: Mercer University Press, 1985), 6.

37. Matthews, *Slavery and Methodism*, 255.

of Bishop Andrew's episcopal supervision to the geographical area in which he was a slaveholder, which would have been Oxford, Georgia. The northern Methodists rejected these proposals: the first failed to address the issue of African enslavement, and the second would constitute a violation of the principles of the itinerancy.

Bishop Andrew decided that because of the controversy he would resign from the office of the episcopacy. However, the southern delegates rejected the idea of Andrew's resigning; the northern Methodists argued that Andrew had violated policy by owning slaves and had embarrassed himself after being nominated and elected as a nonslaveholding southerner. Three-fourths of the general conference delegation voted for the schism between the southern and northern Methodists. The northern Methodists maintained the name Methodist Episcopal Church while the southern Methodists adopted the name Methodist Episcopal Church South (MECS). Thereafter, Bishop Andrew served as the senior bishop of the MECS until his death in 1871. In 1939, the northern and southern Methodists would reunite with the United Brethren to become the United Methodist Church. During this era of uniting and racial segregation, the Methodists formed the Central Jurisdiction, which consisted only of African American congregations, regardless of their geographical location in the United States.[38] The Central Jurisdiction would remain a segregated entity of the United Methodist Church until 1968. Ironically, the spirit of white supremacy that had caused the Methodist schism in 1844 still permeated the reunified denomination.

Black Methodist Denominations

Unfortunately, as is evident in the history of American Methodists, possessing the spirit of abolition did not equate to racial equality. This reality led to the formation of the historical Black Methodist denominations in the United States, which includes the African Methodist Episcopal Church (AME), African Methodist Episcopal Zion Church (AMEZ), and later the Christian Methodist Episcopal Church (CME).[39]

African Methodist Episcopal Church (AME)
The AME Church originated with the rise of its founder and first elected and consecrated bishop, Richard Allen. Allen was a former slave who had purchased his freedom for two thousand dollars in Delaware and thereafter migrated to Philadelphia, the place of his birth. Allen was one of only two

---

38. See James S. Thomas, *Methodism's Racial Dilemma: The Story of the Central Jurisdiction* (Nashville, TN: Abingdon Press, 1992).

39. The CME Church will be discussed later in the next chapter as a product of the Reconstruction era.

African Americans present to witness the birth of American Methodism at the Christmas Conference of 1784. Dennis Dickerson argues that Allen believed in a color-blind Christianity yet possessed a robust Black consciousness, evident in Allen's formation of the Free African Society with Absalom Jones in 1787.[40] The Free African Society, a benevolent organization designed for the social welfare of freed Blacks, was the precursor to the formation of the AME Church and the African Episcopal Church of St. Thomas, the first African American Episcopalian parish in the United States. Ultimately, the AME Church came about because of the white supremacy and racial discrimination at St. George MEC in Philadelphia, particularly an incident related to racially segregated worship space, which prompted Allen to lead the colored members to separate and form the Mother Bethel AME Church in Philadelphia. In 1816, the AME Church held its organizing general conference, becoming the first African American denomination in the United States.

African Methodist Episcopal Zion Church (AMEZ)

The origins of the AMEZ Church resulted from the formation of the Zion Church or "African Chapel" as it is affectionately called in New York City. David Henry Bradley Sr. argues that an enslaved African, Peter Williams, was one of the most respected Negroes in New York City.[41] Williams was a native of the city; he approached the John Street MEC and requested that they purchase his freedom and allow him to repay them. The church obliged, confirming Bradley's argument about the respect Williams had garnered. The tremendous growth of the Negro membership at John Street became a problem for the white members of the congregation. Despite this growth, the congregation had licensed only three Negro preachers and one Negro exhorter. In 1800, the refusal of the New York Conference of the MEC to ordain Black preachers caused Blacks to separate and form the Zion Church. As a trustee of the Zion Church, Williams had the honor of laying the cornerstone for the first erected building in 1801. The charter of the Zion Church dates back to a private meeting Negroes held in 1784. The meeting was private, because New York state law prohibited Negroes from meeting in groups, a result of the New York Slave Revolt of 1712. In 1796, the members of the Zion Church voted to secede from the MEC and form the AMEZ Church, which held its organizing general conference in 1822 and became an official denomination, electing James Varick as its first bishop.

40. Dennis C. Dickerson, *The African Methodist Episcopal Church: A History* (New York: Cambridge University Press, 2020), 25.

41. David Henry Bradley, *A History of the A.M.E. Zion Church, 1796–1872* (Eugene, OR: Wipf & Stock, 1956), 44.

American Baptists

Ironically, the road to schism for the American Baptists in 1845, like that of the American Methodists in 1844, ran through the state of Georgia. In 1812, Baptist missionary Luther Rice, who desired a unified Baptist missionary organization, formed the Triennial Convention, the goal of which was to advance the missionary work of Baptists in America.[42] Another missionary organization in the Baptist denomination, the American Baptist Home Mission Society (ABHMS), was formed as the successor to the Home Mission Society of 1832. In 1844, the Georgia Baptists nominated a slaveholder, James Reeve, as a home missionary to the ABHMS. The ABHMS had remained neutral on the issue of slavery and understood that confirming the nomination of Reeve, a slaveholder who planned to continue owning slaves after his appointment as a home missionary, would cause abolitionists to believe that the ABHMS was no longer neutral.[43] The rejection of Reeve's nomination alarmed Georgia Baptists because their economic interest was fueled by slavery and the preservation of white supremacy.

In the same year, Alabama Baptists challenged the Triennial Convention through the nomination of a slaveholder for appointment to foreign missions. As legitimate members of the convention, Alabama Baptists felt entitled to be a part of decisions regarding missionary appointments and found neutrality unacceptable.

The mastermind behind the separation of the southern Baptists from the Triennial Convention was Baptist cleric, slaveholder, and president of the University of Alabama, Basil Manly Sr. According to religious sociologist Robert P. Jones, Manly was the leading theological apologist in defense of slavery in 1844.[44] He had drafted resolutions from the Alabama state convention demanding that, as financial contributors to the Triennial Convention, slaveholders be eligible for denominational leadership positions and missionary appointments. The Alabama resolutions were rejected, which resulted in southern Baptists withholding funds from the Triennial Convention until the board abandoned its position of neutrality and affirmed the practice of slaveholding. The next year in Augusta, Georgia, southerners of the Triennial Convention met to officially secede from the convention; they formed their own missionary organization known as the Southern Baptist Convention (SBC). As an emblem of southern victory, the SBC elected William Bullein Johnson as their first president—Johnson had been

---

42. The official name of the convention was the General Missionary Convention of the Baptist Denomination in the United States for Foreign Missions.

43. Anthony L. Chute, Nathan A. Finn, and Michael A. G. Haykin, *The Baptist Story: From English Sect to Global Movement* (Nashville, TN: B & H Academic, 2015), 158–61.

44. Robert P. Jones, *White Too Long: The Legacy of White Supremacy in American Christianity* (New York: Simon & Schuster, 2020), 34.

the president of the Triennial Convention from 1841 to 1844.[45] In 1907, the northern Baptists from the Triennial Convention reorganized as the Northern Baptist Convention and in 1972 became the American Baptist Churches USA. Unlike the Methodists, American Baptists have never experienced a reunification.

Black Baptist Congregations

The Black Baptist churches in the United States originated geographically in the South and form the beginning of the Independent Black Church movement. While African American Methodists were the first to form Black denominations in the United States, African American Baptists were the first to form local independent Black congregations, which predate Black denominations.[46] The First African Baptist Church of Petersburg, Virginia, was established in 1774 on the William Byrd Plantation and moved to Petersburg in 1820 after the Byrd Plantation was burned by fire. The African Baptist Church of Williamsburg, Virginia, established in 1776, began as a brush arbor meeting on the Green Spring Plantation held in response to restrained and segregated worship at Bruton Parish. In 1777, George Liele established the First African Baptist Church of Savannah with the assistance of David George, and the First African Baptist Church of Augusta was established in 1787, later changing its name to the Springfield Baptist Church.[47]

In addition to forming independent congregations, African American Baptists established their own associations and conventions. Wayne Croft argues that these "Black Baptist associations originated out of a desire for racial progress and resistance to racist practices within white Baptist churches and associations. Although few white Baptist ministers protested against it." The first association was established in 1834 as the Providence Baptist Association; it consisted of six churches in southern Ohio and focused on antislavery causes, changing their name to the Providence Antislavery (Colored) Baptist Association. The second association was estab-

45. Chute, *The Baptist Story*, 158–61.

46. Love Henry Whelchel, *The History and Heritage of African American Churches: A Way Out of No Way* (St. Paul, MN: Paragon House, 2010), 98–99. There is a historical dispute over whether the African Baptist Church (Bluestone Church) formed on the William Byrd Plantation near the Bluestone River in Mecklenburg, Virginia, or the Silver Bluff Church formed on the Bryan Plantation located on the bank of the Savannah River not far from Augusta, Georgia, was the first independent Black congregation. The Bluestone Church was founded in 1758, and while historical records date the founding of the Silver Bluff Church between 1773 and 1775, established by George Liele, the cornerstone of the church building claims a founding date of 1750.

47. Whelchel, *The History and Heritage*, 97–107. See also Wayne E. Croft Sr., *A History of the Black Baptist Church* (Valley Forge, PA: Judson Press, 2020), 37–56.

lished in 1836 as the Association of Regular Baptist Churches of Color in Ohio; it consisted of five churches focused on missions and social reform and was also known as the Union Association. The third association was established in 1839 as the Wood River Baptist Association of Illinois; it consisted of ten churches focused on consulting churches, ordaining ministers, and organizing the Colored Baptist Home Missionary Society in 1844. The fourth association was established in 1841 as the Baptist Association for Colored People in Amherstburg, Canada; it supported the social welfare of Black Baptists who had migrated to Canada.[48]

The development of predominantly Black Baptist conventions stemmed primarily from the disagreement that Black Baptists had with the white-controlled convention on the issues of slavery and abolition. The first Black Baptist convention was established in 1840 as the American Baptist Missionary Convention (ABMC) at the Abyssinian Baptist Church in New York City. Sampson White, the pastor and a free Black, provided leadership in organizing the convention. The initial membership consisted of the Zion Baptist churches of New York and the Union Church of Philadelphia in addition to Abyssinian Baptist Church. In 1858, White strongly urged churches affiliated with the convention to abandon their affiliations with the white-controlled conventions. Minutes from the convention reflect agreement with White's admonition and the ABMC response that "in view of the wicked prejudice and proscription which exists among our white brethren, we, the churches composing this Convention, withdraw our connexion with different associations, and form one among ourselves."[49] Consequently, the ABMC laid the foundation for the development of independent Black Baptist conventions through the twentieth century.

In 1874, the New England Baptist Missionary Convention was established with a general focus on ministry through the organization of churches and a women's auxiliary in 1892. In 1880, the Baptist Foreign Mission Convention was established at the First Baptist Church of Montgomery, Alabama, and extended the influence and commitment of Black Baptists' missionary work in Africa. In 1886, the American National Baptist Convention was established under the leadership of William J. Simmons with the intent of promoting the unity of Black Baptist churches and the African American race. In 1893, W. Bishop Johnson established the National Baptist Education Convention to educate Black Baptist leaders. In 1895, the National Baptist Convention of the United States of America (NBCUSA) was established at Friendship Baptist Church in Atlanta, Georgia, resulting from a

---

48. Croft, *A History of the Black Baptist Church*, 59–66.
49. James M. Washington, *Frustrated Fellowship: The Black Baptist Quest for Social Power* (Macon, GA: Mercer University Press, 2004), 41. See also Croft, *A History of the Black Baptist Church*, 66–70.

consolidation of the Baptist Foreign Mission Convention, National Baptist Educational Convention, and the American National Baptist Convention. In addition to promoting the national unity of Black Baptists, the NBCUSA organized three new boards, which included the Foreign Mission Board, located in Louisville, Kentucky; the Home Mission Board, located in Little Rock, Arkansas; and the Educational Board, in Washington, DC.[50]

American Presbyterianism

The initial schism within American Presbyterianism occurred in 1837 because of the Old School–New School Controversy. Old School Presbyterianism consisted of traditional and moderate Presbyterians committed to classical Calvinist orthodoxy as reflected in the Westminster Confession. Its leading theologian was Charles Hodge, who was one of the primary architects of the Princeton School of Theology. New School Presbyterianism consisted of revivalists who theologically embraced Edwardsean Calvinism and New Divinity theology. The New School also promoted the "new measures" of Finneyite revivalism as a new interpretation of the theological standards of the Westminster Confession.

Most abolitionists in the Presbyterian Church belonged to the New School faction, which experienced tremendous growth. Consequently, most of the southern Presbyterians aligned themselves with the Old School Presbyterian Church.[51] While this Presbyterian schism was not directly related to the debate over slavery, it established the geographical boundaries regarding the slavery issue, and both the assemblies argued that their assembly was the Presbyterian Church (USA). In 1857, a schism occurred in the New School assembly over the issue of slavery when the southern synods and presbyteries of the assembly established the proslavery United Synod of the Presbyterian Church. The Old School assembly was conservative and rooted strongly in the southern region of the United States; therefore the assembly maintained its unity until the outbreak of the Civil War. In 1861, southern Presbyterians became the Presbyterian Church in the Confederate States of America. Following the Civil War, the Old School and New School Presbyterians of the South reunited to form the Presbyterian Church in the United States. Among the three major denominational traditions in the United States that experienced schisms during the antebellum era, Presbyterians had the most complicated theological issues and controversies leading to various factions through the twentieth century, which eventually resulted in 1973 in the formation of the conservative

50. Croft, *A History of the Black Baptist Church*, 70–85.
51. Goen, *Broken Churches*, 68–78

Reformed alternative to the larger liberal and progressive Presbyterian Church in the United States of America.[52]

Theologies of Blackness and Whiteness

In addition to the financial interest of slaveholders in preserving the institution of slavery, proslavery evangelicals believed that slavery was imperative to the success of the divine economy. Adopting the biblical literalism from the Reformed tradition, they believed that God had sanctioned slavery through the divine revelation of Scripture.[53]

The most respected Presbyterian theologian and cleric in the antebellum South, James Henley Thornwell, believed slavery was good, merciful, and constituted the providential will of God. In 1850, Virginia Baptist cleric Thornton Stringfellow stated that slavery was a biblical institution and therefore concluded that enslaved persons had a biblical obligation to serve their masters.[54] In his overtly racist literature, particularly his work *Slavery as It Relates to the Negro*, published in 1843, Josiah Priest argued that slavery was a biblical practice and therefore not sinful.[55]

Hamitic Curse Myth

The primary biblical text proslavery evangelicals used to justify the sinful and wicked enterprise of chattel slavery in the United States was the supposed curse of Ham (Gen 9:20–27). The curse-of-Ham myth was not only the nucleus of proslavery theology, it also became the determining factor in the antebellum southern culture of honor and dishonor.[56] The institution of slavery dominated southern culture; and therefore, denial of the Hamitic curse myth became an issue of southern respectability. Despite his drunken stupor, which led to his nakedness in the biblical text, Noah was exalted by proslavery theologians as the righteous and obedient patriarch of God.[57] In his interpretation of the passage, Priest characterized Ham's older brothers,

---

52. Randall Balmer and John R. Fitzmier, *The Presbyterians* (Westport, CT: Greenwood Publishing, 1994).

53. Heath W. Carter and Laura Rominger Porter, eds., *Turning Points in the History of American Evangelicalism* (Grand Rapids, MI: Eerdmans, 2017).

54. Luke E. Harlow, "The Civil War and the Making of Conservative American Evangelicalism," in Carter and Porter, *Turning Points*, 112.

55. Emerson B. Powery and Rodney S. Sadler Jr., *The Genesis of Liberation: Biblical Interpretation in the Antebellum Narratives of the Enslaved* (Louisville, KY: Westminster John Knox Press, 2016), 86.

56. Stephen R. Haynes, *Noah's Curse: The Biblical Justification of American Slavery* (New York: Oxford University Press, 2002), 65–67.

57. Haynes, *Noah's Curse*, 69.

Shem and Japheth, as gentlemen who protected their father's and their own honor.[58] Priest situates Ham in the context of a sexual scandal and portrays him as a sexual reprobate. He concludes that Ham's crime against his father could have been an incestuous relationship with his mother.[59] Another interpretation is that Ham attempted the castration of his father.[60] Biblical scholar Randall C. Bailey questions the depictions of Ham related to the Genesis narrative and concludes that there is a polemic in other parts of the narrative, which he argues "has as its agenda the discrediting of the people who are depicted as practicing taboo sexual acts, such that they are dehumanized in the process of labeling."[61] The biblical interpretations of proslavery advocates reflect the psychological fears and fantasies of the slaveholder. In fact, substantial historical evidence exposes the sexual assault of slaveholders against enslaved women, who were raped regularly, and recent historical scholarship reflects the reality of enslaved men being raped by slaveholders with homoerotic desires.[62] The castration of lynched victims lends evidence to white supremacists' fears of the sexual prowess of Black male genitalia.[63] The sexualization of Ham was part of the agenda to sanctify the racism of white supremacists and their apparent obsession with Black male genitalia.

The theological scandal of proslavery evangelicals here was equating the totality of the Black race with Ham and postulating that Blacks were thus cursed with blackness and enslavement. One of the major problems with the proslavery theologians' claim of a curse on Ham was that Noah actually cursed Canaan, the son of Ham, and therefore makes the biblical justification of slavery erroneous.[64]

---

58. Haynes, *Noah's Curse*, 70.

59. Haynes, *Noah's Curse*, 69.

60. Haynes, *Noah's Curse*, 67.

61. Randall C. Bailey, "They're Nothing but Incestuous Bastards: The Polemical Use of Sex and Sexuality in Hebrew Canon Narrative," in Fernando Segovia and Mary Ann Tolbert, eds., *Reading from This Place: Social Context and Biblical Interpretation in the United States*, vol. 1 (Minneapolis, MN: Fortress, 1994), 1:121–38.

62. See Daina Ramey Berry and Leslie M. Harris, *Sexuality and Slavery: Reclaiming Intimate Histories in the Americas* (Athens, GA: University of Georgia Press, 2018). See also Thomas A. Foster, "The Sexual Abuse of Black Men under American Slavery," *Journal of the History of Sexuality* 3 (2011): 445–46.

63. See Ezekiel 23: 19–20, which characterizes the African male as having oversized genitals and ejaculations, as noted in Michael D. Coogan, ed., *The New Oxford Annotated Bible*, 3rd ed. (New York: Oxford University Press, 2001), 1211; Franz Fanon, *Black Skin, White Masks* (New York: Grove Press, 1967), 63–82; Frances Cress Welsing, *The Isis Papers: The Keys to the Colors* (Washington, DC: CW Publishing, 1991), 1–16, 93–100; David Marriott, "Bordering on: The Black Penis," *Textual Practice* 20 (1996): 9–28.

64. Powery and Sadler, *The Genesis of Liberation*, 91. Powery and Sadler conclude that most of the early African American biblical interpreters embraced the notion of Ham as Black but rejected the notion of Ham as cursed. They also viewed Ham as equal with Shem and Japheth.

While this early African American biblical interpretation was imperative to debunking the Hamitic curse myth, it was still insufficient because
it did not address the issue of black skin, which the curse equated with
enslavement. In 1860, Louisiana proslavery physician Samuel Cartwright
published his medical research on the Negro in relation to the institution
of slavery entitled "Slavery in the Light of Ethnology," in which he argued
that the Negro was both heathenistic and intellectually inferior to whites.
Based on his interpretation of Leviticus 5:44–46, which destined the heathen to enslavement, Cartwright argued that enslavement of Africans was
necessary; and based on his interpretation of Genesis 9, he concluded that
enslaved Africans were the American descendants of Canaan.[65]

Bailey strongly challenges this emphasis because of the dangers embedded in theologies of election. He suggests that Black Christians should
equally argue against the curse of Canaan, which he identified as a social
construct, noting that the Black Christian emphasis on the curse of Canaan
implies lack of care for the Canaanites:

> Canaanites shall be slaves to Shemites forever. Even though this is a
> nationalist, as opposed to a racialist claim (Canaanites and Shemites
> are of the same geographical and racial stock, that is Northeastern
> African), the text does sanction one nation enslaving another. Thus,
> the appeal to "This isn't a curse on Ham, it's a curse on Canaan," offers
> no help to practitioners of liberation hermeneutics.[66]

A prevailing argument against the Hamitic curse myth was the one-
blood doctrine based on a verse in Acts that states, "[God] made all nations
to inhabit the whole earth" (Acts 17:26). The one-blood doctrine was central
to antislavery evangelicals' theological argument against the institution of
slavery.[67]

The one-blood doctrine was foundational in the African American belief
that God's original creation of humanity was one race of people. William
Anderson, who had been born free then kidnapped and sold into slavery in
the 1820s, rejected the notion of Ham as the progenitor of the Black race.
Holding a view similar to the one-blood doctrine, Anderson believed that,
based on his interpretation of Genesis 2:7, all humans originated from one

---

65. Sylvester A. Johnson, *The Myth of Ham in Nineteenth-Century American Christianity*
(New York: Palgrave Macmillan, 2004), 41–42.

66. Bailey, "They're Nothing but Incestuous Bastards," 138.

67. Note also that in 1850, Northern antislavery evangelical Moses Stuart contended
that the racism that fueled the heinous and sinful practice of slavery was unbiblical. Quoting
Scripture, Stuart asserted that no slaveholder actually believed that they were fulfilling the
golden rule—"Do unto others as you would have them do until you"—by enslaving others and
emphasized that "God shows no partiality" (Acts 10:34). See Harlow, "The Civil War," 114–15.

race, which he concluded was the Black race.[68] Sylvester A. Johnson argues that, historically, the descendants of Ham represented those who are the antithesis of the people of God, particularly in Jewish and Christian biblical theology.[69] He further suggests that, in the nineteenth century, the Hamitic curse myth was really about racial origins not slave apologetics, and that the curse myth aided proslavery theologians in their goal of equating blackness with evil.[70] However, Anderson counters this idea with his exegesis of 1 Kings 5 concerning the curse of leprosy. Generally, Naaman, the protagonist of this narrative, who is the captain of the Syrian army and was healed of leprosy, is the focus. Anderson shifts the focus from Naaman to Gehazi, who was cursed with leprosy; he concludes that this narrative is much more racialized than that of the Hamitic curse myth.[71] In the text, Gehazi, who was the servant of the prophet Elisha, attempted to deceive Naaman and Elisha in order to gain a profit from Naaman's healing. Gehazi was cursed with the disease of leprosy because of his spirit of greed, and his skin turned white. Anderson argues that Gehazi was born Black but turned white due to the curse of leprosy, which he believes constituted the curse of whiteness.[72]

As White as Snow

In his scholarly article "They Shall Become as White as Snow: When Bad Is Turned into Good," Bailey characterizes the formula "to be made white as snow" as a curse rather than a blessing. While this formula is traditionally interpreted as a blessing (based on the biblical exegesis of Isa 1:18–20), Bailey demonstrates its role as a curse in other parts of the Hebrew Bible. For example, in Exodus 4:6, Moses is cursed with leprosy and turns white for his objection to God's call on his life; and in Numbers 12:10, Moses's sister Miriam is cursed with leprosy and turns white because of her opposition to Moses's marriage to an African woman, Zipporah. Nevertheless, Bailey correctly asserts, "the formula, 'to be made white as snow,' has been used in white supremacist societies as a sign of purity and, thus, as a desirable outcome to which one should strive."

Bailey notes that this white supremacist interpretation has even plagued some of the liturgical hymns that have been popularized in African American worship.

For example, a popular hymn of discipleship within African American spirituality is "Jesus Paid It All," written by Elvina Hall in 1865, which speaks of salvation, repentance, and forgiveness. The hymn's refrain exclaims,

---

68. Powery and Sadler, *The Genesis of Liberation*, 103.

69. Johnson, *The Myth of Ham*, 6.

70. Johnson, *The Myth of Ham*, xiii.

71. Powery and Sadler, *The Genesis of Liberation*, 110.

72. Powery and Sadler, *The Genesis of Liberation*, 104–8.

"Jesus paid it all, All to Him I owe; Sin had left a crimson stain, He washed it white as snow." The refrain reflects the classical hermeneutic of "as white as snow" as a blessing. Yet what is even more striking in this particular hymn is the irony in the second and third stanzas:

> *Lord, now indeed I find Your pow'r, and*
> *Yours a-lone, Can change the leper's spots*
> *And melt the heart of stone.*
>
> *For nothing good have I Where-by*
> *Your grace to claim I'll wash my garments white*
> *In the blood of Calv'ry's Lamb.*[73]

The irony of the second stanza is situated in Hall's claim that God can change the leper's spots; yet she claims that the sinner with leper's spots will be washed white as snow.[74] Even more gruesome is the idea in the third stanza that the sinner's garment is made white when washed in the blood of Jesus. This reflects Riggins Earl's "ideal Christian master type," which we noted earlier as the belief of some Christian slave masters that the soul of enslaved Africans could be saved if washed in the white blood of Jesus.

Another popular hymn sung in African American eucharistic worship is "Nothing but the Blood of Jesus," written by Robert Lowry in 1876 during a camp meeting. The first stanza and refrain proclaim:

> *What can wash away my sin? Nothing but the blood of Jesus;*
> *What can make me whole again? Nothing but the blood of Jesus.*
>
> *Oh! Precious is the flow, That makes me white as snow;*
> *No other fount I know, Nothing but the blood of Jesus.*[75]

Both Hall and Lowry suggest that the blood of Jesus makes the sinner white and the blood of Jesus saves the sinner, thereby emphasizing the idea that whiteness was equated with salvation, an argument that was used to justify white supremacy and white racial superiority.

---

73. Elvina M. Hall, "Jesus Paid It All" (No. 357), in *African American Heritage Hymnal* (Chicago: GIA Publications, 2001). Another example is the hymn "Have Thine Own Way, Lord," published by Adelaide A. Pollard in 1907 as a hymn of discipleship in African American worship.

74. Note that the stanza contradicts the biblical text here. The Mosaic law (Leviticus 14) stipulates that only the temple priest could diagnose leprosy and declare healing of leprosy, which consisted of the white spots having been removed, yet Hall wants to be washed white as snow.

75. Robert Lowry, "Nothing but the Blood of Jesus" (No. 262), in *African American Heritage Hymnal* (Chicago: GIA Publications, 2001).

7

Postbellum Evangelicalism

The principles of Jesus are exemplified in the lives of these newly chosen people of God when they permit their so-called inferiors to eat the crumbs let fall by those whom their idol god has carefully selected as the honor guests at the feast. If the humble Nazarene appeared there disturbing the present caste system, he would be speedily lynched as he was in Palestine.

—Carter G. Woodson

In 1921, African American historian Carter G. Woodson published his work *The History of the Negro Church*, in which he vividly described the state of American Christianity.[1] Woodson's historical and theological analysis exposed the scandalous and corrupt nature of white Christianity in the northern and southern regions of the United States. Woodson's description reflected a form of Christianity that was so distorted that he concluded that white Christians would lynch the very figure on which the religion is based in the same manner that Negroes were being lynched in the name of Christ, particularly in the American South.

Woodson foreshadowed the scholarship of Black theologian James Cone almost a century later in his work *The Cross and the Lynching Tree*. Cone identified the cross as the symbol of Christian faith providing Christians with hope and salvation. The antithesis of the cross is lynching, which Cone argued was a symbol of Black oppression in America resulting from the reality of white supremacy. Cone concluded that, for white supremacists, the cross had become an emblem of cheap grace as opposed to the ultimate model of what German theologian Dietrich Bonhoeffer characterized

---

1. Carter G. Woodson, *The History of the Negro Church* (Suwanee, GA: 12th Media Services, 1921).

as the cost of discipleship that constitutes authentic Christian faith.[2] Cone states:

> The cross has been transformed into a harmless, non-offensive orna-
> ment that Christians wear around their necks. Rather than reminding
> us of the "cost of discipleship," it has become a form of "cheap grace,"
> an easy way to salvation that doesn't force us to confront the power
> of Christ's message and mission. Until we can see the cross and the
> lynching tree together, until we can identify Christ with a "recruci-
> fied" black body hanging from a lynching tree, there can be no genu-
> ine understanding of Christian identity in America, and no deliver-
> ance from the brutal legacy of slavery and white supremacy.[3]

These reflections of Woodson and Cone on the Christian faith—almost a century apart—reflect and confirm the fact that white Christian suprem-acy has been a source of scandal in white American Christianity from its inception in the United States, and the scandal continues to the present day. In other words, white supremacy exists in the DNA of white American Christianity.

Reconstruction

The Reconstruction era (1865–1877) began a few months prior to the Con-federacy's defeat in the Civil War, marked by Confederate Army General Robert E. Lee's surrender to Union Army General Ulysses S. Grant on April 9, 1865. The meeting of Union Army General William Sherman and Secre-tary of War Edwin S. Stanton with twenty African American pastors on January 12, 1865, in Savannah, Georgia, laid the foundation for Reconstruc-tion. President Abraham Lincoln had sent Secretary Stanton to the South to meet with leaders of formerly enslaved Africans to determine the most effective way of rejuvenating the South and governing in the best manner to ensure the welfare of African Americans in the aftermath of the Civil War. Ironically, the state of Georgia, which had been the catalyst for the antebellum schisms in the Methodist and Baptist denominations, was also the state where the spiritual freedom of African Americans occurred along with their emancipation.[4] Having defeated Atlanta, General Sherman became a spiritual liberator of African American Christians in the greater Atlanta area. His actions included preserving the Big Bethel AME Church

---

2. See Dietrich Bonhoeffer, *The Cost of Discipleship* (New York: Simon & Schuster, 1995).

3. James Cone, *The Cross and the Lynching Tree* (Maryknoll, NY: Orbis Books, 2011).

4. Whelchel, *The History and Heritage*, 127–31. See also Love Henry Whelchel Jr., *Sherman's March and the Emergence of the Independent Black Church Movement: From Atlanta to the Sea to Emancipation* (New York: Palgrave Macmillan, 2014).

in downtown Atlanta, liberating Blacks from the control of First Baptist Church in Marietta, which resulted in the formation of the Zion Baptist Church in 1866, and liberating the predominantly Black Bethesda Baptist Church from the control of the First Baptist Church in Stone Mountain.[5]

Special Field Order 15

Reconstruction addressed the secession of the Confederate states and the political, social, and civil rights of African Americans following the Civil War. African Americans had been the victims of chattel slavery, the most heinous form of human enslavement in human history. As enslaved persons they had been the property of their slaveholders with no rights or resources. In addition to liberation, enslaved persons desired self-sufficiency. During their historic meeting with General Sherman and Secretary Stanton, the African American ministers expressed the deep desire of freed Blacks to profit from their own labor and land. Historically, the "forty acres and a mule" promise for freed Blacks following the Civil War has been characterized as a myth, at best, or a false narrative based on the figment of Black folks' imagination, at worst. However, this was no myth or false narrative. It was a government-mandated promise to provide land, resources, and protection to freed Blacks.[6] Unfortunately, this reality has been obscured in historical narrative because of the negligence or racial bias of historians. Immediately following the historic meeting, General Sherman issued Special Field Order 15, which stipulated that coastal lands from Charleston, South Carolina, to the St. John's River in Florida become lands exclusively for the settlement of freed Blacks, including the major cities of Beaufort and Hilton Head in South Carolina, Savannah in Georgia, and Fernandina Beach, Jacksonville, and St. Augustine in Florida. The order stipulated that each freed Black family would receive forty acres of tillable land.[7]

The implementation of Special Field Order 15 was pivotal to the economic welfare and future of freed Blacks. By June 1865, forty thousand freed Blacks had settled new farmlands in the order's stipulated territories, which had been confiscated by Union forces from slaveholders as spoils of war. However, in August 1865, President Andrew Johnson provided pardons for those slaveholders, which essentially restored the land to their ownership and displaced freed Blacks.[8] Many of the freed Blacks became sharecroppers, which was enslavement of a different nature with the only

5. Whelchel, *The History and Heritage*, 125–27.

6. Paul Harvey, *Bounds of Their Habitation: Race and Religion in American History* (Lanham, MD: Rowman & Littlefield, 2017), 101.

7. Whelchel, *The History and Heritage*, 133–34.

8. Whelchel, *The History and Heritage*, 134.

difference being that sharecroppers were not considered the property of the landowner; they were considered the landowner's tenants.

At this point, freed Blacks, against their own volition, had provided approximately 246 years of free labor to white enslavers. Special Field Order 15 was not an act of benevolence for it reflected only a portion of what was owed to freed Blacks after centuries of enslavement. Congress passed legislation allowing freed Blacks to purchase other government lands, but with what resources? This reality exposed how paternalistic whites, who preach racial reconciliation but are opposed to proper reparations for the succeeding generations of enslaved Africans, reflect the disingenuous desire for supposed justice. Reconciliation suggests the restoration of a relationship in which there is mutual respect and equality. This form of relationship definitely did not exist then and exists very scarcely now. Essentially, the failure of Special Order 15 imposed a permanent economic impediment on freed Blacks.

Political and Social Achievements

While the economic prescriptions of Reconstruction failed to free Blacks, there were major political and social achievements. The most prominent was the passage of the Thirteenth, Fourteenth, and Fifteenth Amendments to the US Constitution, which are affectionately characterized as the Reconstruction amendments: the Thirteenth Amendment, ratified in 1865, legally abolished slavery; the Fourteenth Amendment, ratified in 1868, legalized birthright citizenship; and the Fifteenth Amendment, ratified in 1870, legalized the right of Black men to vote.[9] Each of these amendments was crucial to the legal status of African Americans following the Civil War and emancipation.

Furthermore, President Johnson was determined to restore the South to its antebellum state by advocating for the readmission of the Confederate states to the Union. Therefore, in addition to the Reconstruction amendments, Congress passed several legislative measures to ensure the civil rights of African Americans. The Civil Rights Act of 1866 was designed to protect all US citizens under the law, and specifically African Americans. The Civil Rights Act of 1875 prohibited racial discrimination regarding access to all services and public accommodations. These legislative measures were politically expedient in uplifting freed Blacks. In fact, during the Reconstruction era, over two hundred Black ministers held political office.[10] And for the duration of the Reconstruction era, there was a Black majority in the South Carolina state legislature.

---

9. See Eric Foner, *The Second Founding: How the Civil War and Reconstruction Remade the Constitution* (New York: W. W. Norton, 2019).

10. Harvey, *Bounds of Their Habitation*, 102.

Religious Impact

The religious impact of the Reconstruction was most evident in the formation of the Colored Methodist Episcopal (CME) Church in 1870. The CME
Church is the youngest of the three black Methodist bodies and was formed
under completely different circumstances from the AME and AMEZ denominations. Geographically, the CME Church has southern origins through an
agreement between the MECS and its colored members. Prior to the Civil
War, there were 207,000 colored members of the MECS. After the Civil War,
only about 78,000 colored members remained, as many of the colored members abandoned the MECS because of emancipation and joined either the
AME, AMEZ, or MEC denominations. The origin of the CME Church stems
from a mutual desire of the white and colored members of the MECS to
develop an independent Black denomination for its colored members, carried out during the 1866 General Conference of the MECS in New Orleans.
An initial step in establishing this new denomination was the formation
of colored conferences within the MECS. In preparation for the creation of
colored conferences following the 1866 MECS General Conference, regional
annual conferences began ordaining Black preachers; and by the end of 1866
there were twenty-six Black local preachers and two Black presiding elders.
By 1869, there were colored conferences in Tennessee, Kentucky, Mississippi,
Georgia, Alabama, Arkansas, East Texas, and South Carolina.

While the white members of the MECS desired the colored members to
have their own institution, they maintained a paternalistic relationship
with them.[11] Part of the 1866 Plan of Separation consisted in the transfer
of properties—valued at 1.5 million dollars—to the new Black denomination. This caused major conflicts with other Methodist bodies. The AME,
AMEZ, and MEC denominations engaged in evangelistic efforts to include
the colored members of the MECS as their own and to claim the transferred
property. The colored members rejected these efforts from all these entities because they were determined to build their own denomination. On
December 15, 1870, in the basement of the First MECS of Jackson, Tennessee, forty-one delegates from the colored conferences who were all ex-slaves
convened for the organizing general conference of the CME Church, electing William Henry Miles and Richard H. Vanderhorst as their first and second bishops respectively.

Unfortunately, the rich history and heritage of the CME Church have been
obscured by the negligence and false assumptions of historians. These false
assumptions include the claims that the CME Church is a small and insig-

---

11. Love Henry Whelchel Jr., *Hell without Fire: Conversion in Slave Religion* (Nashville, TN:
Abingdon Press, 2002), 93–119. See also Othal H. Lakey, *The History of the CME Church*, rev. ed.
(Memphis, TN: CME Publishing House, 1996).

nificant denomination, historically less politically active, and complacent regarding white supremacy because of its alleged paternalistic relationship with the MECS. One of the stipulations regarding the transfer of properties from the MECS, in fact, was an agreement that the CME Church would not engage in political activity; the agreement remained a clause in the denominational Book of Discipline until the civil rights movement in the 1950s. However, this does not suggest that members of the CME Church adhered to this clause. American historian Elizabeth Jemison strongly argues that the CME Church was not complacent with white supremacy and that clergy and laity of the CME Church indeed challenged white supremacy theologically more so than politically.[12] While some of the earliest mulatto episcopal leaders, such as Lucius Holsey and Isaac Lane, may have exhibited apolitical piety, there were other episcopal leaders, clergy, and laity, in the denomination who challenged the white supremacy and white paternalism of the MECS. For example, the MECS insisted that the new denomination be named the "Colored Methodist Episcopal Church South," which would solidify colored members' identification with the white paternalism of the MECS. Miles brought a resolution from the Kentucky Colored Conference that stated that the new denomination's name shall be "Colored Methodist Episcopal Church in America." Another challenge of Miles to the white paternalism of the MECS was the suggestion that the CME publishing house be located in Nashville, the location of the MECS and SBC publishing houses. By reason of their origins, both publishing houses had been defined by their proslavery apologetics. Miles's rejection of Nashville as the location of the publishing house reflects the independence of the CME Church from the influence of the MECS.

The 1877 Compromise

The Compromise of 1877, which settled the presidential election of 1876 between Samuel Tilden and Rutherford B. Hayes, marked the end of the Reconstruction era. The era ended with white supremacists' glorification of violence against Blacks. To solidify his election to the presidency, the Republican nominee Hayes agreed to the demands of southern Democrats to remove federal troops from the South. These troops had provided protection for Blacks in the South against the violence of white supremacists who were looking to act out their white backlash against the emancipation of Blacks and the defeat of the South in the Civil War. Hayes won the election, gaining the electoral votes of the Democratic stronghold in the for-

---

12. See Elizabeth L. Jemison, *Christian Citizens: Reading the Bible in Black and White in the Post-emancipation South* (Chapel Hill: University of North Carolina Press, 2020).

mer Confederate states of South Carolina, Florida, and Louisiana.[13] There
is no question that violence against Blacks occurred in the South during
Reconstruction, even with the protection of federal troops; but the removal
of these troops assured that violence against Blacks at the hand of white
supremacists, who claimed Christianity as their faith, would become more
widespread. For white Christian supremacists, Reconstruction was the
eradication of the divinely ordained social order. Consequently, they legitimized racial violence to replace Reconstruction with segregation and to
restore the social order controlled through white supremacy.[14] The restoration of the white-supremacist-controlled social order represented southern
redemption following their defeat in the Civil War.

Jim Crow

Southern redemption fostered the rise of Jim Crow, and the Compromise
of 1877 gave birth to the redeemer government through which Jim Crow
would function. Jim Crow was the nickname given to government-imposed
laws that legalized racial segregation, in many instances through threats
and acts of racial violence against Blacks. While Jim Crow was a product
of southern redemption, the phenomenon of racial violence was observed
in both the South and the North. Black codes had been enacted in southern legislatures prior to the end of Reconstruction and were imposed on
Blacks in both regions. Black codes were laws designed to empower former
slaveholders and other white supremacists to control the behavior of freed
Blacks by imposing violent consequences against Blacks who were considered out of order.

Lynching

The most egregious form of Jim Crow violence against Blacks was lynching. The act of lynching was used by white supremacists in the South and
the North to terrorize Blacks. It had originated in Virginia during the
Revolutionary War and gained prominence as a form of white supremacist
backlash following the passage of the Reconstruction Act of 1867, which
stipulated that Confederate states that had seceded from the Union could
be readmitted only after ratification of the Fourteenth Amendment, thus
assuring the citizenship rights of African Americans.

Lynching became the most celebrated religious ritual of white supremacist Christianity. In many instances, white supremacists would gather in

---

13. Henry Louis Gates Jr., *Stony the Road: Reconstruction, White Supremacy, and the Rise of
Jim Crow* (New York: Penguin Books, 2019), 6.

14. Jemison, *Christian Citizens*, 3.

public assembly for the heinous and diabolical spectacle of Negro lynching. It was not uncommon for white Christian supremacists to board trains in the afternoon following their supposed Christian worship services and travel to the next town to witness the terrorist act of lynching. James Cone depicts vividly this public spectacle and time of fellowship for white Christian supremacists:

> By the 1890s, lynching fever gripped the South, spreading like cholera, as white communities made blacks their primary target, and torture their focus. Lynching became a white media spectacle, in which a prominent newspaper, like the *Atlanta Constitution*, announced to the public the place, date, and time of the expected hanging and burning of black victims. Often as many as ten to twenty thousand men, women, and children attended the event. It was a family affair, a ritual celebration of white supremacy, where women and children were often given the first opportunity to torture black victims—burning black flesh and cutting off genitals, fingers, toes, and ears as souvenirs. Postcards were made from the photographs taken of black victims with white lynchers and onlookers smiling as they struck a pose for the camera. They were sold for ten to twenty-five cents to members of the crowd, who then mailed them to relatives and friends, often with a note saying something like this: "This is the barbeque we had last night."[15]

Furthermore, to sanctify lynching as a religious ritual, white clerics would bless the ritual publicly, pronouncing benedictions while white Christian supremacists lynched and burned the bodies of Negroes.[16]

Separate but Equal

The 1896 decision of the Supreme Court in the *Plessy v. Ferguson* case established the constitutionality of racial segregation through the legalization of the "separate but equal" clause. The decision fostered the illusion that Blacks in American society were equal to whites despite being treated differently. The decision ensured that African Americans would be forced to endure separate and fewer facilities, resources, and opportunities. The decision resulted in white children being educated in the best facilities, while Black children were educated in dilapidated schoolhouses; white children being bused from their neighborhood to school, while Black chil-

---

15. Cone, *The Cross and the Lynching Tree*, 9.
16. Harvey, *Bounds of Their Habitation*, 109.

dren walked miles to school; and white supremacists being provided legal protection in their practice of racial discrimination against Blacks in public accommodations.

Love Henry Whelchel claims that "the only equal in the doctrine of separate but equal seems to have been with the collection of taxes, with Blacks being required to pay the same proportion of their incomes in taxes as whites in order to support a system that gave them far less in return."[17] His claim further reflects the disingenuous nature of the racial reconciliation argument without any consideration for suitable and just reparations. Blacks have paid the same taxes as their white counterparts for decades only to receive lesser services and inferior accommodations. Many opponents of the rightful provisions for reparations often claim that they are not liable for the sins of their ancestors who enslaved Blacks; yet they fail to realize or at least acknowledge that they inherited wealth from their ancestors accumulated through chattel slavery and racial discrimination due to the "separate but equal" clause, which makes them just as accountable for the sin that has contributed significantly to the wealth gap between Blacks and whites in the United States.

Racial Segregation and Discrimination

The "separate but equal" clause empowered Jim Crow to create sundown towns and sanction racial segregation in public and private entities throughout the United States. Most sundown towns were not formed until after Reconstruction; they became prominent in the United States between 1890 and 1940. Sundown towns expelled Blacks and prohibited the admission of Black residents.[18] Sociologist James W. Loewen describes the explicit purpose for sundown towns:

> A sundown town is any organized jurisdiction that for decades kept African Americans or other groups from living in it and was thus "all-white" on purpose. There is a reason for the quotation marks "all-white": requiring the towns to be literally all-white in the census—no African Americans at all—is inappropriate, because many towns clearly and explicitly defined themselves as sundown towns but allowed one black household as an exception. Thus, an all-white town may include nonblack minorities and even a tiny number of African Americans.[19]

---

17. Whelchel, *The History and Heritage*, 155.
18. James W. Loewen, *Sundown Towns: A Hidden Dimension of American Racism* (New York: Simon & Schuster, 2005), 9.
19. Loewen, *Sundown Towns*, 4.

Sundown towns were a result of white supremacy in America and fostered racial discrimination. In fact, they promoted discrimination against African Americans in public and private education, public housing, private suburban neighborhoods, local, state, and federal governmental services. Sundown towns fueled the negative stereotypes that whites possessed about Blacks that, in turn, rationalized the existence of these towns. These negative stereotypes consisted of the belief that Blacks were intellectually inferior, indolent, and immoral. Black men, in particular, were erroneously and unjustifiably deemed criminals, sexual deviants, and rapists, who lurked after white women. Consequently, violence was a major factor in the formation and function of sundown towns. There were warning signs posted for Blacks such as "Niggers, Don't Let the Sun Go Down on You," "Whites Only within City Limits After Dark," and "If You Can Read . . . You'd Better Run . . . If You Can't Read . . . You'd Better Run Anyway." The presence of Blacks in these towns, specifically after a certain time of day, would result in angry white mobs terrorizing Blacks and using violence to the point of causing hospitalization and even death.[20]

In addition to the existence of sundown towns, racial segregation and discrimination were rampant even in the supposed more progressive region of New England. The Jim Crow system in New England functioned as a racial caste system. New England had segregated theaters, hotels, and hospitals, and Blacks and whites were separated on stagecoaches and steamboats. There was no law in New England that sanctioned segregated housing, but in the larger New England towns, Blacks were excluded from living in certain neighborhoods. The practice in New England of discriminatory church seating throughout the antebellum era continued through the Jim Crow period, especially in the Reformed Protestant churches. These churches in New England based church seating on one's social status, with the congregants with the highest status sitting closer to the pulpit and Africans Americans being relegated to the farthest point away from the pulpit. Between 1786 and 1820, the New England state legislatures of Massachusetts, Rhode Island, and Maine passed laws prohibiting racial amalgamation between people of color, including Native Americans, and people of European descent.[21] The racially motivated exclusive seating in Reformed Protestant churches reflects the theology of white superiority that was embedded in the Reformed theologies of the Puritans. Racial discrimination has a long history in Massachusetts. The city of Boston was the primary port for slave ships in the Atlantic triangular slave trade in British colonial America, and, during the height of the civil rights movement, Boston was

---

20. Loewen, *Sundown Towns*, 10–12.

21. Richard Archer, *Jim Crow North: The Struggle for Equal Rights in Antebellum New England* (New York: Oxford University Press, 2017), 6–12.

classified as the most racist city in America because of the prevalence of racial segregation.

Lost Cause Religion

The ideology of the Lost Cause was a mythical justification for the Confederate defeat in the Civil War and the spiritualization of white supremacist southern culture. Lost Cause religion was the belief of Confederate Christians that the Confederacy and the Civil War were divinely ordained. Confederate Christians viewed secession from the Union as God's cause in defense of slavery.

In his seminal work *Baptized in Blood*, Charles Reagan Wilson situates the origins of Lost Cause religion in the antebellum era and argues that "it was a Southern civil religion, which tied together Christian churches and Southern culture."[22] White supremacy dominated southern culture; therefore, Lost Cause religion constituted a revival of antebellum white supremacy culture, which Confederate Christians believed had been maligned by Reconstruction.[23] White southerners viewed Reconstruction as the cause of their poverty and the erosion of their social, cultural, and political dominance. They believed that Reconstruction fostered the prosperity and political power of Blacks.[24] Confederate Christians, in particular, viewed Lost Cause religion as their crusade against the demonic forces in the North and within the federal government. As solid southern Protestants, Confederate Christians had once identified the "whore of Babylon" in the Book of Revelation as the Roman Catholic papacy, but the Civil War shifted that identification to the northern churches. Additionally, Confederate Christians viewed the Beast in the Book of Revelation as the federal government. They believed that God had permitted the devil to use the Beast to defeat the Confederacy.[25]

The myth of Lost Cause religion was reminiscent of the puritanical vision of divine election. Confederate Christians believed that they had been chosen by God for the Lost Cause and therefore possessed a southern religious-moral identity.[26] Lost Cause religion epitomized the religion of white Christian supremacy with Confederate Christians regarding themselves as virtuous. This conservative virtue was based on the cultural principles of Dixie.[27] Dixie became the affectionate nickname for the Con-

22. Charles Reagan Wilson, *Baptized in Blood: Religion of the Lost Cause, 1865–1920* (Athens, GA: University of Georgia Press, 2009), 1.
23. Wilson, *Baptized in Blood*, 11–12.
24. Wilson, *Baptized in Blood*, 37.
25. Wilson, *Baptized in Blood*, 64–65.
26. Wilson, *Baptized in Blood*, 13.
27. Wilson, *Baptized in Blood*, 13.

federate states and was fueled by the theology of the Lost Cause. Wilson asserts that "in the theology of the Lost Cause, one can see that Southerners still hoped the spirit of the suffering and dead Confederacy would one day have, in the words from a Confederate monument, a joyful resurrection."[28] The purpose of Lost Cause religion was to foster the rise of the Confederate South from the ashes of their Civil War defeat.

At the heart of Lost Cause theology was the Confederate Christians' interpretation of the Civil War. For them, the Civil War was "redemption from past sins, atonement, and sanctification for the future."[29] They viewed the Civil War sacramentally, which is evident in their theology of atonement. In the Christian tradition, sacraments are the means through which God conveys grace to the believer and provides the healing remedy for the disease of sin. Confederate Christians viewed the bloodshed of the Civil War as atonement for the sins of the Confederacy.[30] Furthermore, they believed that God had ordained the institution of slavery and that their defeat in the Civil War resulted from their failure to civilize the pagan enslaved Africans. whom they viewed as sinful.[31] Due to the sin of the southerners, God shifted the responsibility for civilizing the supposed heathen Africans to northerners.[32] Confederate Christians believed that, through enslavement, they fostered within enslaved Africans the morality needed for virtuous living.[33] As part of their theology of redemption, Confederate Christians correlated the deaths of Confederate army soldiers with the passion of Christ, making their deaths sacrificial and redemptive.[34] Furthermore, being baptized in blood, Confederate Christians believed that they had been baptized with fire, which assured for them the fullness of salvation. By way of atonement and redemption, Confederate Christians believed that baptism in the blood of the Civil War provided justification; baptism in the fire provided sanctification. Therefore, they viewed the Civil War as a sanctifying event that provided the remedy of redemption for their sins and bestowed holiness.[35]

The theology of Confederate holiness in Lost Cause religion is most evident in Confederate hagiography. The members of the Confederate trinity, which includes Robert E. Lee, Jefferson Davis, and Stonewall Jackson, achieved sainthood in Confederate Christianity because of their leadership and service on behalf of the Confederate cause during the Civil War.

---

28. Wilson, *Baptized in Blood*, 58.
29. Wilson, *Baptized in Blood*, 5.
30. Wilson, *Baptized in Blood*, 44.
31. Wilson, *Baptized in Blood*, 68–69.
32. Wilson, *Baptized in Blood*, 69.
33. Wilson, *Baptized in Blood*, 104.
34. Wilson, *Baptized in Blood*, 44–45.
35. Wilson, *Baptized in Blood*, 44–45.

Confederate Christians viewed Lee, the commander of the Confederate Army, as the incarnation of the Lost Cause, and, therefore, he functioned as a typology of Christ.[36] Lee is believed to have been sent by God to save the Confederacy. Confederate Christians correlated the suffering of Davis, the president of the Confederacy, with the suffering of Christ and therefore viewed him as a martyr. Davis's suffering was regarded as redemptive because he was arrested by Union forces. Because of the redemptive suffering of Davis, Confederate Christians believed that they were holy. Davis epitomized Lost Cause religious understanding of holiness. Jackson was a Confederate general known for his strategic warfare tactics, whom Confederate Christians viewed as the prophet-warrior of the Confederacy.[37] This canonization of Lee, Davis, and Jackson reflects the rationale for why Confederate Christians portray the South as the Garden of Eden and the Appomattox Court House, where Lee surrendered to Grant, as Golgotha.[38] As the Garden of Eden, the South was the place of original perfection in its antebellum condition, which, for Confederate Christians, justified the institution of slavery as divinely ordained. As Golgotha, the Appomattox Court House was the place of ultimate sacrifice, where the South atoned for the sins of Confederate Christians in redeeming the Confederacy.

In Lost Cause religion, the saints and martyrs of the faith are at the heart of the holidays, liturgies, and artifacts of Confederate Christianity.[39] The organization most responsible for cultivating Lost Cause rituals was the United Daughters of the Confederacy. The birthdays of Lee and Davis became regional holidays in the South. Decoration of Confederate graves and displaying the Confederate flag became rituals of veneration to the dead, and the dedication of Confederate monuments became holy shrines for the pilgrimages of Confederate Christians. The liturgies of Confederate Christian worship consisted of prayers in the name of Confederate saints. During southern revivalism, the invitation to Christian discipleship constituted an invitation to become followers of Robert E. Lee, Jefferson Davis, and Stonewall Jackson. Southern Baptists and Southern Methodists were the dominant denominations of Dixie; however, Episcopalians proved most active in Lost Cause rituals because the denomination was strongly grounded in antebellum and aristocratic values.[40] While Lost Cause religion was related to race, Wilson notes that race was not the primary moti-

---

36. Wilson, *Baptized in Blood*, 48–49.

37. Wilson, *Baptized in Blood*, 51.

38. Donald G. Matthews, *At the Altar of Lynching: Burning Sam Hose in the American South* (New York: Cambridge University Press, 2018), 43.

39. Wilson, *Baptized in Blood*, 36. Wilson argues that "the religion of the Lost Cause was a cult of the dead, which dealt with essential religious concerns."

40. Wilson, *Baptized in Blood*, 18–36.

vation for its philosophy. He contends that the motivations behind Lost Cause religion were southern religion and southern history, both of which reflect southern identity, noting the claim of southerners that the Civil War was fought not because of slavery but on the principle of preserving Confederate virtue.[41] While Wilson presents an enlightening and significant study of Lost Cause religion, his argument for the motivations behind Lost Cause religion is questionable. The reality is that Lost Cause religion was intentionally designed by Confederate Christians to preserve white supremacy. There is nothing virtuous about white supremacy since it is the emblem of hate and antithetical to virtue. This reality is most evident in the possession and expression of white Christian supremacy demonstrated through the philosophy and actions of the Ku Klux Klan (KKK).

The Ku Klux Klan (KKK)

The 1865 organization of the first Ku Klux Klan (KKK) in Pulaski, Tennessee, was the white supremacist reaction to the emancipation of Blacks and the effects of Reconstruction. Wilson identifies "white supremacy as a key tenet of the Southern Way of Life."[42] White supremacy, however, was not simply a tenet of white southern life, it was its nucleus in both the antebellum and postbellum eras. The unsubstantiated, unjustified, and irrational fear of freed Blacks in society ignited the violent terrorism of the KKK against Blacks. Based on their belief that Blacks were savages and heathens without the civilization of enslavement, Confederate Christians feared that freed blacks would become uncivilized. Blacks gaining civil, social, political, and equal rights to white supremacists constitutes uncivil behavior and was therefore a threat to white society. The KKK consisted of angry white mob vigilantes committing vicious acts of violence, including assassinations, in an attempt to eradicate Black power in America through Reconstruction. The first KKK was dissolved in 1869; however, their terrorist attacks continued. The violent domestic terrorism of the first KKK was so widespread that, in 1871, President Ulysses S. Grant requested Congress to pass the Third Ku Klux Klan Act, which enforced the Fourteenth Amendment by guaranteeing all citizens of the United States the rights afforded by the Constitution and providing legal protection under the law. To take action against this newly defined federal crime, the act empowered the president to suspend habeas corpus, deploy the US military, and use "other means, as he may deem necessary."[43]

---

41. Wilson, *Baptized in Blood*, 117–18.
42. Wilson, *Baptized in Blood*, 100.
43. Wilson, *Baptized in Blood*, 100–112.

The second KKK was formed by a former Southern Methodist circuit rider William J. Simmons in Stone Mountain, Georgia, following the release of D. W. Griffith's white supremacist film, *The Birth of a Nation*, in 1915. The film glorified the KKK as the saviors of the country from the supposed evils of Reconstruction and was based on the 1905 novel *The Clansman*, by Thomas Dixon. In the novel, Dixon, a North Carolina Baptist cleric, portrayed Blacks as dangerous and morally degenerate and praised the KKK for taking vengeance against a Black man accused of raping a southern white woman.

To justify the necessity of law and order, Confederate Christians dehumanized Blacks, especially Black men, characterizing them as violent and dangerous. They even dehumanized Black ministers as hypersexual, self-aggrandizing, and uneducated.[44] Confederate Christians were essentially domestic terrorists who dehumanized Blacks regardless of white violence against Blacks, such as the rape of Black women and the lynching of Black men.

Wilson argues that the second KKK was more Christian than Confederate in its symbolism than the first KKK.[45] However, such an argument is weak in that it constitutes a false alternative since there was no distinction between Christian and Confederate, and Confederate Christians represented the corrupting of authentic Christianity through the scandal of white supremacy. In Lost Cause religion, white southern Protestant Christianity and the Confederacy were not strange bedfellows; they were interdependent.

Finally, the second KKK reflected how Lost Cause religion promoted white Christian supersessionism, which asserted that white Christians had replaced Jewish people in the divine covenant as God's chosen. The promotion of Christian supersessionism explicitly reflects the belief that God's chosen people are whites.[46] That white supremacy and supposed Protestant morality were central to the second KKK is evident in their violent vigilante hate against Jews and Roman Catholics, in addition to Blacks, condemning them all as reprobates. Consequently, members of the KKK were not the progenitors of white supremacy but rather the products of the Lost Cause religion of white Christian supremacy.

---

44. Jemison, *Christian Citizens*, 78–79.

45. Jemison, *Christian Citizens*, 117. The fact that Dixon was a Southern Baptist cleric and Simmons was a Southern Methodist cleric might explain Wilson's conclusion.

46. Matthews, *At the Altar of Lynching*, 38.

8

White American Fundamentalism

Does this present civil rights program promote the Love of God? The lead-
ers are always crying out against prejudice and hate. They are always
talking about love.... Love cannot be legislated. Love is found in a Per-
son—His Name is Jesus Christ. The church needs to become dedicated
once again to the task of preaching Christ. Education, medicine, social
reform, and all the other external ministries cannot meet the needs of
the human soul and spirit.

—Jerry Falwell

On March 21, 1965, at the height of the civil rights movement, Jerry Falwell preached his sermon "Ministers and Marches" at the Thomas Road Baptist Church in Lynchburg, Virginia, the church he founded in 1956.[1] In his sermon, Falwell berates civil rights leaders such as Martin Luther King Jr. for teaching love in their quest to achieve equal rights for Blacks in American society and shamefully questions their motives, accusing them of hypocrisy. He further expresses his fear and outrage regarding peaceful protests, which he characterizes as riots, and diabolically accuses the civil rights activists of inciting violence. Falwell's false claims regarding Black riots and violence reflect the reality that, even though the Confederate Christians were defeated in the Civil War, their Lost Cause religion was victorious. Falwell perpetuates the Lost Cause belief that Blacks were uncivilized simply because they dared to challenge racial injustice.[2]

---

1. Jerry Falwell, "Ministers and Miracles," in Matthew Avery Sutton, *Jerry Falwell and the Rise of the Religious Right: A Brief History with Documents* (Boston: Bedford/St. Martin's, 2013).

2. As we noted in the last chapter, Confederate Christians believed that Blacks were civilized through the institution of slavery and then, after emancipation, became heathen savages again. Falwell's sermon reflects a person so warped with the racial hate of Lost Cause religion that he questions the reality of racial discrimination against Blacks.

The victory of Lost Cause religion is evident because even some abolitionists were unconvinced of the full equality of Blacks and whites. Abraham Lincoln, the enemy of the Confederacy, denounced slavery as sin and argued that the entire nation—both South and North—had engaged in sinfulness in having enslaved persons. Therefore, Lincoln declared that the Civil War was necessary in order overcome America's original sin of slavery.[3] However, even Lincoln believed in the superiority of the white race.[4] His advocacy for the liberation of enslaved persons and the passage of the Emancipation Proclamation in 1863 were necessary politically to preserve the Union.[5] Lincoln really did not feel a moral or spiritual obligation to emancipate enslaved persons; his wife had enslaved Africans. Indeed, Lincoln's belief in Negro inferiority and the abolitionist concessions of Weld and Garrison, the publisher of the abolitionist newspaper *The Liberator*, reflect Mark Noll's argument that proslavery apologists had won the battle of the Bible.[6] Therefore, while Confederate Christians lost the Civil War, their Lost Cause religion won the war of theology.

Dwight Moody

The most influential American revivalist of the nineteenth century, Dwight Moody, was influenced by Lost Cause religion. Modern white evangelicalism stems from the evangelicalism of postwar evangelists such as Moody, who emphasized personal piety, which propelled white Christian supremacist piety. White evangelicals, many of whom had been slaveholders or advocates of slavery, promoted proslavery theology, which fueled their sense of Confederate redemption and the rise of Jim Crow. They chose the white supremacist form of evangelicalism rather than Christian perfectionist evangelicalism. The latter, as we have explored, fostered social justice and social holiness through the vision of Charles Finney and emphasized the transformation of society. Moody's vision of personal piety and spirituality was a corrupted version of Christian piety and a scandalous form of Christian spirituality.

Businessmen Revivalism

Moody's revivalism was primarily influenced by the Great Revival of 1857–1858, which was a religious awakening of businessmen primarily affiliated

---

3. Harlow, "The Civil War," 109.

4. Powery and Sadler, *The Genesis of Liberation*, 97.

5. Lincoln's advocacy reflects the political behavior of Constantine, who in AD 313 ended the persecution of Christians in the Roman Empire with the Edict of Milan. Constantine ended the persecution of Christians, and Lincoln emancipated enslaved persons, primarily for political expediency.

6. Powery and Sadler, *The Genesis of Liberation*, 96.

with northern Protestantism. This revival shifted the emphasis from an evangelical revivalism based on inner piety and social reform to a socially conservative revivalism.[7] The problem here was that its ethical ethos was completely antithetical to the social reforms related to racial equality. Social conservatism was an integration of personal piety and antebellum white Protestantism that was essentially proslavery, and it constituted the spiritualization of white supremacy.

Another major influence on Moody's revivalism was the Keswick movement. In 1871, Moody had an experience that reflected Keswick teachings.[8] The Keswick movement originated among Anglican evangelicals during the Holiness movement, and its theology became an alternative to the perfectionism taught by Oberlinism and the Holiness doctrine of eradicationism, or the belief that sin was eradicated through sanctification. Keswick teachers were suppressionists in that they believed that sin was suppressed through sanctification but not completely destroyed.[9] The revivals of the nineteenth century had been Arminian in nature; however, the Great Revival of 1857–1858 had a Calvinist revival influence: Arminians viewed revivalism as the providential work of God; Calvinists viewed revivalism as the surprising work of God.[10] The revivalism of the businessmen created a Calvinist subculture that influenced Moody's revivalism. Significantly, the Calvinist doctrine that propelled Adam Smith's economic philosophy of laissez-faire, or free-market, capitalism would prove extremely appealing to the capitalist businessmen. As a result, some of the key features of Moody's revivalism were laissez-faire economic principles and individualism.

Theology

The focus on laissez-faire philosophy and individualism was imperative to Moody's soteriology, which promoted Christian conversion as the path to prosperity. Moody emphasized the Puritan work ethic in his revival preaching; however, he built on the Puritan doctrine cultivating a theology-of-prosperity gospel. He believed that salvation through the blood of Jesus delivered prosperity, which gave the convert a respectability, as opposed to

---

7. Kathryn Teresa Long, *The Revival of 1857–58: Interpreting an American Religious Awakening* (New York: Oxford University Press, 1998), 124.

8. Frances Fitzgerald, *The Evangelicals: The Struggle to Shape America* (New York: Simon & Schuster, 2017), 91.

9. Donald W. Dayton, *Theological Roots of Pentecostalism* (Seoul: Christian Literature Society of Korea, 1993), 104–5.

10. Kathryn Long, *The Revivals of 1857–58: Interpreting an American Religious Awakening* (New York: Oxford University Press, 1998), 19–23.

being considered a charity case.[11] His theology suggests that wealth is the symbol of the converted, and poverty the symbol of the unconverted.

Historically, the origin of the prosperity gospel, or Word of Faith movement, has been situated in the positive confessional teaching of Essek William Kenyon. In the late nineteenth century, Kenyon embraced the New Thought movement of Phineas Quimby, which the American philosopher and psychologist William James called the "mind-cure movement."[12] New Thought philosophy taught that all disease had a mental origin and that the remedy for the disease is right thinking. Essentially, persons who believe that they are suffering from illness are not really sick; they only think they are sick. Sickness is in the mind. Consequently, Kenyon developed positive confessional teaching based on his interpretation of Scripture, through which he concluded that the word of God was more powerful than the presence of God. He connects the word of God with the creative power of God in that nothing was created in Scripture until God spoke.[13] Therefore, making positive confessions or positively speaking the word of God assured health and wealth—the features of prosperity. Positive confessional teaching became the foundation for the Word of Faith movement.

Moody's revivalism focused on the faith of the individual, and it became the model for the revivalism of Billy Sunday and Billy Graham in the twentieth century. As a revivalist, Moody desired to reach the masses. However, his revivalism appealed mostly to those in the white middle and upper classes—white-collar Protestants.[14] Moody's theology was strongly aligned with that of Calvinism in that the salvation of an individual was based on economic status. In Moody's theology, it is clear that whites in the middle and upper classes of society constituted God's elect, while those in poverty, regardless of race, were those whom God had damned. Blacks, however, were in the worst state of damnation, solely because of the color of their skin. Moody preached about the ethical duty of northern and southern whites to reconcile in the postbellum era, and held segregated revivals in the South.[15] Segregated revivalism was emblematic of Moody's white Christian supremacism, which rejected social reform and social justice. Appalled by these segregated revivals, African American abolitionist Frederick

---

11. Fitzgerald, *The Evangelicals*, 90.

12. See William James, *Varieties of Religious Experience: A Study in Human Nature* (New York: Random House, 1929).

13. See Kate Bowler, *Blessed: A History of the American Prosperity Gospel* (New York: Oxford University Press, 2013).

14. Fitzgerald, *The Evangelicals*, 86–87.

15. Alan Jay Richard, "A War of Aggression: The Moody Formation of American White Christian Nationalism," in Jeffery W. Robbins and Clayton Crockett, *Doing Theology in the Age of Trump: A Critical Report on Christian Nationalism* (Eugene, OR: Cascade Books, 2018), 14.

Douglass declared, "Of all the forms of negro hate in the world, save me from the one which clothes itself in the name of the loving Jesus."

Premillennial Dispensationalists

Moody was the progenitor of the fundamentalist movement, and the Moody Bible Institute was the training center for premillennial dispensationalist teachings. The institute was designed as a Bible training school for working-class lay Christians to become city lay missionaries. The teachings of premillennial dispensationalism integrated white American nationalism and the theologies of the Civil War and were pivotal in the development of white American Christian nationalism and white American Christian supremacy.[16] The teaching offered theological justification for the rejection of equal rights and social justice for Blacks in the postbellum era. In the late nineteenth and early twentieth centuries, advocacy for social justice through social reform was characterized as theological liberalism and condemned by premillennial dispensationalists as false teaching. George Marsden provides a clear and excellent depiction of this reality:

> Dispensationalism, or dispensational premillennialism, was the fruit of renewed interest in the detail of biblical prophecy which developed after the Civil War. Rejecting the prevailing post-millennialism which taught Christ's kingdom would grow out of spiritual and moral progress of this age, dispensational premillennialists said that churches and the culture were declining and that Christians would see Christ's kingdom only after he personally returned to rule in Jerusalem. They thus offered a plausible explanation of the difficulties the church was facing . . . now that was being made apparent by the secularization of the culture and the apostasy (liberalism) within the churches themselves. Yet the Bible also provided firm hope for the coming of the kingdom.[17]

Postmillennialists believed that Christ would return after the transformation of society through the salvation of souls and social reform. Essentially, they believed that the world was sinful and would only be redeemed at Christ's return.[18]

---

16. Richard, "A War of Aggression," 8.

17. George Marsden, *Understanding Fundamentalism and Evangelicalism* (Grand Rapids, MI: Eerdmans, 1991), 39–40.

18. Jones, *White Too Long*, 93.

American Pentecostalism

Historically, the origins of American Pentecostalism are greatly debated. At the heart of the debate is the issue of race, centering on the white Pentecostal Charles Fox Parham and the Black Pentecostal William J. Seymour.

Charles Parham

Charles Parham was born in Muscatine, Iowa, in 1873, with an ailment that hindered his physical growth. In 1891, he was healed of his illness and answered the call to ministry. In 1893, Parham was licensed to preach in the Methodist Episcopal Church but became disenchanted with the episcopal polity of the denomination. Parham became attracted to the Holiness movement because of the emphasis on divine healing, which he had experienced himself.[19] In 1898, Parham formed the Bethel Healing Home in Topeka, Kansas, and two years later formed Bethel Bible College to train missionaries.[20] During the inaugural year of the college in 1900, Parham led his students in a study of the Book of Acts, seeking to discover the definitive evidence of Spirit baptism. After asking for prayer from Parham through imposition of hands, one of his students, Agnes Ozman, was Spirit baptized on January 1, 1901, and spoke in the Chinese language, which was a language she had never learned. Consequently, some scholars, such as Parham's biographer, James R. Goff, and African American Pentecostal historian Leslie Callahan, have argued that Parham became the theological progenitor of Pentecostalism through the development of his "initial evidence" theory, which suggested that *xenolalia* (tongues for foreign mission and world evangelization) was the initial physical evidence of Spirit baptism.[21] Parham's theological emphases included salvation, Spirit baptism, the advent of Christ, and water baptism through immersion.[22] Additionally, Parham rejected the doctrine of hell, believing that unredeemed bodies would experience annihilation, affirmed premillennialism, and was an advocate of Christian Zionism, which resulted in his belief that Orthodox Jews did not have to convert to Christianity for salvation.[23]

---

19. See Kimberly Ervin Alexander, *Pentecostal Healing: Models in Theology and Practice* (United Kingdom: Deo Publishing, 2006).

20. James R. Goff Jr., *Fields White unto Harvest: Charles F. Parham and the Missionary Origins of Pentecostalism* (Fayetteville, AR: University of Arkansas Press, 1988), 1–86.

21. Goff, *Fields White unto Harvest*, 67–86. See also Leslie Callahan, "Charles Parham: Progenitor of Pentecostalism," in Henry Hal Knight, ed., *From Aldersgate to Azusa Street: Wesleyan, Holiness, and Pentecostal Visions of the New Creation* (Eugene, OR: Pickwick Publications, 2010), 210–17.

22. Callahan, "Charles Parham," 210–17.

23. Goff, *Fields White unto Harvest*, 101.

William J. Seymour

William J. Seymour was baptized as a Roman Catholic in 1871 as a result of the legal requirements of residency in the parishes of the Roman Catholic dominated state of Louisiana. Seymour was raised in deep poverty as both of his parents had been former slaves. After migrating to the North, Seymour converted to the Methodist Episcopal Church but was sanctified through his affiliation with the Holiness group the Evening Light Saints in Cincinnati, Ohio. Seymour became an evangelist in this Holiness tradition and adopted the doctrine of sanctification through the evidence of holy living and belief in the necessity of a second experience after conversion as final salvation. He was influenced by the teachings of Martin Knapp that emphasized racial integration.[24] After migrating to Texas, Seymour was introduced to Charles Parham by Lucy Farrow, who had been a former slave from Virginia and had received Spirit baptism in one of Parham's revivals. Seymour initially accepted Parham's views on Spirit baptism and speaking in tongues wholeheartedly. He and Parham began conducting revivals together among Blacks. Parham was a blatant racist who practiced racial segregation in his revivals and classroom. While in Houston, Parham allowed Seymour to attend classes at his Houston Bible School on the stipulation that Seymour would sit outside the classroom in the hallway, which fulfilled Parham's own segregationist practices and those of the Jim Crow laws in the South. Despite the fact that Parham's practices were antithetical to Martin Knapp's vision of racial integration, Seymour embraced Parham's teachings on Spirit baptism and divine healing.[25]

On April 6, 1906, after migrating to Los Angeles and affiliating with some adherents of the Holiness movement, Seymour called for a ten-day fast. Edward Lee and Jennie Seymour were baptized in the Spirit with the physical evidence of *glossolalia*. On April 12, Seymour finally experienced the Spirit baptism that he had been teaching but had not yet experienced at a makeshift altar in the home of Richard Asberry, alongside a white man who had experienced Spirit baptism simultaneously. These simultaneous interracial Spirit baptisms violated Parham's insistence on segregation.[26] However, they foreshadowed Seymour's revivalism during the Azusa Street revival. Seymour's prayer meeting in the Asberry home on Bonnie Brae Street in an African American neighborhood became a massive revival of people of all races experiencing Spirit baptism. As a result, Seymour led

---

24. Gaston Espinosa, *William J. Seymour and the Origins of Global Pentecostalism: A Biography and Documentary History* (Durham, NC: Duke University Press, 2014), 47–49.

25. Espinosa, *William J. Seymour*, 49–50. See also Estrelda Y. Alexander, *Black Fire: One Hundred Years of African American Pentecostalism* (Downers Grove, IL: InterVarsity Press, 2011), 110–58.

26. Espinosa, *William J. Seymour*, 53–58.

the new congregation that had developed out of revivalism in purchasing a building at 312 Azusa Street, which had been the Stevens AME Church. Gaston Espinosa argues that the Azusa Street revival was a congregation that was nurtured in the womb of the Black church.[27]

Azusa Street Mission

The congregation at Azusa was multiracial and multicultural, consisting of Blacks, whites, Latinos, Asians, and Native Americans. The only prerequisite for leadership in the Azusa Street Mission was an experience of Spirit baptism. Worship at Azusa Street consisted of interracial fellowship, spiritual warfare at the altar, glossolalia, being slain in the Spirit, singing in the Spirit, writing in the Spirit, prophecy, revelation, visions, and the laying on of hands.[28] Vinson Synan highlights the significance of the global missionary work produced through the Azusa Street Mission and contends that the premillennial beliefs of early Pentecostals caused them to provide Pentecostal missionaries working globally with a one-way ticket.[29] The racial integration at Azusa caused Pentecostal historian Frank Bartleman to declare that "the color line had been washed away in the blood." However, the washing away of the color line was temporary.

After arriving at the Azusa Street Mission, Parham condemned and criticized Seymour's leadership. Parham accused the mission of spiritualism, hypnotism, mesmerism, engaging in fetish worship, orgies, and free loveism. In addition to these condemnations, Parham identified the spiritual ecstasy at Azusa as "Negroisms" and classified the revival as a "darky camp meeting." These condemnations resulted from Parham's racial bigotry, which he justified through his theological and ideological affirmation of the British-Israelism theory. This theory suggested that Adam and Eve were white, and therefore whites were superior to Blacks, Latinos, Asians, and Native Americans.[30] In his biographical account of Parham, Goff contends that, prior to his Azusa experience, Parham was not a blatant racist; he only suffered from paternalistic racism. Goff argued that prior to his Azusa experience, Parham stood somewhere between the social segregation of theory of W. F. Carothers and the racial integration theory of Alexander Dowie. Carothers

---

27. Espinosa, *William J. Seymour*, 58.

28. Cecil Roebuck, *The Azusa Street Mission and Revival: The Birth of the Global Pentecostal Movement* (Nashville, TN: Thomas Nelson Publishers, 2006), 129–86. The modern-day Pentecostal movement became a global phenomenon as a result of aggressive evangelism and global appeal of the Azusa Street revival.

29. Vinson Synan, *The Holiness-Pentecostal Tradition: Charismatic Movements in the Twentieth Century* (Grand Rapids, MI: Eerdmans, 1997), 129–42.

30. Roebuck, *The Azusa Street Mission and Revival*, 168–72. See also Espinosa, *William J. Seymour*, 96–106.

argued that Blacks needed to respect social segregation, even within revivalism. Goff concludes that after his Azusa experience, Parham became more blatant in his racism, using theology and racist ideology to justify his support of Jim Crow, Manifest Destiny, rejection of interracial marriage, and his encouragement of Pentecostals to support the Ku Klux Klan.[31] The suggestion of paternalistic racism is erroneous, because Parham was a blatant racist prior to Azusa and thereafter. Furthermore, his embrace of the white supremacist British-Israelism theory, segregationist practices, condemnation of Azusa revivalism, and advocacy for the oppression of Black people confirms his support of white Christian supremacy.

After experiencing the racial bigotry of Parham at Azusa, Seymour's theology of Spirit baptism shifted. Initially, Seymour had fully affirmed Parham's theology of Spirit baptism but shifted to the belief that divine love, not the initial physical evidence of speaking in tongues, was the true evidence of Spirit baptism. Historical theologian Dale Coulter has identified the Catholic spirituality of early Pentecostalism and argues that Seymour situated Spirit baptism in the affective transformation of love and therefore identified Spirit baptism as a baptism of love.[32] Seymour adopted Wesleyanism, which he believed was the foundation of Pentecostalism. The spirit of divine love as understood in Wesleyanism prompted Seymour's utilization of bridal imagery in his theology. Spirit baptism constituted marriage to Christ, and union with Christ produced tongues, prophecies, revelations, visions, and loving actions.[33] Due to white Christian supremacy, the first, second, and third generations of white Pentecostal scholarship tended to favor Parham over Seymour as the founder of Pentecostalism.[34] Walter Hollenweger, however, traces the origins of Pentecostalism to African spirituality based on the Black root, which he attributes to the growth of global Pentecostalism. The features of the Black root are orality of liturgy, narrativity of testimony and witness, reflection, prayer, reconciliatory community, inclusion of visions in worship, and the close relationship between the body and mind.[35] Third generation Black Pentecostal scholars, such as Leonard Lovett, James S. Tinney, David Daniels, and Estrelda Alexander, affirm Hollenweger's notion of the Black root and conclude that Seymour is the founder of modern global Pentecostalism with Azusa Street revivalism as the catalyst.

---

31. Goff, *Fields White unto Harvest*, 128–32.

32. Dale Coulter, "The Spirit and the Bride Revisited," *Journal of Pentecostal Theology* 21, no. 2 (2012): 298–319.

33. Coulter, "The Spirit and the Bride Revisited."

34. Espinosa, *William J. Seymour*, 8–18.

35. Walter Hollenweger, *Pentecostalism: Origins and Developments Worldwide* (Peabody, MA: Hendrickson Publishers, 1997), 18–25.

White Christian Supremacy

White Christian supremacy continued to plague the Pentecostal movement in the United States following the racism leveled against the Azusa
Street revival. Nevertheless, many Pentecostal denominations developed
across the country as a result of Azusa. Among these denominations was
the Church of God in Christ (COGIC). The COGIC was initially chartered
as a Holiness denomination in 1897 through the spiritual partnership of
Charles Harrison Mason and Charles Price Jones.

There are two prominent examples of the influence of white Christian
supremacy in American Pentecostalism. The first example is the formation
of the Assemblies of God (AG) denomination. In 1907, the COGIC became
the first official Pentecostal denomination chartered in the United States.
Therefore, from 1907 to 1914, the COGIC was the only Pentecostal body in
the country registered with the US government to grant ministerial credentials. The COGIC had just as many white ministers as Black ministers.
Mason prayed for the Christianity of his enslaved ancestors and practiced
conjuration. Estrelda Alexander notes that Jones had a major issue with
Mason's practice of African spirituality:

> Though not denying the authenticity of the experience, Jones saw the
> experience of tongues as only one possible evidence of Holy Spirit bap-
> tism. Mason, on the other hand, viewed his Azusa Street experience
> as essential to his personal quest to preserve elements of slave reli-
> gion in African American worship and make its presence felt within
> the COGIC experience. But not only did Jones reject Mason's conten-
> tions; but also, mainline pastors ridiculed Mason's prayer and heal-
> ing rituals, especially his display of misshaped roots as "magic" and
> pure superstition. . . . Mason, however, sought to give both a biblical
> and cultural interpretation to elements of Pentecostal worship, and
> the more his detractors protested, the more tenaciously he held on
> to these practices and his interpretation of them as rooted in African
> spirituality.[36]

In 1914, the white ministers of the COGIC succumbed to the white Chris-
tian supremacy widespread in American society and particularly the Jim
Crow South and separated from the COGIC to form the AG denomination in
Hot Springs, Arkansas. Another example of the influence of white Christian

---

36. Alexander, *Black Fire*, 176–77. See also Vinson Synan, *The Century of the Holy Spirit:
100 Years of Pentecostal and Charismatic Renewal* (Nashville, TN: Thomas Nelson Publishers,
2001), 101. See also Yvonne Chireau, *Black Magic: Religion and the African American Conjuring
Tradition* (Berkeley: University of California Press, 2003), 111.

supremacy is the formation of the United Pentecostal Church. At the 1916 General Council of the Assemblies of God, 156 pastors separated and formed the Pentecostal Assemblies of the World denomination (PAW), which had initially begun as a trinitarian denomination but after the development of the Oneness issue, or "Jesus-only" doctrine, quickly adopted Oneness theology. Its most influential pastor was Garfield T. Haywood, an African American pastor of a racially integrated congregation in Indianapolis, Indiana. From the beginning, the PAW was racially integrated, with nearly three-fourths of the initial membership being white. In 1919, Haywood was elected as the general secretary, a role that gave him the responsibility of signing ministerial credentials. PAW continued as an integrated body until 1924 when a separation occurred due to the feeling of whites in the PAW that a racially integrated church would hinder the denomination's growth, and the white ministers became concerned that their credentials, signed by a Black man, would not be accepted in the Jim Crow South. Therefore, whites in the PAW abandoned the denomination to form the predominantly white Oneness denomination, the United Pentecostal Church (UPC).

The actions of the pioneers of the AG and UPC are indicative of the modus operandi of white Christian supremacy. Despite claims of a monopoly on God and supernatural knowledge through divine revelation and prophecies, white Christian supremacists tend to engage in behavior that is antithetical to the Spirit of God and the gospel of Jesus Christ. In the case of the AG and UPC, white Pentecostals chose to succumb to the demonic spirit of white supremacy. Such behavior raises the question of whether they had really been regenerated, truly been sanctified, and whether their Spirit baptism had been authentic.

Jerry Falwell

Jerry Falwell was the driving force behind the formation of the Moral Majority and the Reagan Revolution. Falwell was born in Lynchburg, Virginia, in 1933, to an agnostic businessman father who bootlegged liquor during Prohibition and a religious mother. In 1952, after his conversion experience, Falwell committed himself to a career of fulltime ministry. He enrolled at Baptist Bible College, a fundamentalist school in Springfield, Missouri, and adopted militant separatism, which was the far-right position of fundamentalism that advocated for separation from mainstream American culture.[37] Falwell correlated American evangelicalism with the Crusades, asserting that God had endowed white evangelicals with the burden of capturing

---

37. Matthew Avery Sutton, *Jerry Falwell and the Rise of the Religious Right: A Brief History with Documents* (Boston: Bedford/St. Martin's, 2013), 1–10.

America for Christ in the same manner as the Crusades had been committed to capturing Jerusalem for Christ.[38] Ironically, he based the majority of his sermons on the Pauline epistles rather than the Gospels, which reflected the life and ministry of Jesus.[39] Interestingly, white American evangelicals generally develop their moral standards and cultivate their holiness codes following the guidance of Paul rather than the guidance of Jesus. Paul even warns Christians at the church of Corinth against making demigods out of certain spiritual figures, even biblical characters (cf. 1 Cor 3:6–7). Regardless, Pauline theology coupled with Reformed theology has been the nucleus of the fundamentalist-evangelical biblical impulse.

Segregation

Fundamentalist theology was pivotal to white Christian supremacist's opposition to racial integration, as evident in Falwell's early ministry. He was a racial segregationist who fought vehemently against the implementation of integration. He condemned President Lyndon Baines Johnson's civil rights legislation and accused civil rights leaders such as Martin Luther King Jr. as being the pawns of communists who intended to ruin what he considered were good race relations during the 1950s. Following the 1954 Supreme Court decision in the *Brown v. Board of Education,* which mandated the desegregation of public schools in the United States, white Christian supremacists developed segregation academies. These segregation academies were founded throughout the South by white Christian supremacists to protect their children from attending public school with Black children and essentially became educational factories for the production and development of future generations of white Christian supremacists. In 1967, Falwell founded Lynchburg Christian Academy, which was a segregationist academy. A year later, Falwell admitted three Black students, which some historians have characterized as his concession to desegregation. However, his action appears much more an attempt to safeguard against the charge of racism.[40]

The Moral Majority and the Religious Right

In the 1970s, Falwell led in the fundamentalist-evangelical hardline separation between church and state. As a transition into this major shift in his view of American civil religion, Falwell denounced his past segregationist sermons as "false prophecy" and expressed his resolve to follow the model of

---

38. Fitzgerald, *The Evangelicals,* 284.
39. Fitzgerald, *The Evangelicals,* 266.
40. Fitzgerald, *The Evangelicals,* 284–87.

Martin Luther King Jr. and other civil rights activists whom he had demonized.[41] However, Falwell's epiphany on his racist theology was either short-lived or completely inauthentic, as white Christian supremacy continued to plague him. Some historians have erroneously situated the origins of the Moral Majority in religious opposition to the 1973 Supreme Court decision in *Roe v. Wade*, which legalized abortion in the United States. While there was some controversy over this decision, it emanated from Roman Catholics, for whom abortion had always been a violation of Catholic doctrine. In fact, white evangelicals were initially not interested in the legality of abortion, which they viewed as a Catholic issue. Therefore, the notion that the Moral Majority was formed due to white evangelical opposition to the legalization of abortion is completely erroneous.[42]

The Moral Majority grew out of the white Christian supremacy of the religious right and can be traced back to the formation of segregation academies. Bob Jones University was formed in 1927 by the racist fundamentalist Bob Jones Sr. following the Scopes Monkey Trial, a landmark legal battle in the state of Tennessee over the controversy of teaching Darwinism, or human evolution, rather than creationism based on the biblical narrative. This legal battle was a concern for early-twentieth-century fundamentalist evangelicals who feared the supposed corruption of secular education. Jones and his presidential successors were racial segregationists who, until 1971, enforced racist policies, such as prohibiting the admission of African American students and the practice of racial amalgamation, forbidding students from engaging in interracial relationships.

In 1971, however, based on the ruling in that same year of the court case *Green v. Connally*, any institution practicing segregation was no longer considered a charitable not-for-profit organization and therefore would lose its tax-exempt status. Consequently, Bob Jones University lost its tax-exempt status. While this ruling had occurred during the Nixon administration, final action on the case took place in January 1976 on the eve of Jimmy Carter's inauguration as president. Nevertheless, part of the political strategy for developing the Moral Majority was ensuring that Carter, a devout Southern Baptist Sunday School teacher, suffered undue blame for the revocation of tax-exempt status for segregated Christian schools. White evangelicals became disenchanted with Carter because they viewed his presidential agenda and actions as liberal and progressive and felt that he had ignored them in his administration's policies. Falwell founded the

---

41. Fitzgerald, *The Evangelicals*, 287.

42. See Randall Balmer, *Thy Kingdom Come: How the Religious Right Distorts the Faith and Threatens America* (New York: Basic Books, 2006), 12. Balmer has characterized this as the abortion myth.

Moral Majority in 1979, with Paul Weyrich as the mastermind of the abortion myth.[43]

The catalyst for the Moral Majority was the court ruling in *Green v. Connally* and not the Supreme Court decision in *Roe v. Wade*; consequently, the formation of the Moral Majority centered on racial ethics not sexual ethics.

Weyrich had been engaged in conservative political activism since the 1964 presidential campaign of Barry Goldwater and was committed to garnering white evangelical attention and activism on the issues of abortion, school prayer, and the proposed Equal Rights Amendment.[44] He convinced Falwell and other white evangelical leaders that the abortion myth was the cause for launching a defense against the federal government regarding the threat to white Christian supremacy. White Christian supremacists even characterized themselves as the "new abolitionists," correlating the supposed cause for abolition of abortion with the cause of the abolition of slavery. Balmer provides a scathing depiction of the racist origins of the Moral Majority based on the abortion myth:

> The abortion myth serves as a convenient fiction because it suggests noble and altruistic motives behind the formation of the Religious Right. But it is highly disingenuous and renders absurd the argument of the leaders of the Religious Right that, in defending the rights of the unborn, they are "new abolitionists." The Religious Right arose as a political movement for the purpose, effectively, of defending racial discrimination at Bob Jones University and at other segregated schools. Whereas evangelical abolitionists of the nineteenth century sought freedom for African Americans, the Religious Right of the late twentieth century organized to perpetuate racial discrimination.[45]

Balmer accurately situated the roots of the Moral Majority in the fundamentalist premillennial dispensationalism of the evangelicalism that emerged from Dwight Moody and meditated through Confederate Christianity rather than the Oberlin perfectionism and postmillennial abolitionist evangelicalism of Charles Finney.

The agenda of the Moral Majority consisted of defeating the proposed Equal Rights Amendment, emphasizing family values, resisting the encroachment of secular humanism, abolishing the Department of Education, and outlawing abortion. As the principal founder of the Moral Majority, Falwell viewed the agenda of the organization as a holy war against the agenda of liberals and secularists.[46]

---

43. Balmer, *Thy Kingdom Come*, 1–34.

44. Balmer, *Thy Kingdom Come*, 15.

45. Balmer, *Thy Kingdom Come*, 16–17.

46. Fitzgerald, *The Evangelicals*, 292.

Equal Rights Amendment

Falwell and other white Christian supremacists believed that America had been corrupted and had fallen into the abyss of moral degeneracy, but they were evidently spiritually blind to the evil of the white supremacy that fueled their racist motivations. In addition to blatant racism, the agenda of the Moral Majority suffered from blatant sexism. The Equal Rights Amendment (ERA) was first proposed in 1923 to ensure equal legal rights for all Americans regardless of gender. In addition to white Christian supremacists' organizations such as the Moral Majority, historically a major hindrance to the adoption of the ERA has been the opposition of conservative white women. By 1977, thirty-five of the required thirty-eight states had ratified the proposed amendment to the Constitution. However, Phyllis Schlafly led a crusade of conservative white women in blocking the ratification in gender-discriminatory-friendly state legislatures. The Moral Majority was attempting to reclaim America for the Christ of Lost Cause religion.[47] Ironically, as we have seen, Lost Cause religion through the development of the second KKK discriminated, sometimes violently, against Jews and Catholics, yet Falwell saw the political expediency of including in the Moral Majority other religious traditions that white Christian supremacists had historically rejected—Catholics, Jews, and Mormons.[48] American Catholicism had gained more acceptability and respectability in the landscape of American religiosity with the 1960 election of John F. Kennedy, and including them in the Moral Majority built on this reality, as Falwell found in Catholics allies who would help legitimize the abortion myth.

Abortion Myth

The abortion myth motivates white evangelicals politically and theologically. The abortion myth also consists of the supposed "pro-life" theology that considers all life as sacred and to be preserved from conception. However, what makes this so-called pro-life theology mythical in the context of white evangelical religion is the reality that this has nothing to do with God. If the supposed pro-life theology were motivated by the belief that life is the product of God's creation and therefore should be preserved, then the so-called pro-life folks would also be against capital punishment. A pro-life theology consists of protecting all life, whether that life is considered innocent or guilty. Furthermore, an authentic pro-life theology consists of protecting and preserving all life regardless of race, gender, social location, economic class, etc., which means advocating for the welfare and quality of every aspect of life for every person. There cannot be a declaration that "All

---

47. John Fea, *Believe Me: The Evangelical Road to Donald Trump* (Grand Rapids, MI, Eerdmans, 2018), 34.

48. Fitzgerald, *The Evangelicals*, 304.

Lives Matter" until there is an authentic pro-life theology. The folks who are characterizing themselves as pro-life in the white evangelical movement are not pro-life; they are pro-birth. And not just pro-birth generically, but specifically they are pro-white birth. If a person cannot bring oneself to the affirmation and declaration that "Black Lives Matter" in light of the historic oppression of Black people in the United States at the hands of white people then they don't believe and can't believe that "All Lives Matter." This reality results not from a pro-life theology but a pro-white-birth theology.

The so-called pro-life movement is not motivated by what we discover in the Scriptures; this pro-white-birth movement is motivated by the desire to ensure that the white race in the United States remains the majority race, and hence the label Moral Majority, which was formed for racist purposes. This pro-white-birth theology is grounded in white superiority, white privilege, white supremacy, and white nationalism.

While there is no doubt that there are persons within the evangelical movement who morally oppose abortion, these convictions can be pro-life only if the death penalty is rejected and the full humanity and quality of every life are affirmed, regardless of race or ethnicity.[49] If many of these white evangelicals are in fact pro-life, it is not pro-life in general but pro-white life. In essence they are only concerned about the value and welfare of white life. Furthermore, to support political candidates based only on their view regarding abortion and without taking into account their dehumanizing actions such as racism, oppression of the poor, oppression of the uninsured, and policies that favor the wealthy for the sake of the underprivileged strongly suggests that one is not pro-life. In other words, if a person does not value the dignity of every life, then the person's claim to be pro-life is difficult to validate. It is sinful and disgraceful for people who claim to be followers of Christ to actively oppress and persecute those who as Christians are supposed to be their neighbors. Christians supporting Donald Trump's anti-immigration policies exhibit behavior and practice a form of corrupted Christianity that is antithetical to the gospel and ministry of Jesus Christ and therefore antithetical to authentic Christianity.

The Reagan Revolution

The Moral Majority aimed to shape American civil religion grounded in American white Christian nationalism, which was achieved through the Reagan Revolution. This process consisted in equating religious faith and patriotism.[50] The Moral Majority achieved this objective in the 1980 presi-

---

49. Catholics, for example, have always been against abortion but not the death penalty. Since 2018, the *Catechism of Catholic Church* clearly rejects the death penalty as well.

50. Fea, *Believe Me*, 48.

dential election, making them a powerful voting bloc in American politics. Following their disenchantment with President Jimmy Carter, white evangelicals shifted their support to the governor of California, Ronald Reagan. Historically, white evangelicals have often adopted the candidate with a lifestyle and values that are contrary to their supposed moral values and supposed religious codes. On the one hand, President Carter was the paragon of the Christian faith, yet he lost the support of white evangelicals especially when he agreed to an interview with *Playboy* magazine for a candid discussion of his views on sex. On the other hand, Reagan was completely antithetical to the moral and religious codes of white evangelicals. He had been divorced and remarried, was a former Hollywood actor, and, as the governor of California, had signed legislation legalizing abortion; and to add insult to injury, Reagan was not religious. Initially Reagan did not find favor with Jerry Falwell; however, his adoption of Richard Nixon's southern strategy proved appealing to white evangelicals. A major aspect of Reagan's southern strategy was robust support for states' rights, which reflected the agenda of the Confederacy.[51] Obery Hendricks argues that Reagan's declaration "I believe in states' rights" affirmed "the euphemism long used by segregationists to justify their legacy of institutionalized racial violence."[52] Therefore, Reagan's southern strategy was a reawakening of white Christian supremacy, which was reminiscent of the Lost Cause religious myth.

In addition to Reagan's southern strategy, the 1980 Republican National Convention (RNC) fueled Reagan's campaign. The Republican platform opposed the Equal Rights Amendment and advocated for a constitutional amendment to overturn *Roe v. Wade*, abortion litmus tests for judges nominated to the federal bench, tax reduction, tax tuition credits, voluntary school prayer, and the eradication of the IRS vendetta against private schools.[53] Falwell concluded that the Republican platform reflected the constitution of a fundamentalist Baptist Church.[54] As the Republican presidential nominee in 1980, Reagan ran on the campaign slogan "Make America Great Again." Following his nomination, Reagan launched his official campaign as the Republican nominee at the Neshoba County Fair in Philadelphia, Mississippi. This was pivotal to Reagan's southern strategy, for this was a clear signal to white supremacists that he was the candidate of white supremacy. Philadelphia was the city in which three civil rights workers— James Chaney, Michael Schwerner, and Andrew Goodman—were brutally

---

51. Fitzgerald, *The Evangelicals*, 312.

52. Obery M. Hendricks Jr., *The Politics of Jesus: Rediscovering the True Revolutionary Nature of Jesus' Teachings and How They Have Been Corrupted* (New York: Doubleday, 2006), 198.

53. Fitzgerald, *The Evangelicals*, 313.

54. Fitzgerald, *The Evangelicals*, 313.

murdered by the KKK in 1964. Reagan also spoke at Bob Jones University to promote tax credits for private school tuition and decried the Supreme Court for "expelling God from the classroom."[55]

Part of Reagan's appeal to white Christian supremacists was his embrace of the puritanical notion of white American superiority. As noted earlier, Puritan theology has fueled the erroneous notion of American exceptionalism and the dangerous implementation of white American Christian nationalism. Reagan exploited this reality to clinch the Republican nomination and win the presidency. Hendricks asserts that "Reagan is honored for restoring America's pride and waking the nation from what some called a spiritual malaise. Invoking the imagery of Matthew 5:14–16, he called America a shining city on a hill and imparted to Americans the sense that they were favored by God."[56]

The catalyst for the revolution of white Christian supremacy known affectionately as the Reagan Revolution was the white evangelical realization that they were a powerful voting bloc. During the 1980 presidential election, televangelist Pat Robertson declared, "we have enough votes to run this country." Reagan's presidency brought to fruition this white evangelical declaration, and Reagan viewed his presidency as his service to the kingdom of God.[57]

The irony of the white evangelical political epiphany is that, historically, the separation of church and state had been held sacred in many Protestant traditions. The Anabaptists were the radical reformers of the Protestant Reformation in the sixteenth century, and their most prominent influence was their insistence on the church and state being independent entities in society. The framers of the US Constitution had created the disestablishment clause, which prohibited the establishment of an official religion in the new American republic in order to combat the prevalence of ecclesiastical authority and influence in the affairs of the state. Yet, modern white American evangelicals have demonized the separation of church and state and accused those attempting to preserve the principles and religious protections in the Constitution of being secular humanists attempting to eradicate Christian values.[58]

White Christian Supremacy

The Reagan presidency was mired in white Christian supremacy, which was evident in Reagan's policies. At the height of the heinous practice of apart-

---

55. Fitzgerald, *The Evangelicals*, 313.
56. Hendricks, *The Politics of Jesus*, 196.
57. Hendricks, *The Politics of Jesus*, 197.
58. Fea, *Believe Me*, 49.

heid in South Africa, Reagan supported the racist Afrikaner-dominated South African government, despite evidence of the violent atrocities leveled against South African natives.[59] In 1994, following the end of apartheid, the Truth and Reconciliation Commission was formed to hold the Afrikaners accountable for their crimes against humanity. The leader of the commission, South African Anglican archbishop Desmond Tutu, characterized Reagan as "a racist pure and simple."

Another racist strategy Reagan utilized to appeal to white Christian supremacists was declaring himself the "law-and-order" candidate. Law-and-order language has historically been oppressive language used against Blacks in America, and it needs to become "safety-and-security" language. Law and order is a racist trope that has been used to sanction state-sponsored violence and terrorism against Blacks. During the institution of slavery in British colonial America, the slave patrols and militias in the colonies were deputized to maintain law and order should enslaved Africans step out of order and were considered the first line of defense against slave rebellions.[60] The racist trope of law and order was also used during the civil rights movement against peaceful protesters. It was the language used by Bull Connor, Jim Clark, Lester Maddox, George Wallace, Orval Faubus, Ross Barnett, and many others in their racist policing of American cities and towns.[61]

Reaganomics

The economic policies of Reagan's presidency exposed the spiritual hypocrisy of white Christian supremacists. Reaganomics constituted the implementation of supply-side economics, or supposed trickle-down economics. Hendricks defines this economic theory as "the elitist belief that the increased riches of the wealthiest Americans and the largest corporations that result from lower taxes will trickle-down to less-well-off Americans in the form of more jobs."[62] The 1981 Economic Recovery Tax Act was promoted as a middle-class tax cut yet ended up being a heavy burden on the middle class. The tax act cut the taxes of wealthy Americans by 60 percent.[63] The wealth of the richest Americans does not trickle down to lower economic classes. In many instances, wealth is acquired through the exploitation of lower economic classes who are overworked and underpaid.

---

59. Hendricks, *The Politics of Jesus*, 203.

60. See Sally E. Hadden, *Slave Patrols: Law and Violence in Virginia and the Carolinas* (Cambridge, MA: Harvard University Press, 2001). Any attempts of enslaved persons to challenge the institution of slavery and achieve freedom was unlawful and out of order.

61. See Silvan Niedermeier, *The Color of the Third Degree: Racism, Police Torture, and Civil Rights in the American South, 1930–1955* (Chapel Hill: University of North Carolina Press, 2019).

62. Hendricks, *The Politics of Jesus*, 199–200.

63. Hendricks, *The Politics of Jesus*, 199–200.

Reagan's economic philosophy and practice reflect the charge of the 1980 Republican presidential primary candidate George H. W. Bush, who characterized Reaganomics as "voodoo economics." Balmer characterizes this economic philosophy and practice as spiritualized Reaganomics since the implementation of tax cuts that benefit the affluent reflects the essence of the prosperity gospel.[64]

There was an intimate relationship between Reaganomics and racism. Reagan's tax cut resulted in major corporations not paying taxes for three years, from 1981 to 1983.[65] Reagan provided corporations with welfare while succumbing to the worst of his white supremacy. He leveled racist attacks against Black women—characterizing Black women on welfare as "welfare queens"—and ignored the reality that there were far more white women receiving welfare.[66] Additionally, Reagan's deepest domestic spending reductions were in low-income housing subsidies, which were cut in half during this first year in the White House. Furthermore, Reagan desired and attempted to eradicate federal funding for the poor completely.[67] In relation to Reagan's white Christian supremacy, Hendricks argues, "despite his [Reagan] repeated declarations that racism was a sin and a moral evil that he saw as his Christian responsibility to oppose with all his might, his actions made a different statement."[68] Reagan constantly attempted to portray his supposed Christianity and ideal of American exceptionalism using the "city-on-a-hill" motif from the Gospel (see Matt 5:14), while he and his white Christian supremacist supporters in the Moral Majority completely rejected Jesus's words:

> Come, you that are blessed by my Father, inherit the kingdom prepared for you from the foundation of the world; for I was hungry and you gave me food, I was thirsty and you gave me something to drink, I was a stranger and you welcomed me, I was naked and you gave me clothing, I was sick and you took care of me, I was in prison and you visited me. (Matt 25:34–36)

Reagan's exploitation and oppression of the poor proved antithetical to the gospel of Jesus Christ. The nefarious relationship between Reagan and the Moral Majority epitomized the corruption of authentic Christianity through the scandal of white Christian supremacy.

---

64. Randall Balmer, "Donald Trump and the Death of Evangelicalism," in Ronald J. Sider, ed., *The Spiritual Danger of Donald Trump: 30 Evangelical Christians on Justice, Truth, and Moral Integrity* (Eugene, OR: Cascade Books, 2020), 85.

65. Hendricks, *The Politics of Jesus*, 199–200.

66. Hendricks, *The Politics of Jesus*, 202.

67. Hendricks, *The Politics of Jesus*, 200.

68. Hendricks, *The Politics of Jesus*, 202.

9

Modern White Christian Supremacy

Just as the election of Barack Obama thrilled the nation, imbuing us with civic pride in the seeming achievement of a post racial society, birtherism signaled that it was permissible for America, deep in its soul, to continue harboring and nursing the historic racial prejudice. It said that a black president could not be legitimate, and so the factual reality of his very birth on American soil had to be denied.

—Luba Kessler

In 2017, thirty-seven psychiatrists and mental health professionals published *The Dangerous Case of Donald Trump*, a collection of essays on the dangerous and dysfunctional nature of Donald Trump's malignant narcissism.[1] These psychiatrists and mental health professionals believed that they possessed a moral and civic duty to warn the country of the trauma and consequences that would result from the Trump presidency, which attempted to normalize unethical behavior, alternate reality, authoritarian rule, and white supremacy. The most dangerous consequence of the normalization of Trump's deranged behavior was the fostering of the Trump cult. Psychiatrist and psychoanalyst Luba Kessler claims that the Trumpian mindset is rooted in the bigotry of the Trump-generated birther movement.

Theologically, the term "cult" has positive and negative connotations. Positively, it generally refers to the early stage of a religious movement becoming a denomination. The word "cult" is derived from the words "culture" and "cultivate," and, in Western theology, generally denotes a specialized form of worship within a religious tradition, rather than a sect, which refers to a group of believers who have become disenchanted with the beliefs and practices of their parent religious body and usually separate to form

---

1. Brandy X. Lee, ed., *The Dangerous Case of Donald Trump: 37 Psychiatrists and Mental Health Experts Assess a President* (New York: St. Martin's Press, 2017).

a new religious group, often resulting in a new denomination.[2] The most prominent example of a cult evolving into a larger mainstream religious body is Christianity. In its early stages, Christianity was considered a cult in the Roman Empire. It began as an underground movement, and Christians were persecuted through to the fourth century for their refusal to worship the Roman emperor. Early Christianity was also considered a sect of Judaism, and most early Christians were Jewish Christians who became followers of Christ and remained faithful to their Jewish religion and culture.

A cult in the negative sense is usually considered unchristian, unscriptural, spiritually corrupt, dangerous, deviant, unorthodox, and the product of false prophecy. The cult of Trump definitely fits this understanding of a cult. The primary ingredient in the establishment of the cult is the malignant narcissism of the cult leader. Clinical psychologist Elizabeth Mika asserts:

> Narcissistic psychopaths turned tyrants possess the right combination of manipulativeness, self-control, and intelligence to convince others to support them long enough to put their grandiose ideas to work on a large scale. They also appear to possess skills that are seen as charisma, the most frequent of which is the ability to deliver public speeches that inspire others to follow them. More often than not, however, this "charisma" is simply their ability to tell others what they want to hear (i.e., to lie), to make them go along with whatever scheme they've concocted for the moment. Their glibness is something that easily fools normal people, who do not understand the kind of pathology that results from a missing conscience. Once in positions of power, tyrants can fully unleash their sadism under the cloak of perverted ideals, which they peddle as a cover for their primitive drives.[3]

Indeed, Trump's behavior epitomizes that of a narcissistic psychopath, and the behavior of his cult followers reflects his influence. Trump influenced his cult followers using brainwashing and mind-control techniques. He controls how his cult followers act; what they read, watch, and listen to; how they think, and how they feel.[4] On January 6, 2021, Donald Trump Jr. declared just two weeks prior to the end of his father's presidency, "This isn't

---

2. John A. Saliba, *Understanding New Religious Movements* (Lanham, MD: Altamira Press, 2003), 1–24.

3. Elizabeth Mika, "Who Goes Trump? Tyranny as a Triumph of Narcissism," in Brandy X. Lee, ed., *The Dangerous Case of Donald Trump: 37 Psychiatrists and Mental Health Experts Assess a President* (New York: St. Martin's Press, 2017), 303.

4. Steven Hassan, *The Cult of Trump: A Leading Cult Expert Explains How the President Uses Mind Control* (New York: Free Press, 2019), 13.

their Republican Party anymore! This is Donald Trump's Republican Party." Ironically, on January 15, 2021, diehard Republican, former Oklahoma Congressman Mickey Edwards abandoned his membership in the Grand Old Party and declared, "It's no longer a political party, it's a cult." On the eve of the presidential inauguration of President Joseph R. Biden and Vice President Kamala Devi Harris, on January 20, 2021, 75 percent of Republicans believed that Biden and Harris had been elected illegitimately, embracing Trump's blatant false propaganda of election fraud. Indeed, the Republican Party had become the cult of Trump.

The Cult of Donald Trump

Donald Trump's appeal to white American Christian nationalism mired in white supremacy has resulted in a religious and political cult driven by his personality. His followers have fallen prey to a demagoguery that has fueled the religion and politics of white Christian supremacy in the United States since the proslavery theologies of the antebellum era.

Narcissistic personality disorder consists of the following psychological characteristics: grandiose self-centered behavior; fantasies of power, success, and attractiveness; a need for praise and admiration; a sense of entitlement; and a lack of empathy.[5] All these characteristics accurately describe the behavior of Donald Trump, whose political rise fostered the emergence of his cult, which was initially driven by "whitelash" and the spirit of anti-blackness following the 2008 election and 2012 re-election of the first African American president, Barack Hussein Obama.

The Tea Party

President Obama inherited the worst economic recession in the United States since the Great Depression of 1929 and immediately began working with Congress to develop solutions to address the economic problems. Following Obama's inauguration, the Tea Party movement was formed and placed the blame for the economic recession squarely on Obama—even though he had only been in office a month—and accused him of promoting socialism in his solutions to restore economic security to the American economy and people.[6] The Tea Party had begun as a far-right, politically conservative fringe movement within the Republican Party. Its stated agenda was opposition to government spending, taxation, and regulation.[7] The Tea

---

5. Hassan, *The Cult of Trump*, 41.

6. Tony Keddie, *Republican Jesus: How the Right Has Rewritten the Gospels* (Oakland: University of California Press, 2020), 108.

7. The Tea Party correlated its protest with that of the 1773 Boston Tea Party, which was the protest of colonists in British colonial America who considered themselves American patriots

Party embraced the common ideology of the religious right, libertarians, and white nationalists.[8] It consisted predominately of white persons over the age of forty-five, mostly male, middle-class, educated, wealthy, with 39 percent being evangelicals and 22 percent Catholic.[9]

White Christian supremacy and conservative politics dominated the Tea Party. Despite the claims of Tea Party adherents, their activism was not motivated by the taxation of the Obama administration, but rather was a form of "whitelash" against the reality of the Black presidency. The Tea Party laid the foundation for the eventual white supremacist birther movement against Obama. The Tea Party activists claimed that Obama was born in Kenya and raised a Muslim. Based on their white supremacist hate of African people and of the Muslim faith, they believed that Obama and his supporters were attempting to implement socialism in America.[10] The "movement" became a caucus in the US Congress, and Republican Representative Michelle Bachmann of Minnesota, the leader and chair of the caucus, demonstrated the depth of her white Christian supremacy through her attempted rationalization of historical falsehoods. She erroneously argued that slavery had been good for African Americans because the institution of slavery promoted family values. She also claimed that slavery had Christianized and civilized African Americans, directly implying that African Americans should possess an attitude of gratitude for their paternalistic, benevolent white Christian enslavers.[11] Bachmann's sentiments exposed her shameful ignorance or diabolical denial of the reality of chattel slavery in the United States. Slavery in America was the most heinous form of slavery in history. Bachmann was oblivious to the fact that enslaved Africans were forbidden from conversion to American Christianity for the first 150 years of American enslavement because canon law prohibited Christians from enslaving other Christians. White Christian supremacist enslavers were not inclined to engage in slave conversions until they established that Christianity saved the soul of the enslaved not the body. Bachmann was oblivious to the historical fact that unlike the slavery practiced in the biblical text, which emphasized the illegality of separating enslaved families, enslaved families in America were separated regularly, and in many instances enslaved Africans were forbidden marriage.

and opposed to the Tea Act, which imposed taxes on them and was initiated by the British Parliament. American colonists believed that the Tea Act violated their rights, as they were not represented in the British parliament and therefore concluded that the act constituted "taxation without representation."

8. Keddie, *Republican Jesus*, 110.
9. Fitzgerald, *The Evangelicals*, 594.
10. Fitzgerald, *The Evangelicals*, 593.
11. Keddie, *Republican Jesus*, 111.

Tea Party activists supported legislation that provided benefits for Social Security, Medicare, and Veterans' programs, which they viewed were for hard-working white citizens. They vehemently opposed other social-safety-net programs designed to provide services to those in the lower economic classes. Tea Party activists attacked the Affordable Care Act, affectionately dubbed "Obamacare," and viewed social welfare programs as government handouts to those they perceived as freeloaders on American society, which included African Americans and Latinx immigrants.[12] The legislative strategy of the Tea Party had the political and financial backing of the rank and file of Republican lawmakers, lobbyists, and financiers on national, state, and local levels through the American Legislative Exchange Council (ALEC), a white supremacist conservative organization that specializes in influencing the passage of legislation in state legislatures such as anti-immigration laws and racist voter-identification laws designed to suppress the votes of minorities.

The Tea Party, with its appeal to white Christian supremacists, was shifting the emphasis from the Moral Majority's focus on eradicating the supposed threat of secularization to that of socialism. Its activists were able to disguise their racism in erroneous economic rationalizations and found a spiritual ally in supporters of the prosperity gospel.

The Protestant Work Ethic

The prosperity gospel is antithetical to the gospel of Jesus Christ in that it advocates for health and wealth while simultaneously condemning the poor as cursed. Ironically, those who subscribe to such theology have attained their wealth on the backs of the poor, whom they disparage and dehumanize. One of the theological architects of the prosperity gospel, Norman Vincent Peale, served as Donald Trump's pastor and characterized him as his "greatest student of all time."[13] Peale attempted to spiritualize the laissez-faire capitalistic principles of Adam Smith and taught that words and thoughts could transform into health and wealth.[14] New Testament scholar Tony Keddie argues that "Peale's eclectic self-help theology combined New Thought and Christian Science philosophies with Baptist, Methodist, and Calvinist beliefs."[15] As examined in the first chapter, Adam Smith's notion of the invisible hand of God working in the economy determines those who would experience economic prosperity and those who suffer economic depression. American Puritans, as noted, adopted Smith's

---

12. Keddie, *Republican Jesus*, 108.

13. Keddie, *Republican Jesus*, 115.

14. See Norman Vincent Peale, *The Power of Positive Thinking* (Upper Saddle River, NJ: Prentice Hall, 1952).

15. Keddie, *Republican Jesus*, 116.

philosophy as their Protestant work ethic, which they believed fueled the success of American capitalism and also influenced the prosperity gospel, which was the theological foundation of the white supremacist Trump presidential campaign, which built on the Tea Party fallacy that white people were the hard-working elect and nonwhite people the freeloading damned in the divine economy of the United States. These same white Christian supremacists seem oblivious to the reality that the capitalistic success of this country from 1619 until now has been situated solidly on the hard work of poor people, especially Blacks. As Martin Luther King Jr. exclaimed:

> We have deluded ourselves into believing the myth that capitalism grew and prospered out of the Protestant ethic of hard work and sacrifice. The fact is that capitalism was built on the exploitation and suffering of black slaves and continues to thrive on the exploitation of the poor both black and white, here and abroad.[16]

The white Christian supremacist attacks on nonwhites, coupled with whitelash resulting from the election and presidency of the first African American president, propelled the political rise of Trump.

The Birther Movement

The Trump cult originated in the birther movement, which was promoted by Donald Trump in 2012 as an attempt to delegitimize the presidency of Barack Obama. At the time, Trump was contemplating his run for president and developed white supremacist propaganda to exploit and promote racist hate against the first African American president. The then-chief justice of the Alabama Supreme Court, Roy Moore, instigated the racist tribalism of the birther movement in 2008 with erroneous claims concerning Obama's place of birth.[17] His claim that Obama was not a natural-born citizen and therefore not qualified for the office of president became the primary conspiracy that drove Republican politics.[18] Obama had become the object of white evangelicals' political fears, and Trump capitalized on these fears, utilizing the dangerous narcissistic tactic of fearmongering. Trump stoked

---

16. Martin Luther King Jr., "The Three Evils of Society," speech delivered on August 31, 1967, at the National Conference of New Politics.

17. Fea, *Believe Me*, 18.

18. In 2003, Moore had become a celebrated martyr for the white Christian supremacists and the Republican Party after he was removed from his position as chief justice because he refused to remove a monument of the Ten Commandments that he had installed in the rotunda of the Alabama Judicial Building. Moore's gesture of posting the Ten Commandments proved sacrilegious, as he blatantly and consistently broke one of those commandments by engaging in falsehoods concerning Obama's qualifications to occupy the office of the presidency.

the racial fears of white Christian supremacists and garnered their support as a voting bloc. He initiated his campaign for president in 2015, demeaning and dehumanizing people of color, characterizing Mexicans as rapists, and stereotyping people of color as criminals. Like Richard Nixon, Ronald Reagan, and even George Herbert Walker Bush with the Willie Horton ad of 1988, Trump invoked historic racist rhetoric of "law and order" to instill fear of widespread violence of minorities against whites in America.

Trump adopted the Reagan campaign slogan, "Make America Great Again" (Make America White Again), as an attempt to re-emphasize and restore antebellum, proslavery white Christian supremacy, with Trump, whose election represented the redemption and resurrection of the Confederate South, as the modern-day Jefferson Davis. White Christian supremacists, who are the religious and cultural descendants of the crusading Confederate Christians, believed that the Confederacy had risen from the dead after eight years of modern-day Reconstruction in the presidency of Obama. This Confederate resurrection is apparent in Trump's calling white supremacists at a rally in Charlottesville, Virginia, "very fine people" and in Trump's instructing the Proud Boys (modern-day white supremacists reminiscent of the KKK without white sheets and burning crosses) to "stand down and stand by." Following his inauguration in 2017, Trump continued to exploit the politics of fear, falsely characterizing refugees and immigrants as criminals and imminent threats to white people.

The appeal of Trump to white Christian supremacists was his promise to dismantle the legacy of Obama. Fea outlines how Trump has kept his promises in order to appease white evangelicals and preserve the support of his political cult.[19]

Spiritual Hypocrisy

Many of the promises that Trump made to white evangelicals reflect the political ploys of the Moral Majority. The problem, however, is that these promises expose the spiritual hypocrisy and scandalous nature of the white American evangelical movement. White evangelicals claim to have a monopoly on God and impose their sacrilegious and sanctimonious moral codes on people in society. However, they were willing to support the most unethical, ungodly, and immoral candidate for president in modern history. They overlooked and excused Trump's debauchery and hedonistic living in order to secure seats on the Supreme Court and swing the court far right ideologically and theologically, particularly regarding the supposed pro-life agenda. Even former chair of the New Hampshire GOP, Jennifer Horn, in an opinion piece for *USA Today* wrote:

---

19. Fea, *Believe Me*, 5.

To be pro-life means to care for all life, at all stages, in all conditions. Trump's assaults on life are egregious and daily. He demeans and degrades minorities, women, the elderly, immigrants and the disabled. The concepts of empathy, sanctity and dignity are foreign to him. Under this president, the weakest and most vulnerable among us are at risk, and a culture of disregard for life is on the rise.[20]

The irony is that white evangelicals who constitute a major stronghold of the pro-life movement have strongly fostered a culture of disregard for life through their unwavering support for Donald Trump. White Christian supremacists feared the influx of immigrants that resulted from the Hart-Celler Act of 1965, which ended immigration quotas imposed in 1921 based on national origins. White Christian supremacists especially feared non-immigrants who practiced religions other than white Christianity. Their racial discrimination against immigrants from non-Western countries explains how they, as evangelical Christians, could still strongly support Trump, even after he characterized African countries as "shit-hole" countries.

Religious liberty in white evangelical circles has taken on a racist form of religious bigotry in that white Christian supremacists believe that only they have the right to religious liberties in America. Through this dangerous ideology, white Christian supremacists have demonized all Muslims as radical Islamists. Prominent white evangelical and pastor of the historically fundamentalist-evangelical First Baptist Church of Dallas, Texas, Robert Jeffress has declared that "we do not restrict other people's worship however they choose to worship, but that doesn't mean we treat all religions equally. This is a Christian nation! Every other religion is an imposter, an infidel."[21] This ideology is not only a form of religious bigotry; it also constitutes racial bigotry, a reality that is evident in the white Christian supremacist version of Christian Zionism, which is grounded in Calvinistic millenarianism. Christian Zionists believe that the United States' re-creation of the state of Israel with the help of allies fulfills biblical prophecy, and some even predicate the second coming of Christ on the existence of this settled land. Ongoing conflict between the Israelis and Palestinians over the rightful settlement of the land has persisted for decades. This conflict has resulted in Christian Zionists from the religious right blindly supporting any policy that favors the Israelis, even when those policies are oppressive to Palestinians. The religious right form of Christian Zionism is

20. Jennifer Horn, "Texas lawsuit was the last straw. I'm leaving the Republican Party: Former NH GOP chair," *USA Today*, December 17, 2020, https://www.usatoday.com/opinion/.

21. Fea, *Believe Me*, 161.

devoid of justice, even when fellow Christians are affected. Many Palestinian Christians are oppressed because of the white Christian supremacist practices of religious right Christian Zionism.[22] Ironically, there are some white Christian supremacists who reflect these right-wing Christian Zionists who seek to protect and preserve Israel to their own theological peril, and there are others who harbor anti-Semitic beliefs.

One of the most glaring spiritual hypocrisies of white evangelicals has been their attempted spiritualization of Trump's character, such as correlating him with King Cyrus of Persia, despite his many moral failures and character flaws. In the Book of Isaiah, King Cyrus conquers Babylon and delivers the Israelites, who had been taken captive by the Babylonians (see Isa 45:1–19). King Cyrus is not an Israelite and does not worship the God of Israel. In fact, King Cyrus is considered a pagan, and yet God uses Cyrus to deliver the Israelites. The King Cyrus and Trump correlation enables white evangelicals to justify Trump's presidency as divinely ordained and therefore his election as the will of God. White evangelical leaders such as Robert Jeffress, Jerry Falwell Jr., and Franklin Graham have been pivotal to the evangelical legitimization of Trump. All three have been more than complicit in Trump's political and religious strategy of race baiting for political gain. They have all fully embraced and promoted the birther conspiracy and condemned the Islamic faith as wicked and evil. All three have theologically stoked Trump's ethno-nationalistic racism against immigrants and especially Muslims.[23]

The development of the Tea Party, the birther movement, and chants such as Trump's campaign slogan, "Make America Great Again," all reflect the white supremacist sentiment of white Christians in the South who celebrated the violent end of Reconstruction as the divine work of God to restore the white supremacist social order. Trump's campaign slogan, in particular, was the signal that his presidency would restore the dominance of white supremacy to its former antebellum glory. Owning slaves in the South during the antebellum era became the symbol of white southern respectability. The institution of slavery was a product and symbol of white supremacy, which, especially in the southern region of the United States, has traditionally been the symbol of white southern respectability symbolized by the Confederate flag—a symbol of hate.

It is no accident that Lyndon Baines Johnson declared that the Democratic Party had lost the South for a generation because of the passage of civil rights legislation, for this legislation violated southern respectability. When the Republican Party caters to white supremacists and harbors

---

22. See Naim Stifan Ateek, *A Palestinian Cry for Reconciliation* (Maryknoll, NY: Orbis Books, 2008).

23. Keddie, *Republican Jesus*, 120–22.

white supremacists, they are engaged in the politics of southern respectability, which is white supremacy. This was evident in Reagan's presidential campaign launch for the 1980 presidential election, and it was evident in Trump's presidential campaign launch for the 2016 presidential election. And it was most evident in Trump's refusal to condemn white supremacists in his first presidential debate with Joe Biden when asked directly by Chris Wallace to condemn white supremacists. Reagan and Trump both intentionally attempted and succeeded in appealing to white supremacists and proudly became the candidates of white supremacists in the modern era. Had Trump condemned white supremacy, he would have lost white southern respectability as well as the diabolical prestige of being the white supremacist in chief.

The Original Sin of White Christian Supremacy

Even before the presidential election of 2020, Trump cultivated the fallacy of election fraud to infuriate his political base. It has been estimated that throughout his presidency, Trump made over twenty thousand false or misleading claims. Despite his compulsive and blatant falsehoods, Trump's political base—his cult—believes whatever he claims, regardless of rationality. Trump even has a tendency to make a particular claim one day and the exact opposite claim the next, yet his cult followers believe and embrace his claims no matter when the claim is made and how often the claim may change.

Ideological Factions

Trump's cult constitutes the unification of like-minded ideological factions. Harvard Medical School mental health expert Steven Hassan identifies these factions as the Christian right, the New Apostolic Reformation, the white working class, the Republican Party, the Jewish right, the alt-right, QAnon, and the National Rifle Association (NRA).[24] With the exception of the Jewish right, the common denominator among these factions is white Christian supremacy. Naturally one would not expect the Jewish right to be here, but the Christian Zionism of the Christian right and the view of Trump as the modern King Cyrus, deliverer of Israel, solidly situates the Jewish right within this group. The cult of Trump epitomizes white Christian supremacist hegemony, which specializes in the production of white superiority, white privilege, and white power. This is most evident in alt-right ideology, which perpetrates extreme violent terrorism in order to exert white power and the agenda of preserving white domination. Therefore, Trump's racist ethno-nationalist white supremacist rhetoric, which dehu-

---

24. Hassan, *The Cult of Trump*, 177–93.

manizes nonwhites and non-Christian people, appeals to white nationalist groups such as the alt-right.

On June 17, 2015, Dylann Roof was inspired by the alt-right movement to murder nine people during a Bible study being held at the historic Emmanuel AME Church in Charleston, South Carolina. The alt-right movement was also behind the "Unite the Right" violent white supremacist rally that turned deadly in August 2017 in Charlottesville, Virginia, as well as the anti-Semitic attack on the conservative Tree of Life Jewish synagogue in Pittsburg, Pennsylvania, on October 27, 2018, which resulted in the death of eleven people. The alt-right movement influenced the racist terrorist attacks on two mosques in Christchurch, New Zealand, during Islamic Friday prayer on March 15, 2019, resulting in the death of fifty-one people. Alt-right forces had a direct influence on Trump's presidential campaigns and his presidency. Steve Bannon, who was the former chief executive of the racist, far-right Breitbart News Network, served as Trump's White House chief strategist, and well-known white nationalist Stephen Miller served as Trump's White House chief advisor for policy. The influence of the alt-right explains the rationale behind the racist elements embedded in many of Trump's presidential policies.

The impact of the white Christian supremacy movement, which had been brewing since the inception of the Tea Party in 2009, occurred on January 6, 2021, during the constitutionally mandated congressional certification of the president and vice president in a joint session of Congress. After many failed and even criminal attempts to overturn the 2020 presidential election results in his favor, Trump summoned his cult followers to Washington, DC, for a rally scheduled on the day of the certification. The event was advertised through social media and other outlets as the "Stop the Steal" rally to reinforce Trump's claims of election fraud and his claim that he had won the election by a landslide. The rally reflected the sights and sounds of the generic Trump rally, which functions as white Christian supremacy revivalism fueled with racist, divisive, and treasonous rhetoric. During these rallies Trump becomes a divine figure for his cult, with the cult followers worshiping him at his altar.

Trump's altar is the altar of white superiority, white privilege, white nationalism, and white supremacy. The "Stop the Steal" event functioned as a pep rally at which followers of the Trump cult were strongly encouraged to engage in warfare for the correct certification of the election—that is, the certification of Trump as president and Mike Pence as vice president. During the "Stop the Steal" rally the worship leaders committed sedition by inciting the MAGA mob of angry Trump cultists to commit crimes against the United States. Republican representative Mo Brooks of Alabama stated that "today is the day that American patriots start taking down names and kicking ass." Trump's personal attorney, Rudy Giuliani, declared, "Let's have trial by combat"; and Donald Trump Jr. proclaimed, "You can be a hero, or you can be a zero. And the choice is yours. But we are all watching. The whole world is watching, folks. Choose wisely." Trump declared to the MAGA mob, "You will never take back our country with weakness," and then instructed the angry mob of his followers to march up Pennsylvania Avenue to the Capitol and demand certification of the election for Trump. He immediately lied to his cult followers, stating that he would be at the Capitol fighting with them.

Hassan has outlined five main types of cults: religious cults, which exploit religious dogma to justify their actions; political cults, which are built on a specific political dogma; psychotherapy/education cults, which convince followers that the cult will help them achieve enlightenment; commercial cults, which exploit people's desire for power and wealth; and personality cults, which are driven by charismatic figures who gain celebrity status and control the psyche of followers.[25] The events following the "Stop the Steal" rally reveal that the cult of Trump was an integration of personality, political, and religious cults and that these white Christian supremacist terrorist organizations are its key stakeholders.

Domestic Terrorists

White Christian supremacists have condemned jihad as terrorism and stereotyped all Muslims as terrorists. Ironically, many white Christian supremacists believe that they can never be considered terrorists because they are white. Legal scholar Caroline Mala Corbin explains the rationalization of this white privilege in the United States:

> Even if I use violence within the United States to intimidate a civilian population, odds are I will not be called a terrorist. Rather than immediately becoming a demonized "other," I would remain an individual, albeit a deeply troubled one. The dehumanization of the Muslim perpetrator happens in an instant. . . . With non-Muslims, the media bends over backwards to identify some psychological traits that may have pushed them over the edge. Whereas if it's a Muslim, the assumption is they must have done it because of their religion. As a white terrorist, the main assumption made about my motive is that some personal trauma must have triggered my violence. In contrast, like a stock villain in a movie, the Muslim perpetrator has no backstory, no grieving family, his motive is clear enough. My argument is not that white terrorists are never mentally ill; many are. But

25. Hassan, *The Cult of Trump*, 15–21.

so too are many Muslim terrorists. However, the presumption of white innocence means that for white terrorists we look to mental illness for explanations in a way that we do not for nonwhite terrorists. The bottom line is that white Christian extremists remain individuals— "lone wolves" suffering in some individualized way—as opposed to an interchangeable member of a terrorist conspiracy.[26]

As the domestic terrorists of the Trump cult, white Christian supremacists employed Jewish rituals, such as the blowing of the shofar horn, a major symbol of Rosh Hashanah and Yom Kippur. In addition, alongside signs and flags depicting Christian messages and the Bible, they carried the Confederate and Trump flags, waving them as emblems of victory when they violently stormed the Capitol. After injuring Capitol police officers, they penetrated the building, some armed with weapons and wearing military and law-enforcement attire, forcing open the doors with metal barrels, breaking windows, and literally climbing the building's outer walls and scaffolds.

Once inside the building, these Trump terrorists vandalized the Capitol building, trashing congressional offices. They stole laptops, other electronic devices, and possessions containing sensitive governmental information. Many photographs, selfies, and videos show these domestic terrorists hanging from the balcony of the Senate chambers, sitting in the chairs of the House speaker and the presiding officer in the Senate chambers. Noticeably, they desecrated the monument honoring the life and service of representative John Lewis, who epitomized the fight for civil and voting rights, having being beaten by Alabama state troopers almost to the point of death during the march from Selma to Montgomery on March 7, 1965. White supremacist Kevin Seefried committed one the most heinous and treasonous acts when he carried the Confederate flag, which symbolizes the terrorization of African Americans and the veneration of Confederates in their crusade to preserve the institution of chattel slavery in America during the Civil War, into the Capitol rotunda.

Historian Terry Bolton, an observer of the insurrection, described this mixed Trump mob as "preppy looking country club Republicans, well-dressed social conservatives, and white Evangelicals in Jesus cap . . . standing shoulder to shoulder with QAnon cultists, Second Amendment cosplay commandos, and doughy, hardcore white nationalists."[27] Among the Trump

---

26. Caroline Mala Corbin, "Terrorists Are Always Muslim but Never White: At the Intersection of Critical Race Theory and Propaganda," *Fordham Law Review* 86, no. 455 (2017): 466–72.

27. Philip Gorski, "White Christian Nationalism: The deep story behind the Capitol insurrection," ABC.net.au, January 13, 2021, https://www.abc.net.au.

terrorists, however, were well-respected members of American society, such as active and retired law enforcement officers, military personnel, fire fighters, Olympic athletes, chief executive officers, attorneys, teachers, and many other middle- to upper-class white Christian supremacists. The most notable of these domestic terrorist caricatures was the self-proclaimed QAnon shaman Jacob Anthony Clansley (aka Jake Angeli), who, as a robust enthusiast of the QAnon conspiracy theory, attends Black Lives Matter protests, declaring that Q sent him, which might explain his self-identification as a shaman. The symbolism of white supremacy signifies their belief in the violent struggle to protect the superiority of whiteness in the world.

These Trump cult followers erroneously equate patriotism with white supremacy. There is nothing patriotic about the MAGA mob that attacked the Capitol; these people are domestic terrorists. In the aftermath of the attack on the Capitol, there were five causalities, including Capitol police officer Brian Sicknick, who died. The unfortunate, senseless, and absolutely outrageous irony of Officer Sicknick's death speaks volumes about the hypocrisy of the Trump cult. As an affront to the affirmation that "Black Lives Matter," Trump's followers have stated that "Blue Lives Matter," yet during the insurrection they resolved to hurt, harm, injure, and even take the lives of those whom they claim matter.

The insurrection was an unprecedented domestic terror attack on the Capitol. During the War of 1812, British troops stormed the Capitol and the president's house, setting fire to both in 1814, but never has there been a successful domestic attack that breached the security of the Capitol and penetrated both houses of Congress. In the political reckoning of attempting to determine how insurrectionists could storm the Capitol, the most prominent question came from African Americans, who pointed out the blatant racial bias and double standard in policing that was most evident in the extreme incompetence of law enforcement in response to the criminal activity of white supremacists.

The Critical Questions

Blacks reflected on the National Guard officers being strategically posted with military attire, military artillery, military tanks, and being unduly attacked with tear gas during their peaceful protests. They reflected on Trump ordering the vile removal of peaceful Black Lives Matter protestors outside the White House so that he could walk across the street shamelessly as one of the most ungodly, unholy, and immoral people in human history and hypocritically stand in front of St. John's Episcopal Church for a photo-op holding a Bible to appeal to his cult of white Christian supremacists. They reflected on the governmental response during the 2020 summer Black Lives Matter protests for justice in response to the killing of

George Floyd by the Minneapolis policeman Derek Michael Chauvin, which prompted Trump to declare an age-old racist trope, "when the looting starts the shooting starts," and saying that anyone who destroys property will be prosecuted to the fullest extent of the law. They angrily reflected on the fact that had the Capitol insurrectionists been peaceful Black protestors they would have been met with the full force of law enforcement who would not have hesitated to restrain them, wound them, and even take their lives unjustifiably—the modus operandi of how this country responds to the protests of Blacks. Yet in his feeble and futile attempt to calm his cult followers and stop their heinous criminality, Trump characterized them as special people and expressed his undying love for them. The Trump terrorists' storming of the Capitol further exposed the depth of white Christian supremacy embedded in the DNA of the United States.

Another critical question that naturally arose following the failed attack concerned the treasonous actions of the Trump insurrectionists and the identification of those members of Congress, law enforcement officers, or federal employees in the Trump administration who were complicit in the event. In their attempt to appeal to their mostly white Christian supremacist followers, the overwhelming majority of Republicans in both the Senate and House of Representatives promoted the dangerous and deadly falsehood that there was widespread election fraud because Trump lost the election. Through their diabolical actions and outright lies, the Republicans in Congress have become a seditious caucus. Following the heinous attack on the Capitol, several Republican senators, including Ted Cruz, Josh Hawley, Rick Scott, Cynthia Lummis, Roger Marshall, Tommy Tuberville, John Kennedy, and Cindy Hyde-Smith, still voted against certifying the election results. Their votes are really acts of sedition. At least two-thirds of the Republican lawmakers in the House of Representatives, totaling 147 members, voted against the election certification.

The seditious ring leaders in the Senate were Cruz and Hawley, who both shamelessly advocated for the Compromise of 1877, which delivered the electoral votes of three southern states to Rutherford B. Hayes in exchange for the removal of federal troops from the South, which ended Reconstruction and fostered the terrorization and disenfranchisement of African Americans.

Finally, another critical question following the carnage of the domestic terrorist attack on the Capitol was whether the attack was a coup attempt from inside the government, and if so, whether members of Congress, law enforcement officers, or federal employees in the Trump administration were part of the coup. In the aftermath of the Capitol insurrection there was a great reckoning on the reality that the insurrectionists could not have breached the security of the building and penetrated the Capitol without

assistance from people with keen knowledge of its floor plan and operations. For example, there were some Capitol police officers who seemed to
allow the domestic terrorists through the barricades and doors and even
took selfies with them while their heroic colleagues protected congressional members and staff. Republican representative and QAnon conspiracy
promoter Majorie Taylor Greene declared that the insurrection had been
waged in the spirit of 1776, as if the insurrection was reminiscent of the
Revolutionary War. Republican Lauren Boebart, who is associated with
right-wing groups that supported the insurrection, disclosed the location
of House Speaker Pelosi during the siege. Democratic representative Mikie
Sherill has requested an investigation into what she characterized as suspi-
cious behavior of visitors touring the Capitol the day before the insurrection. Furthermore, while the Capitol was under siege, several members of
Congress attempted to contact Trump, soliciting his authorization to send
the National Guard to the Capitol to help end the insurrection, but their
requests were ignored and even denied while Trump watched with pleasure
scenes of the carnage and anarchy being unleashed on the Capitol. Former
Capitol police chief Steven Sund expressed his view that the insurrection
was a planned attack on the Capitol and said that he requested additional
law enforcement assistance of the National Guard from former sergeant at
arms of the House and the Senate Paul Irving and Michael Stenger respectively, but his requests were denied with the excuse that this was to avoid the
optics of military-style law enforcement in the Capitol. Interestingly, optics
are never a concern for law enforcement regarding Black Lives Matter protests. Sund, Irvin, and Stenger all resigned in disgrace following the Capitol
insurrection. The FBI is also investigating bitcoin payments in the amount
of $500,000 to far-right-wing activists with ties to the siege of the Capitol
just a month prior to the insurrection; they were believed to have been paid
by foreign instigators who knew the mutual affinity between white supremacists and enemies of the United States. There were even plans to execute
the insurrection in such a manner that Black Lives Matter and Antifa protestors would be blamed for the attack. Republican senator Marco Rubio
shamelessly blamed the media for the insurrection rather than admit to his
seditious acts and acknowledge his role in enabling the dangerous behavior
of the Trump terrorists through his own promotion of Trump propaganda
and falsehoods. All evidence points to the reality that the deadly siege on
the Capitol was a well-planned, well-coordinated, and well-funded attack
instigated and fostered by Trump and his Republican allies.

More Spiritual Hypocrisies

Spiritual hypocrisy is the typical result of white evangelical guilt. Following
the Capitol insurrection, white evangelical leaders unleashed their brand

of Christian piety with statements condemning the violent attacks against the government and even words of repentance. The president of the Family Research Council, Tony Perkins, who had strongly supported and promoted Trump's falsehoods, claimed, "this is what happens when you take God out of the courts and from the schools." Perkins further asserted, "I would be hard-pressed to find Bible-believing Christians that would be Ok with what took place at the Capitol." He attempted to shift the blame to legal and educational institutions instead of identifying the real culprit—white evangelical Christianity. These white Christian supremacist terrorists were carrying Bibles and praying to the white Christ who has been taught and perpetuated in white evangelical Christianity. As theologian Eric Weed asserts:

> The soteriology of white flesh as symbolized in the image of the white Christ brings the American experience to its natural *raison d'être* by creating the systems and matrices of power and meaning that make whiteness and salvation synonymous. For this reason, the white Christ is not here to save nonwhite bodies because they are beyond salvation in the U.S. psyche. Whiteness is the only marker by which soteriological grounding makes sense in the American experience.[28]

In response to the Capitol insurrection, Russell D. Moore, president of the Southern Baptist Convention's Ethics and Religious Liberty Commission and an outspoken "Never Trumper," claimed that "it was a moral abomination incited by the president." He further exclaimed that "it's one thing to defend conservative values, which I still hold, which I share with many who voted for President Trump. . . . But nothing we've witnessed today is conservative." While Moore has been a critic of Trump's behavior, he has stated that he does not regret his vote for Trump. Moore cites conservatism but fails to acknowledge that the conservatism that the SBC has espoused since its inception has been deeply complicit in driving the moral abomination that he cited. The president of Southern Baptist Theological Seminary, Albert Mohler, who did not vote for Trump in 2016 but did vote for him in 2020, stated, "I do not follow a cult of personality. . . . I am committed as a Christian to certain moral principles . . . that I believe are derived from biblical Christianity." The problem here is that Mohler cites biblical Christianity as the source of his conviction but fails to realize that it is the brand of biblical Christianity he espouses that drove the insurrection on the Capitol. To be clear, the problem is not the biblical text; the problem is the white Christian supremacist interpretation of the text that corrupts Christianity.

---

28. Eric A. Weed, *The Religion of White Supremacy in the United States* (Lanham, MD: Lexington Books, 2017), 32–33.

The Critical Race Theory

Mohler's brand of biblical Christianity is the same that proslavery theologians used to justify slavery. This reality is evident in the November 30, 2020, statement of the National Council of Seminary Presidents of the SBC that rejected the Critical Race theory. Mohler had a key role in this rejection, which occurred just a month prior to the violent white Christian supremacist attack on the US government. Essentially, the Critical Race theory holds that racism against people of color is the normal experience of people of color; racism against people of color advances the interests of both white elites and the white working-class; race and races are products of societal invention and manipulation; and the voices of color reflect the histories and experiences of oppression endured by people of color.[29]

In response to the insurrection, Franklin Graham claimed that he did not support violence from the right or the left, and tweeted that "we need God's healing and we need God's help." However, following the second impeachment of Trump in the House of Representatives, which was the most bipartisan vote on impeachment in US history with ten House Republicans voting with the Democrats to impeach, Graham condemned the vote and likened the ten Republicans to Judas, who betrayed Jesus, stating that those ten Republicans had sold themselves to Speaker Pelosi for twenty pieces of silver.

The expressions of condemnation of the insurrection and criticism of Trump from white evangelical leaders are disingenuous at best and, at worst, constitute a blatant spiritual abomination. The presidents of SBC seminaries rejected the Critical Race theory based on their argument that it does not address sin and does not constitute a solution based on the gospel. The racism that these white evangelical leaders harbor in their scriptural interpretations, theologies, and denominational polity and fellowship is sinful, and their so-called biblical Christianity is not based on the gospel of Jesus. While some white evangelical leaders and institutions are releasing statements of repentance, any act of repentance without accountability and adequate restitution in the form of just reparations is cheap. Without an acceptance of the truth and justice, the healing that white evangelicals claim they desire will not occur. Critical Race theory is the truth; so if white evangelical leaders continue to reject that which is the truth and refuse to deal with the white supremacists that they have aided and abetted theologically and otherwise, healing will never occur.

---

29. Richard Delgado and Jean Stefancic, *Critical Race Theory: An Introduction*, 3rd ed. (New York: New York University Press, 2017), 8–11.

Conclusion

White Christian supremacy is a loathsome disease that has infected American society since the arrival of the Puritans and is indeed America's original sin, based on the Christian doctrine of original sin that the actual sins of humans result from the sinful condition in humans. Therefore, it is imperative that white evangelicals experience an authentic conversion, regeneration, sanctification, and that an authentic Spirit baptism eradicate the original sin of white supremacy. It is not the responsibility of nonwhites, especially Blacks, to save white Christian supremacists. Blacks have the almost impossible psychological burden of dealing with the trauma of being Black in a white-supremacist-driven society.

The domestic terrorists of the Trump cult who attacked the Capitol believed that they were the victims in American society fighting for justice. Trump successfully convinced his followers that they were victims. These people are indeed victims, but they are not victims of a supposed oppressive society driven by socialism and full of nonwhites, feminists, secular humanists, liberals, progressives, Democrats, and radical Islamic terrorists who are infringing on their religious liberties. They are victims of their cult leader, Trump, who is their narcissistic, dishonest, and false messiah. When they attacked the Capitol, they were fighting for a justice that is nonexistent, because there is nothing just about white supremacy, and there is nothing just in promoting falsehoods. The Trump terrorists intended to ignite a second civil war for the same purpose as the first Civil War—to preserve white supremacy. They descended on the Capitol mimicking the Lost Cause religious myth of Confederate Christians crusading as wicked warriors for the cause of Trump.

Part IV

THE WAY FORWARD

10

The Social Gospel

The basic fact is that Christianity as it was born in the mind of this Jewish teacher and thinker appears as a technique of survival for the oppressed. That it became, through the intervening years, a religion of the powerful and dominant, used sometimes as an instrument of oppression, must not tempt us into believing that it was thus in the mind and life of Jesus.
—Howard Thurman

In 1949, the mystic, prophet, and Black social gospeler, Howard Thurman, published his seminal work, *Jesus and the Disinherited,* which revealed his theology, philosophy, and ethics, based on the life and teachings of Jesus.[1] In this work, Thurman addresses the realities of white supremacy and poverty; he concludes that the traditional Christian soteriology lacked the capacity to alleviate the pain and suffering that these oppressive realities imposed on the disinherited in American society. Classical Christian soteriology limited the capacity of salvation to the justification of the soul in preparation for eternal bliss in the heavenly realm. However, this limited soteriology fails to address the earthly problems that plague humanity. The social, economic, and racial problems in American society require a more holistic soteriology that addresses the totality of humanity's existence. As the solution, Thurman's soteriology highlighted the teachings of Jesus as reflected in his life and ministry. As such, Thurman identified the problem of white supremacy and poverty caused by fear, deception, and hate and suggested that the solution was the love ethic exhibited in the life of Jesus. Thurman outlined three enemies to whom Jesus applied the love ethic: personal enemies; enemies who inflict shame and humiliation; and political enemies.[2] At the heart of the social gospel tradition is the love ethic of Jesus, which leads to a holistic Christian understanding of salvation.

---

1. Howard Thurman, *Jesus and the Disinherited* (Boston: Beacon Press, 1976), 18.
2. Thurman, *Jesus and the Disinherited*, 79–99.

The White Social Gospel

The social gospel movement originated in the theological presuppositions and actions of socially-conscious-minded Christians who were intent on addressing the social, racial, and economic issues of the postbellum era. This movement took root within major Christian traditions in America, initially among the state church traditions of the Unitarians, Congregationalists, and Episcopalians, and later among the pietist-separatist traditions of the Methodists and Baptists.[3] African American social ethicist and Martin Luther King Jr. scholar Rufus Burrow identifies five primary themes of this social gospel: the centrality of the doctrine of divine immanence; the communal view of society, with an emphasis on the independence and interrelatedness of persons in the world; an emphasis on the higher criticism of the biblical text, which is grounded in the social teachings of Jesus; an emphasis on the ethical achievement of the kingdom of God; and an emphasis on the role of sociology or actual state of social reality.[4] In 1894, American Congregationalist cleric Washington Gladden published *The Church and Kingdom*, in which he argued that Jesus stood in the prophetic tradition.[5] Social gospelers based their theology and social action on the historical Jesus rather than the creedal Jesus taught in classical Christian thought. Gladden was shaped theologically by the Burned-Over district of upstate New York, the bedrock of enthusiastic religious experience and the seedbed of social Christianity. As a pastor, Gladden would preach sermons tailored to classical Christian theology in the morning and sermons tailored to the social gospel in the evening. In addition to Gladden, among the white social gospelers were Josiah Strong, Lyman Abbott, and Walter Rauschenbusch, who was the most prominent systematic theologian of the group.

Walter Rauschenbusch

Rauschenbusch was a Baptist cleric whose attraction to the social gospel grew out of his experience serving as the pastor of the Second German Baptist Church in the Hell's Kitchen community of Manhattan, New York, from 1886 to 1892. In addition to the spiritual welfare of his congregation, Rauschenbusch was equally concerned about the social ills of society. At the time, Hell's Kitchen embodied human suffering, being plagued with unemployment, poverty, disease, starvation, and injustice. After initially preaching an individualistic evangelical gospel, Rauschenbusch experienced an

---

3. Rufus Burrow Jr., *God and Human Dignity: The Personalism, Theology, and Ethics of Martin Luther King Jr.* (Notre Dame, IN: University of Notre Dame Press, 2006), 35.

4. Burrow, *God and Human Dignity*, 35–36.

5. See Washington Gladden, *The Church and the Kingdom* (New York: Fleming H. Revel, 1894).

epiphany that convinced him that the evangelical gospel was inadequate for meeting the spiritual and social needs of oppressed people in America. He realized that the stereotypical belief that oppressed people were lazy and had been chosen for suffering was wrong.

Theology

In 1917, Rauschenbusch published his systematic theological work, *A Theology of the Social Gospel,* in which he characterized Jesus as the initiator of the kingdom of God. Rauschenbusch argued that the gospel of Jesus offered a new kind of humanity and that Jesus was the real revelation of God.[6] He asserted that "we have in Jesus a perfect religious personality, a spiritual life completely filled by the realization of a God who is love."[7] Therefore, possession of Christ's personality was the key to human salvation.[8] Rauschenbusch connected the kingdom of God to the ethics of Jesus, which he situated in the virtue of love. He believed that the social gospel promoted an ethic of love. Earlier in 1907, Rauschenbusch had published *Christianity and the Social Crisis,* in which he analyzed the Hebrew prophets and concluded that they demonstrated mercy and executed justice. He also examined the life and ministry of Jesus and concluded that Jesus revealed the life of God and divine love. The ethic of love became the heart of Rauschenbusch's understanding of the social gospel:

> The fundamental virtue in the ethics of Jesus was love, because love is the society-making quality. Human life originates in love. It is love that holds together the basal human organization, the family. The physical expression of all love and friendship is the desire to get together and be together. Love creates fellowship. In the measure in which love increases in any social organism, it will hold together without coercion.[9]

Social gospelers viewed the social gospel as the doctrine of the kingdom of God. In his theology of the social gospel, Rauschenbusch contrasted the kingdom of God with the kingdom of evil. On the one hand, he argued that the kingdom of God, divinely initiated by Jesus Christ and sustained through the Holy Spirit, consists of peace, justice, and love. He viewed the social gospel as the teleological objective of Christianity. On the other hand,

---

6. Walter Rauschenbusch, *A Theology of the Social Gospel* (Louisville, KY: Westminster John Knox Press, 1997), 152.

7. Rauschenbusch, *A Theology of the Social Gospel,* 155.

8. Rauschenbusch, *A Theology of the Social Gospel,* 151.

9. Walter Rauschenbusch, *Christianity and the Social Crisis in the 21st: The Classic That Woke Up Christianity* (New York: HarperCollins, 2007), 55.

the kingdom of evil possesses injustice, hate, and crime, and is antithetical to the kingdom of God.[10]

Social gospelers redefined the doctrine of sin as the power of the kingdom of evil. The demonic character of social institutions, social classes, and social groups constituted the kingdom of evil. They defined sin as selfishness. Rauschenbusch asserted that "sin is essentially selfishness; this definition is more in harmony with the social gospel than any individualistic type of religion. The sinful mind, then, is the unsocial and anti-social mind."[11] He accused the Christian tradition of emphasizing the biological transmission of sin from generation to generation through original sin while ignoring the social transmission of sin.[12] Social sin is transmitted through social assimilation to what Rauschenbusch characterized as superpersonal forms of evil, which are communities, institutions, and social customs.[13] Social gospelers believed that attaining the kingdom of God was the chief aim of the gospel; however, the church had become a meager substitute for the kingdom. A contemporary of Rauschenbusch, French Roman Catholic priest and theologian Alfred Loisy, who was excommunicated in 1908 after his writings were condemned by the Roman Curia, declared, "Jesus came proclaiming the kingdom, and what arrived was the church."[14] Nevertheless, Rauschenbusch situated salvation from the kingdom of evil in the church, which he characterized as the social factor of salvation.[15] Social gospelers believed that the church was the institution designed for the socialization of the soul, which constitutes salvation. The church is empowered to socialize the soul through the revolutionary power of Christ as realized through the kingdom of God present in the church.

Critiques

One of the most scathing critiques of the white social gospel is the claim that white social gospelers were only concerned with issues of economic class and ignored the reality of white supremacy. Rauschenbusch argued that God was the bond of racial unity as evident in the social gospel and attempted to address the reality of European imperialism through religion. He asserted that "those who adopt the white man's religion come under the white man's influence, Christianity is the religion of the domi-

10. Rauschenbusch, *A Theology of the Social Gospel*, 139–40.
11. Rauschenbusch, *A Theology of the Social Gospel*, 50.
12. Rauschenbusch, *A Theology of the Social Gospel*, 59–60.
13. Rauschenbusch, *A Theology of the Social Gospel*, 69–76.
14. See Alfred Loisy, *The Gospel and the Church* (New York: Charles Scribner's Sons, 1904).
15. Rauschenbusch, *A Theology of the Social Gospel*, 118–30.

nant race."[16] Rauschenbusch's conclusion reflects the white Christian supremacist corruption of the Christian faith through colonization and Christianization. Burrow, however, accused the white social gospelers of failing to reject white supremacy, embracing the notion of Black inferiority, and denying Black moral agency.[17] Josiah Strong adopted the racist and imperialist notion of "Anglo Saxon triumphalism,"[18] and Lyman Abbott embraced gradual abolition rather than immediate abolition and believed that white southerners would treat freed Blacks right in the postbellum era.[19] Social ethicist Gary Dorrien argued that the earlier Rauschenbusch was silent on issues of racial justice but later addressed the issue through his emphasis on the spirit of Jesus.[20] In 1995, though, Dorrien conceded that Rauschenbusch was unwilling to alienate his white liberal disciples by addressing white supremacy. Rauschenbusch had employed racially offensive language in his discussion on immigration to express his preference for European immigrants to the United States.[21] Rauschenbusch had a profound intellectual influence on Martin Luther King Jr. regarding the social gospel.[22] King was attracted to Rauschenbusch's emphasis on the communalism of the kingdom of God in Jesus's prophetic and social teachings rather than individualism.[23] While King seemed to have overlooked Rauschenbusch's racial proclivities, he still engaged in critical constructive critique of the white social gospel. Burrow identified the following four criticisms of King regarding the white social gospel: its aggressively ethical approach, which resulted in moral discontent; identifying the kingdom of God with social or economic particularity; the idea of inevitable progress; and the miscalculation of sin on personal and collective levels.[24] The clear failure of the white social gospelers to address issues of racial justice adequately and provide a robust theological offense against white supremacy based on the prophetic, social, and ethical teachings of Jesus necessitated the Black social gospel, which, with its emphasis on the social and ethical teachings of Jesus and the Black church, had a transformative influence and effect on King's life.

---

16. Rauschenbusch, *A Theology of the Social Gospel*, 185.

17. Burrow, *God and Human Dignity*, 45.

18. Burrow, *God and Human Dignity*, 42.

19. Burrow, *God and Human Dignity*, 43–44.

20. Gary Dorrien, *Breaking White Supremacy: Martin Luther King Jr. and the Black Social Gospel* (New Haven: Yale University Press, 2018), 35.

21. Gary Dorrien, *Soul in Society: The Making and Renewal of Social Christianity* (Minneapolis: Fortress Press, 1995), 43–44.

22. Dorrien, *Breaking White Supremacy*, 18.

23. Burrow, *God and Human Dignity*, 60.

24. Burrow, *God and Human Dignity*, 37–38.

The Black Social Gospel

The Black social gospel grew out of the prophetic tradition of the Black church. Dorrien characterizes the Black social gospel as a form of liberation theology situated in the spirituality of Black abolitionists.[25] In 2015, he accurately argued that the Black social gospel had been erroneously ignored to the peril of historical and theological scholarship in the American Christian tradition. He claimed that at the heart of this intellectual and spiritual maleficence was the reality of white Christian supremacy:

> The founders of black social Christianity were distinct and marginalized in their interactions with the white social gospel movement and within Afro-American Christianity. They were marginalized ecumenically because white American Protestantism was as segregated and as prone to white supremacism as the rest of American society.[26]

Dorrien characterizes the Black social gospel as a new abolitionism, asserting that "the black social gospel affirmed the dignity, sacred personhood, creativity, and moral agency of African Americans and responded to racial oppression."[27] He identifies four ideological streams that shaped the Black social gospel tradition. The first was centered on the political accommodationist principles and economic philosophy of Booker T. Washington. The second centered on the African American nationalist theology and philosophy of Bishop Henry McNeal Turner of the AME Church, which emphasized the need for Blacks to have their own nation. The third was a robust rejection of Washington's accommodationist strategy through the advocacy of notable activists such as AME cleric Reverdy C. Ransom and Ida B. Wells, who were protesting racial and social injustice against Blacks. The fourth synthesized the anti-Washington militant activism of W. E. B. Dubois and the pro-Washington political efforts of leading figures such as Baptist educator Nannie H. Burroughs, Baptist cleric Adam Clayton Powell Sr., and Bishop Alexander Walters of the AMEZ Church.[28]

In the era between the formation of the National Association for the Advancement of Colored People (NAACP) in 1909 and the genesis of the civil rights movement in 1955, a second abolitionist movement grew out of the Black social gospel tradition. This second abolitionist iteration of the Black social gospel was crucial theologically, intellectually, and socially to the shaping and success of the civil rights movement and its influence on

---

25. Dorrien, *Breaking White Supremacy*, 1–2.

26. Gary Dorrien, *The New Abolitionist: W.E.B. Dubois and the Black Social Gospel* (New Haven: Yale University Press, 2015), 11.

27. Dorrien, *The New Abolitionist*, 2.

28. Dorrien, *The New Abolitionist*, 2–4.

Martin Luther King Jr. Those people most influential in shaping the theology of King include Howard University president Mordecai Johnson, Morehouse College president Benjamin Mays, and Howard Thurman.

Mordecai Johnson

Morehouse College and Howard University were the theological and intellectual centers of the Black social gospel. Mordecai Johnson was a native of Paris, Tennessee, where he was born in 1891 and reared in the home of a strict Baptist cleric father who had been enslaved. Prior to his tenure as the first African American president of Howard University, Johnson had served as the pastor of First Baptist Church, the leading Black congregation in Charleston, West Virginia. He had also served on the faculty of Morehouse College as professor of economics and history. Theologically, Johnson emphasized the historical Jesus over the Christ of faith. The historical Jesus practiced humility and was self-sacrificing, which, Johnson believed, reflected the kingdom of God. Johnson prioritized the kingdom of God over racial pride based on his premise that authentic Christian faith consisted of prioritizing Christ over everything in one's life. He developed a robust theology of selfishness and ingratitude and concluded that Blacks owed gratitude to American whites, even considering their justified protests against racial injustice. Otherwise, Johnson concluded, Blacks would suffer from selfishness, ingratitude, and a mentality of victimization. He asserted that orthodox Christian teaching had erroneously made God the problem and postulated that the problem of sin was bondage to selfishness. Johnson wholeheartedly embraced the love ethic of the social gospel of Rauschenbusch, but rejected Rauschenbusch's adoption of the substitution theory of the atonement. He concluded that the substitution theory was not salvific. Building on Rauschenbusch's notion of the kingdom of evil, Johnson believed that God had designed salvation to defeat the kingdom of evil, which consisted of humans polluting the human race.[29] Johnson's characterization of the kingdom of evil epitomizes the spirit of white Christian supremacists, that is, humans who pollute the human race.

Benjamin Mays

The most prominent concept of God in the Black social gospel tradition is found in the theological presuppositions of Benjamin Mays. In 1894, Mays was born in Ninety-Six, South Carolina. Both of his parents had been enslaved and were freed following the Emancipation Proclamation of 1863.

Mays graduated from South Carolina State College in 1916 and then traveled north to matriculate at Bates College and the University of Chicago,

---

29. Dorrien, *Breaking White Supremacy*, 24–49.

where he earned a masters of arts degree in 1925 and a doctor of philosophy degree in 1935. During his graduate studies, Mays studied under American liberal Christian theologian Shailer Matthews, who was a white social gospeler and author of *The Social Teachings of Jesus.*[30]

Mays also studied under American philosopher and theologian Henry Nelson Wieman, who was a scholarly expert in the process and metaphysical teachings of Alfred North Whitehead. The liberal theology and philosophy of Matthews and Wieman influenced Mays master's thesis, "Pagan Survivals in Christianity," in which he challenged the hypocrisy of the orthodox Christian tradition for its demonization of pagan practices. In his thesis, he systematically demonstrated the ways in which core Christian rituals such as the sacrament of baptism had originated in pagan religion and survived in the Christian faith.[31]

Robert Ezra Park

Mays completed his doctoral dissertation under the mentorship and supervision of American sociologist Robert Ezra Park, who had studied race relations with Booker T. Washington at the Tuskegee Institute; later, at the University of Chicago, he developed his "race relation cycle," which consisted of the four stages of contact, conflict, accommodation, and assimilation.[32] In 1963, Frazier wrote *The Negro Church in America*, in which he challenged the presuppositions of German anthropologist Melville Herskovits regarding the survival of African retentions in North America. In 1941, Herskovits authored *The Myth of the Negro Past*, in which he attempted to discredit the myth that African Americans had no cultural past by concluding that there was indeed a survival of African retentions in North America. He concluded that if enslaved Africans lacked ancestral practices that were not robust enough to survive North American enslavement such would suggest Negro inferiority.[33] Frazier disagreed with Herskovits, arguing that the cultural and religious heritage of enslaved Africans was not able to survive the horrific process of North American enslavement. He notes that the loss of social cohesion on American plantations made the survival of significant African retentions impossible and that the empty social vacuum had been

---

30. Shailer Mathews, *The Social Teaching of Jesus: An Essay in Christian Sociology* (New York, Macmillan, 1897).

31. Dorrien, *Breaking White Supremacy*, 96–107.

32. See Robert Ezra Park, *Race and Culture* (Glencoe, IL: Free Press, 1950). In addition to Mays, Park mentored African American sociologists E. Franklin Frazier, Charles Johnson, and Bertram W. Doyle.

33. See Melville J. Herskovits, *The Myth of the Negro Past* (New York: Harper & Brothers, 1941).

filled with the culture of the slaveholder, which was most prevalent in white American Christianity as the new bond of social cohesion.[34] In 1930, Charles Johnson wrote *The Negro in American Civilization* and, in 1946, became the first African American president of Fisk University. In 1937, Doyle published *The Etiquette of Race Relations in the South,* in which he analyzed the social control of Negroes in the antebellum South fostered through slave codes and concluded that these codes still dominated the proper conduct of Blacks in relation to whites in the South following the Emancipation Proclamation and abolition of slavery.[35] In 1950, Doyle was elected the twenty-fifth bishop in the episcopacy of the Colored Methodist Episcopal Church.

In 1933, prior to the completion of his doctoral program, Mays completed *The Negro's Church,* which he co-authored with CME cleric Joseph Nicholson. This publication was ground breaking and dominated the field of Black religious sociology for three decades. The major critique of the sociological study was its failure to examine Black churches in the Holiness-Pentecostal traditions. This omission possibly resulted from Park's influence on the study. Park felt that the emotionalism and spontaneous nature of Black churches hindered the churches' ability to produce effective leadership necessary for social change.[36] In 1938, Mays published his doctoral dissertation, *The Negro's God as Reflected in His Literature,* a theological analysis of God influenced by the philosophical theology of Henry Weiman, particularly his theology of creative process, which was based on Whitehead's view of events possessing creative authority. Wieman viewed God as a structured event and defined theology as the analysis of the total event that constitutes religious experience.[37] Mays argued that all ideas of God are constructs based on social circumstances.[38] He believed that Blacks cultivated ideas of God out of their experience of oppression and their desire for justice. He viewed Black religious experience as compensatory, concluding that Black spirituality equipped oppressed Blacks to survive. Significantly, he connected his view of Black religion as compensatory to the idea of the Negro God as reflected in Negro spirituals:

> Clearly the ideas of God in the Spirituals adhere to the traditional, compensatory pattern. For the most part the authors of the Spirituals appropriated the idea of God found in the Bible, particularly the

---

34. See E. Franklin Frazier, *The Negro Church in America* (New York: Schocken Books, 1963).

35. See Bertram W. Doyle, *The Etiquette of Race Relations in the South: A Study in Social Control* (Chicago: University of Chicago Press, 1937).

36. Dorrien, *Breaking White Supremacy,* 112.

37. Dorrien, *Breaking White Supremacy,* 113–14.

38. Dorrien, *Breaking White Supremacy,* 116.

magical, spectacular, and miraculous ideas of the Old Testament; either that or the ideas of God in the Spirituals were stimulated by those contained in the Bible. They adhere to the compensatory pattern because they are ideas that enable Negroes to endure hardship, suffer pain, and withstand maladjustment, but they do not necessarily motivate them to strive to eliminate the source of the ills they suffer.[39]

Based on his argument related to cultivating ideas of God based on social context, Mays concluded that the Negro's God in the antebellum era was the liberating God and the Negro's God in the postbellum era was the God of racial equality.[40] In 1934, Mays was appointed the first dean of the School of Religion at Howard University, and, in 1940, the board of trustees of Morehouse College appointed Mays the sixth president of the institution, which he led successfully for three decades.

Howard Thurman

All three of the Black social gospel theologians—Johnson, Mays, and Thurman—promoted the nonviolent philosophy of Mahatma Gandhi, which would develop into the nonviolent religion of the civil rights movement. However, its most prominent advocate was Howard Thurman.

Thurman was born in Florida in 1899 and reared in Daytona Beach, Florida. His father died of pneumonia when he was seven years old; therefore, most of his upbringing was shaped by his mother, Alice Thurman, and grandmother, Nancy Ambrose, who were both devout Christians in the Black Baptist tradition. Thurman attended the Florida Baptist Academy in Jacksonville, Florida, which at the time was one of only three high schools for Negroes in Florida. He matriculated at Morehouse College, graduating as the valedictorian in 1923. Thurman also graduated from Rochester Theological Seminary in 1926 as the valedictorian of his class after writing his master's thesis on the issues of sexual morality with an emphasis on the ethics of premarital sex. He concluded that sexual desire represented an expression of God's Spirit and that women had been sexually repressed through the sexual code that limited premarital chastity to women in order to keep them subordinated to men.[41] Based on Thurman's sexual ethics, which have been correlated with the ideas of free loveism, some Thurman scholars have characterized him as a feminist. Thurman's views on sexual morality represent a departure from the views of fellow Black social gospel theologian Mordecai Johnson. Johnson had serious concerns about the

---

39. Benjamin Mays, *The Negro's God: As Reflected in His Literature* (Eugene, OR: Wipf & Stock Publishers, 2010), 23–24.

40. Dorrien, *Breaking White Supremacy*, 116.

41. Dorrien, *Breaking White Supremacy*, 129–30.

welfare of children who had been orphaned and even condemned as selfish and ungrateful couples who did not desire children. He maintained that the plight of abandoned children evident in orphanages and hospitals originated with the sin of sexual immorality.[42]

Commitment to Nonviolence

Thurman's commitment to nonviolence was the nonviolent anticolonial cause of Gandhi in India, which exposed the complicity of white Christian supremacy in the colonial oppression of Indian people. Based on the horrors and trauma of colonialism in India, Gandhi contended that the greatest threat to Jesus Christ in India was the Christian religion. He believed that the colonial scheme of white Christian supremacy was the greatest enemy of Jesus.[43] Thurman stipulated that the necessary response to the oppression of imperialism and colonialism on the plight of the disinherited was nonviolent resistance. He rejected armed resistance, asserting that "armed resistance is apt to be a tragic last resort in the life of the disinherited. Armed resistance has an appeal because it provides a form of expression, of activity, that releases tension and frees the oppressed from a disintegrating sense of complete impotency and helplessness."[44] Thurman believed that the teachings of Jesus were designed to alleviate human suffering. He concluded that the Christian religion had corrupted the true gospel of Jesus and, therefore, had eradicated the dreams of the disinherited. At the heart of white Christian supremacy's corruption of the Christian faith was hate. Thurman exclaimed:

> Christianity has been almost sentimental in its effort to deal with hatred in human life. It has sought to get rid of hatred by preachments, by moralizing, by platitudinous judgments. It has hesitated to analyze the basis of hatred and to evaluate it in terms of its possible significance in the lives of the people possessed by it. This reluctance to examine hatred has taken on the character of a superstition. It is a subject that is taboo unless there is some extraordinary social crisis such as war involving the mobilization of all the national resources of the common life to meet it. There is a conspiracy of silence about hatred, its function and its meaning.[45]

Thurman here exposes the complicity of silent white Christianity in light of the hate prevalent within its ranks because of the presence and power of

---

42. Dorrien, *Breaking White Supremacy*, 40–42.
43. Dorrien, *Breaking White Supremacy*, 144–45.
44. Thurman, *Jesus and the Disinherited*, 15–16.
45. Thurman, *Jesus and the Disinherited*, 65.

white Christian supremacy. White Christianity has used its brand of morality as a veneer for its complicity in white Christian supremacists' expressions of hate against humanity, and specifically people of color. This veneer
of morality is inadequate and ineffective because of its spiritual hypocrisy.

Theology

In his proposal to overcome hate, Thurman emphasized the love ethic,
which he believed was central to the teachings of Jesus. He was most concerned with the toxicity of hate possessing and plaguing the disinherited
and asserted that "hatred makes this sort of profound contribution to the
life of the disinherited, because it establishes a dimension of self-realization
hammered out of the raw materials of injustice."[46] Thurman concluded that
hate gave the disinherited a false sense of righteousness. He argued that
"when hatred serves as a dimension of self-realization, the illusion of righteousness is easy to create. Often there are but thin lines between bitterness, hatred, self-realization, defiance, and righteous indignation."[47] Hate
results from the bitterness of the disinherited, and Thurman believed that
Jesus rejected hate, and that it caused the death of the mind, spirit, and
communion with God.[48] Rather than applying hate, Thurman promoted
applying the love ethic—the model of Jesus—to the enemy, who was the
perpetrator of the oppression being imposed on the disinherited. Therefore,
Thurman's theology was strongly rooted in Jesus's command to love and
forgive one's enemies—a command that he regarded as mandatory for the
disinherited and as the work of divine grace:

> In Jesus' insistence that we should forgive seventy times seven, there
> seems to be the assumption that forgiveness is mandatory for three
> reasons. First, God forgives us again and again for what we do inten-
> tionally and unintentionally. There is present an element that is con-
> tingent upon our attitude. Forgiveness beyond this is interpreted
> as the work of divine grace. Second, no evil deed represents the full
> intent of the doer. Third, the evildoer does not go unpunished. Life is
> its own restraint.[49]

The source and function of the love ethic are best understood in Thurman's pneumatology, in which he maintained that possessing the spirit of
Christ was an impossibility for those who practiced, proved complicit, or

---

46. Thurman, *Jesus and the Disinherited*, 71.
47. Thurman, *Jesus and the Disinherited*, 72.
48. Thurman, *Jesus and the Disinherited*, 77–78.
49. Thurman, *Jesus and the Disinherited*, 98.

felt indifferent to racial oppression.[50] For Thurman, the Spirit of God is the unifying principle of all life that, as a mystic, fueled his mysticism, which he defined as the unity of all things.[51] In 1932, Thurman had been appointed the first dean of Rankin Chapel at Howard University and then, in 1953, the dean of Marsh Chapel at Boston University, where he served as the first African American spiritual guide for an all-white educational institution in the United States. However, his greatest achievement in the cause of racial integration occurred in 1944 when he established the Church for the Fellowship of All Peoples in San Francisco as the first racially integrated congregation in the United States. Thurman believed that segregated Black churches were an obstacle for the success of the civil rights movement.[52] His commitment to nonviolent resistance and promotion of racial integration had such a profound influence on Martin Luther King Jr. that, in addition to the Scriptures, King traveled with a copy of Thurman's *Jesus and the Disinherited.*

---

50. Dorrien, *Breaking White Supremacy*, 127.
51. Dorrien, *Breaking White Supremacy*, 167.
52. Dorrien, *Breaking White Supremacy*, 168.

11

Social Resistance

Any law that uplifts human personality is just. Any law that degrades the human personality is unjust. All segregation statues are unjust because segregation distorts the soul and damages the personality. It gives the segregator a false sense of superiority and the segregated a false sense of inferiority.

—Martin Luther King Jr.

On April 16, 1963, Martin Luther King Jr. wrote his "Letter from Birmingham Jail" after being incarcerated on Good Friday that year for civil disobedience.[1] King had been leading civil rights demonstrations in Birmingham, Alabama, since April 3, which infuriated many of the city's white citizens, especially the white supremacist police chief, Theophilus Eugene "Bull" Conner. King's letter was in response to a publicized letter of eight white Christian supremacist clergypersons in Alabama that criticized the efforts of the civil rights movement and urged Blacks to abandon their support for King and the movement.

In his letter, King exposed the complicity of white Christians in the structural system of white supremacy that was embedded in American society and most evident in the unjust laws that justified racism and segregation. Building on the theological presuppositions of major Christian theologians such as St. Augustine, Thomas Aquinas, and Paul Tillich, King emphasized the responsibility of Christians to challenge these unjust laws. He argued that unjust laws distort the human personality and that, since humans are created in the *imago Dei*, anything that distorts the human personality, such as racism, sexism, or xenophobia, is indeed sinful because it distorts the image of God. King, who was influenced by the Black social gospel, was

---

1. Martin Luther King Jr., "Letter from Birmingham Jail," in Milton Sernett, *African American Religious History: A Documentary Witness*, 2nd ed. (Durham, NC: Duke University Press, 1999), 524.

the principal leader, prophetic voice, and champion for social justice of the movement.

The Theology of Martin Luther King Jr.

King witnessed and became attracted to the Black social gospel during his childhood. His grandfather, Adam Daniel Williams, and his father, Martin Luther King Sr., served as the second and third pastors respectively of the historic Ebenezer Baptist Church in Atlanta, and both had a profound influence on King as pioneers of the Black social gospel movement. Williams integrated Booker T. Washington's emphasis on Black vocational skills with Black entrepreneurship and W. E. B. Dubois's strategy of civil rights activism. Williams was one of the pioneer founders of the local Atlanta branch of the NAACP and served as the president. Traditionally, some scholars characterize Daddy King as a Black fundamentalist preacher. Certainly, many Black ministers subscribed to a conservative theology; however, those such as Daddy King were liberal socially and politically, and his ministry and civic activism in Atlanta reflected the principles of the Black social gospel.

In addition to the impact of his father and grandfather, King was also attracted to the ministry of William Holmes Borders, the pastor of Wheat Street Baptist Church in Atlanta. Borders's ministry also reflected features of the Black social gospel. Like Williams and Daddy King, Borders focused on the salvation of the holistic person—body and soul—and not merely the salvation of the soul, which was the common focus of white evangelicals.

Personalism

Building on this holistic salvation, King embraced the philosophy and theology of personalism. Among the leading thinkers of personalism were Edgar Brightman, Harold DeWolf, and Walter Muelder, all of whom served on the theology faculty of Boston University and had a profound influence on King during his doctoral studies. They emphasized the value, dignity, and sacredness of human personhood based on the belief that humans are created in the *imago Dei*. Burrow defines personalism as "any philosophy that stresses God as personal and human beings as innately precious because they are summoned into existence, sustained, and loved by God."[2] It focuses on the personality of the individual, not regarding the benefit of one's self-interest, but rather the community. The key features of personalism are moral autonomy, human freedom, and communalism.[3] Burrow identifies the four fundamental themes of King's personalism as God as personal and loving; the inherent dignity of persons; the impor-

2. Burrow, *God and Human Dignity*, 70.
3. Burrow, *God and Human Dignity*, 70.

tance of personal-communal spirit; and the need to protest injustice and social evil in order to cultivate the beloved community, which constitutes the kingdom of God.[4]

Personalism had a direct influence on King's view of God, Christology, and theological anthropology. Black theologian Noel Leo Erskine linked a personal and loving God with the natural moral order in the universe that is rooted in the nature of God. Based on this natural moral order, humans have an ethical responsibility to execute justice on behalf of the oppressed. For King, God is an active participant in the struggle of the oppressed against injustice as executed through the structures of social evil, and therefore linked justice for the oppressed with the love of God as manifested supremely in the cross of Christ.[5]

Theologian Peter Heltzel maintains that King's Christology reflects Martin Luther's theology of the cross.[6] Luther recognized the dichotomy of the theology of glory and the theology of the cross. On the one hand, the theology of glory constitutes a rational effort to prove the existence of God; on the other hand, the theology of the cross is the paradoxical revelation of God as a suffering human being. In line with Heltzel's assertion, King's personal God is both immanent, that is, active in the world, and transcendent, that is, working outside the world. Furthermore, as Heltzel contends accurately, King was calling white evangelicals back to the gospel of Jesus Christ and the commandment to love one's neighbor.[7] Theologically, the foundations for white evangelicalism are the principles of the Protestant Reformation, and specifically the doctrine of justification. As Rauschenbusch accurately argued, the Protestant Reformation had in essence celebrated Pauline doctrine and ignored the spirit of Jesus.[8]

Freedom is imperative in King's theology, for creation in the *imago Dei* stipulates human freedom. King identified three moments in human life that constitute freedom: (1) freedom to deliberate; (2) freedom to make decisions; and (3) freedom to act responsibly.[9] Consequently, he believed that there are several forms of sin against the human personality, including segregation, racism, war, and poverty, since these evil forces distort the human personality and eradicate human freedom.[10] King's understanding

4. Burrow, *God and Human Dignity*, 80.

5. Noel Leo Erskine, *King among Theologians* (Cleveland, OH: Pilgrim Press, 1994), 141–47.

6. Peter Goodwin Heltzel, *Jesus and Justice: Evangelicals, Race and American Politics* (New Haven: Yale University Press, 2009), 47.

7. Heltzel, *Jesus and Justice*.

8. Dorrien, *Breaking White Supremacy*, 33.

9. Martin Luther King Jr., "The Ethical Demands of Integration," in James M. Washington, ed., *A Testament of Hope: The Essential Writings of Martin Luther King, Jr.* (San Francisco: Harper & Row, 1986), 120.

10. Erskine, *King among Theologians*, 147–48.

of sin was completely antithetical to that of white evangelicals, which was most evident in their revivalism.

Billy Graham

Billy Graham, possibly the most prominent white evangelical revivalist in modern American evangelicalism, was a contemporary of King. Historian Grant Wacker has identified Graham as "America's Pastor," a title that stems from Graham's many crusades, which attracted millions of people with his message of accepting Jesus Christ as one's personal Lord and Savior.[11] Realistically, such a title should reflect a spiritual leader who has served the best interests of all Americans. Graham's work as an evangelist, however, served only the interests of white American evangelicals. Historically, Graham has been hailed as an apolitical figure, and yet, he provided spiritual advice to several US presidents following his role as Dwight Eisenhower's presidential counselor. Steven Miller concedes that Graham was not merely a spiritual advisor to presidents but also functioned as a political strategist. He notes that Graham was the political force that brought an end to legalized Jim Crow practices in the South and ended the Democratic Party's dominance there. He characterized Graham's political influence as the *politics of decency*.[12] The political reality, however, is that during this time of Graham's influence, the Republican Party became the party of Jim Crow through the infiltration of the Dixiecrats; and despite the 1954 Supreme Court ruling in *Brown v. Board of Education*, the racist and segregationist practices of white supremacy in the South still reigned. There is no question that the history of the Democratic Party in the antebellum era through to the 1960s was mired in white supremacy, yet this reality does not absolve the white supremacist actions of the Republican Party and the fact that the modern-day Grand Old Party serves as the political refuge for the cause of white supremacy in the United States. Ultimately, civil rights legislation that ended Jim Crow practices in the South were formulated and passed under the Democratic presidents John F. Kennedy and Lyndon B. Johnson respectively.

Graham was born in 1918 in Charlotte, North Carolina, and raised in the Associate Reformed Presbyterian Church, which was affiliated with a very conservative synod and possessed a very strict adherence to the Westminster Confession.

After graduating from high school in 1936, Graham enrolled at the racially segregated Bob Jones College, matriculating for one semester and

---

11. See Grant Wacker, *America's Pastor: Billy Graham and the Shaping of a Nation* (Cambridge, MA: Belknap Press, 2014).

12. Steven P. Miller, *Billy Graham and the Rise of the Republican South* (Philadelphia: University of Pennsylvania Press, 2009), 64–88.

then transferring to the Florida Bible Institute in Temple Terrace, Florida. During his matriculation in Florida, Graham preached his first sermon and was eventually baptized again and ordained a minister in the Southern Baptist Convention, completing his undergraduate studies in 1943 at Wheaton College. As a revivalist, Graham belonged to the fundamentalist evangelical revivalist tradition of Dwight Moody. However, while Moody's revivalism appealed to northern upper- and middle-class whites, Graham's revivalism appealed to the masses from different socio-economic backgrounds as well as some people of color in the northern and southern regions of the United States.[13]

A Crisis of Faith

Graham robustly advocated the white evangelical agenda that limited the capacity of salvific power to the human soul, but he had a crisis of faith related to the nature of the Christian faith in practice. Historically, the scandal of the white evangelical faith stems from the dichotomy of proclaiming the gospel of Jesus but having difficulty fulfilling and living out that gospel. For Graham, this crisis came down to whether the purpose of the Christian faith is the fulfillment and living out of the gospel or appeasing people—specifically those who represent white Christian supremacy. The scandal of white evangelical faith, as we noted earlier, has been the preservation of white cultural ethics mediated through a false interpretation of Pauline theology that is erroneously characterized as the gospel of Jesus Christ.

The essence of Christian discipleship is the command to take up one's cross and follow Jesus in daily living—the living out of one's salvation and sanctification. Heltzel accurately maintains that white evangelicals view this command as a struggle for moral purity. Those situated in the social gospel, specifically the Black social gospel, such as King, understood taking up one's cross as being committed to love and justice both personally and politically. Indeed, King's theology and practice of bearing one's cross resisted white supremacy through nonviolent love.[14] The question of whether the Christian faith constituted a struggle and commitment to love and justice, specifically resistance to white supremacy or a struggle for white evangelical moral purity, was at the heart of Graham's crisis of faith.

In 1955, the liberal ministers of the Protestant Council of the City of New York invited Graham to hold a crusade in 1957 at Madison Square Garden. Graham included local civil rights leaders and invited King to share the platform with him and offer prayer. Graham was also accepting invitations to speak at liberal seminaries, which infuriated his fundamentalist evan-

---

13. Fitzgerald, *The Evangelicals*, 169–99.
14. Heltzel, *Jesus and Justice*, 67–68.

gelical base who claimed that Graham was shifting from fundamentalist evangelicalism to a neo-evangelicalism. When Graham spoke at Union Theological Seminary, which was considered the bedrock of liberal theology, fundamentalist evangelical leaders Carl McIntire and Bob Jones Jr. condemned Graham for having fellowship with those in the bastion of theological apostasy in the viewpoint of fundamentalist evangelicals.[15] In 1963, after the bombing of the Sixteenth Street Baptist Church in Birmingham, Alabama, Graham intentionally held integrated crusades there on Easter Sunday.[16] He also privately advised King and other civil rights leaders in the Southern Christian Leadership Conference.[17]

Despite Graham's ecumenical interactions with liberal theologians and his friendship with King and other civil rights leaders, his crisis of faith reflects his theological ambiguity. Graham adopted Moody's version of Adam Smith's laissez-faire, free-market capitalism, which influenced his emphasis on the individualism of personal faith in Christ. As we have noted, this economic philosophy was severely complicit in the selfishness and economic injustice of American culture, which solidified the poverty of certain people and wealth of others in American society based on race, class, and socio-economic status.

Even after his decision to end the practice of segregated crusades, Graham still maintained his fellowship with segregationists. In 1958, King wrote to Graham regarding his planned crusade to be held in San Antonio, Texas, where Graham was to be introduced by the segregationist Texas governor Price Daniel. King implored Graham not to share the platform with this governor, asserting that such would signal his support for racial segregation and discrimination; but, under the advice of his advisor Grady Wilson, Graham ignored King's wisdom and request. Furthermore, Graham proposed overcoming racial discrimination through neighborly love rather than the passage of civil rights legislation. In addition to his rejection of the Civil Rights Act of 1964 and Voting Rights Act of 1965, Graham intentionally avoided the term "integration." Graham evidently suffered from the illusion that white Christian supremacists, who were the perpetrators of racial segregation and racial discrimination, had the capacity to demonstrate neighborly love to racial others even under the diabolical influence of

---

15. Fitzgerald, *The Evangelicals*, 190–91.

16. See Edward L. Moore, "Billy Graham and Martin Luther King Jr: An Inquiry into White and Black Revivalistic Traditions" (PhD diss., Vanderbilt University, 1979).

17. See Moore, "Billy Graham and Martin Luther King Jr." See also Gary Dorrien, "Niebuhr and Graham: Modernity, Complexity, White Supremacism, Justice, Ambiguity," in Michael G. Long, ed., *The Legacy of Billy Graham: Critical Reflections on America's Greatest Evangelists* (Louisville, KY: Westminster John Knox Press, 2008), 150–51. Some historians see evidence of Graham and King's friendship in their travels together to Baptist conferences and Graham's posting bail for King after being imprisoned in Albany, Georgia, and Birmingham, Alabama.

their racist ideologies and theologies, including the illusion of white Christian supersessionism and the belief that only white people were recipients of salvation and that only they were Christians. Graham obviously rejected this notion, evident in his integrated crusades; however, he failed to condemn these beliefs. In 1965, Graham equated some activists in the Alabama campaign of the civil rights movement with the domestic terrorists in the Ku Klux Klan and concluded that the violence, which resulted in the brutalization and death of Black bodies, was the fault of activists protesting for voting rights rather than the authoritarian terrorism and police brutality of Alabama state troopers.

Graham's crisis of faith exposes at least two conflicting approaches to the Christian faith: the white evangelical approach for moral purity that included white Christian supremacy and its struggle for racial purity, and the approach of the Black social gospel of King and the Black church tradition in the struggle to love and achieve justice. Ultimately, Graham chose the struggle for moral purity, which represented a corruption of the gospel of Christ. Furthermore, Graham emphasized an individual, personalized faith, which occurs when one accepts Jesus Christ as one's personal Lord and Savior. Therefore, the only concern should be the salvation of the soul, which will assure one citizenship in the heavenly kingdom. Miller identifies Graham's soteriological model as *evangelical universalism*. This social ethic asserts that "the individual soul is the primary theological and political unit in society; that relational solutions greatly surpass legislative ones in resolving social problems; and that Christians should, in most cases, acquiesce to ordained governmental authority."[18] Graham's model for salvation ignored racism, sexism, and all other forms of oppression and injustice in American society. His plan of salvation reflects the plan of salvation that Christian slaveholders created for enslaved Africans, one that saved only the soul of the enslaved, not the body, and assured only spiritual salvation, not physical salvation.

The Beloved Community

As a Black social gospeler, King emphasized the notion of the kingdom of God, which he concluded was the already and the not yet.[19] The kingdom of God not yet constitutes the heavenly realm, and the kingdom of God already—the Beloved Community—represents the earthly realm. King's Beloved Community was a plan of salvation that not only assured citizenship in the heavenly kingdom but also assured a quality life for citizens in the earthly kingdom. In addition to the salvation of the soul through accep-

18. Miller, *Billy Graham and the Rise of the Republican South*, 9.
19. Erskine, *King among Theologians*, 146.

tance of Jesus Christ, it assured salvation from poverty, hunger, and homelessness, whereby all citizens benefit from the wealth of the earth. It also assured salvation from racism, bigotry, prejudice, discrimination, and all forms of oppression.[20]

The freedom and moral agency of humans were imperative in achieving King's Beloved Community. King believed that humans were not born with moral agency but were born with the freedom that empowered them to be responsible and intellectual moral agents through education and socialization.[21] Moral agency is essential to the free expression of *agape* love, the practice of which grounded King's vision of the Beloved Community. He believed that the civil rights movement was a microcosmic reflection of the Beloved Community.[22]

The Civil Rights Movement

Following the Supreme Court decision in *Brown v. Board of Education* that would integrate Blacks into the institutions of exclusive white American society, white backlash, specifically in the South, resulted in the terrorization of Blacks through the burning of their homes and churches.

On August 24, 1955, while fourteen-year-old Emmett Till of Chicago was visiting family in the Mississippi Delta, he and several other Black boys were gathered in front of Bryant Grocery and Meat Market in Money, Mississippi. A twenty-one-year-old white woman, Carolyn Bryant, accused Till of flirting with her, suggesting that he had whistled at her. The accusation had grave consequences for Till, resulting in Bryant's husband, Roy Bryant, and brother-in-law, J. W. "Big" Milam, kidnapping Till from his relative's home in the middle of the night, brutally beating him, and drowning him in the Tallahatchie River. After Till's dead, brutalized body was discovered with a seventy-pound cotton gin tied around his neck with barbed wire three days after his murder, Bryant and Milam were arrested and brought to trial. In her court testimony, Carolyn Bryant testified that Till had not just whistled at her, but that he had a picture of a white girl and boasted about having sexual relations with her. Carolyn Bryant further accused Till of stretching his arms across the counter and grabbing her by the waist. Based on Carolyn's testimony, Till had violated the rules of sexual etiquette in the

---

20. Burrow, *God and Human Dignity*, 161–67. American personalist Josiah Royce was the first to coin the phrase "Beloved Community," which he understood as a principle of Christian morality through which the morality of every action is judged based on the teachings of Jesus concerning the kingdom of God; Boston personalist Edgar Brightman correlated the notion of Beloved Community with his own phrase, "the Community of Love"; and Black social gospeler Howard Thurman believed that God created humans to love in community.

21. Burrow, *God and Human Dignity*, 173.

22. Burrow, *God and Human Dignity*, 168.

Jim Crow South, which forbade any activity of a sexual nature, even flirtation, between Black men and white women. The Jim Crow South continued to perpetuate the Lost Cause myth of Black men as Black beasts who would eradicate through sexual activity the purity of supposed pristine, pure, southern-belle white women. The two men charged in the murder of Emmett Till were acquitted, something that was common with all-white juries dominated by white supremacy.

Half a century later, Carolyn Bryant admitted that her accusations were fabricated and based on a southern racist horror film about a Black beast rapist and had the gall to declare "nothing that boy did could ever justify what happened to him."[23] The horrors of the Till murder became the case that shifted the psyche of some in white America and was the catalyst for the most transformative movement in American history. The driving force behind Till's murder becoming an international outrage was his mother, Mamie Till-Bradley. Her tenacious and courageous decision to have an open casket nationally televised with her son's brutalized body on view— particularly his disfigured face—created the much needed social change in American society. Till-Bradley's appearances at rallies advocating for justice drew thousands of outraged sympathizers who heard her declare, "Lord you gave your only son to remedy a condition, but who knows but what the death of my only son might bring an end to lynching."[24] On September 25, 1955, at least sixteen thousand people gathered at a rally in Harlem, New York City, at Williams Institutional CME Church. It was organized by A. Phillip Randolph as a public demonstration for justice for Till, whose lynching shocked the world and led to the civil rights movement.

The Montgomery Bus Boycott in December of 1955 marked the official beginning of the civil rights movement. Rosa Parks's refusal to give up her seat for a white person on a Montgomery city bus and her arrest propelled the boycott. Earlier that year, on March 2, 1955, fifteen-year-old high school student Claudette Colvin had refused to give up her seat for a white passenger and was arrested and literally dragged from the bus by a police officer, which caused outrage in the Black community of Montgomery. Community activist Jo Ann Robinson, who became a key figure in the civil rights movement, led calls for protests against the segregated bus system in Montgomery, but some of the Black leaders caved to the politics of respectability and prevented the protests because of rumors suggesting that Colvin, an unmarried teenager, was in the early stages of pregnancy. Therefore, the Parks's incident became strategic in the cause for civil rights since she was

---

23. See Timothy B. Tyson, *The Blood of Emmett Till* (New York: Simon & Schuster, 2017).

24. Mattie Smith Colin, "Mother's Tears Greet Son Who Died a Martyr," *Chicago Defender*, September 10, 1955.

regarded as a respectable figure who was married, worked as a professional tailor at the largest department store in Montgomery, and served as the secretary of the local chapter of the NAACP. A year later, the boycott ended in victory after it caused significant economic devastation for the city of Montgomery; and in December of 1956 the Supreme Court upheld the ruling of the federal courts that the city's segregated buses policy was unconstitutional. Ultimately, civil rights activists had successfully desegregated the Montgomery city bus system.[25]

As the leader of the civil rights movement, King traveled with activists throughout the South leading nonviolent protests and other acts of civil disobedience. The boycott had laid the foundation for the successful organization of other campaigns in numerous southern cities. One of the most controversial was the Children's Crusade organized by the Alabama Christian Movement for Human Rights (ACMHR) and the Southern Christian Leadership Council (SCLC).[26] The Children's Crusade consisted of African American school children peacefully protesting for desegregation. Initially, the campaign was viewed as unsuccessful because the crusade had not drawn the kind of national attention necessary to expose the Jim Crow South's terrorization of Blacks, including children. However, on May 3, 1963, Bull Conner directed police officers to unleash high-pressure water hoses and attack dogs on the children, who were between the ages of seven and eighteen; the action resulted in the arrest of seventy children. The most heinous crime of the Birmingham campaign occurred on September 15, 1963, when white supremacists Thomas Edwin Blanton Jr., Herman Frank Cash, Robert Edward Chambliss, and Bobby Frank Cherry bombed the Sixteenth Street Baptist Church, killing four Black girls attending Sunday School. While the diabolical nature of this crime caused international outrage, white supremacists celebrated the deaths of the four Black girls, declaring "four less niggers."[27] The Kennedy administration immediately sent federal law-enforcement agents to Birmingham to investigate the bombing, and on June 11, 1963, President John F. Kennedy addressed the nation declaring civil rights and racial equality moral issues and his commitment to the passage of civil rights legislation. After Kennedy's assassination two months later, on November 22, 1963, President Lyndon Johnson affirmed his commitment to the legislation. On July 2, 1964, the Civil Rights Act of 1964 was

---

25. Whelchel, *The History and Heritage*, 187–205.

26. The ACMHR had been formed in 1956 under the leadership of civil rights leader Fred Shuttlesworth in Birmingham. The SCLC had been formed in 1957 under the leadership of King in Atlanta, Georgia. Both civil rights organizations were committed to the desegregation of segregated public spaces, public modes of transportation, and businesses.

27. Sara Bullard, *Free at Last: A History of the Civil Rights Movement and Those Who Died in the Struggle* (New York: Oxford University Press, 1993), 63–64.

enacted, outlawing racial segregation in public accommodations and racial discrimination based on race, gender, or national origin.[28]

Affirmative Action and Atonement

An outgrowth of civil rights legislation is the mandate for affirmative action. This mandate originated with an executive order by President Kennedy on March 6, 1961, to hinder discriminatory practices in employment, wages, and access to education based on race, gender, and national origin. Another executive order by President Johnson in 1965 reaffirmed this mandate. Opponents of affirmative action generally accuse African Americans of suffering from a victim mentality. On the contrary, African Americans more than any other race are not only survivors; they are also victors. They have survived and overcome systematic oppression in the United States many times over and continue to overcome oppression from white supremacy.

An early model of the atonement emphasizes Christ's death as a ransom through which Christ was victorious over the powers that held humans in bondage to sin, death, and the devil. Gustaf Aulen's reinterpretation of this theory of atonement is known as *Christus Victor*, in which the central idea, Aulen argues, is "the view of God and the kingdom of God as fighting against evil powers ravaging in mankind. In this drama Christ has the key role."[29] Now, affirmative action is a form of victory atonement through which African Americans gain victory over white supremacy, white privilege, white superiority, and white oppression perpetuated through colonialization, imperialism, slavery, Jim Crow, racial segregation, lynching, redlining, reverse redlining, gerrymandering, gentrification, and many other forms of racial discrimination and racial injustice that constitute systematic racism in the history of the United States.

There are many forms of this victory atonement, such as the Civil Rights Act of 1964 and the Voting Rights Acts of 1965. However, unlike Christ's atonement on the cross, which was a one-time act, full victory and liberation for African Americans over white supremacy and white oppression has required many acts of atonement and will require many more, such as reparations. These acts of atonement for white supremacy are imperative until white supremacy, the primary cause of systematic racism, is completely eradicated and African Americans are liberated and vindicated from white supremacy and oppression, and affirmed in their full humanity.

---

28. This act was the most significant piece of civil rights legislation passed in the United States since the Civil Rights Act of 1875.

29. Guslaf Aulen, *Christus Victor: An Historical Study of the Three Main Types of the Idea of Atonement* (New York: Macmillan, 1969), ix.

Furthermore, persons who have been martyred through peaceful protest and marching at the hands of white supremacists are martyrs for the cause of liberation, and, as such, their lives have become atoning sacrifices. Not all the martyrs are Black; some are from different races or ethnicities. But they are all allies in the cause of liberation and victory for the oppressed according to the gospel of Jesus Christ.

Nonviolent Atonement

In addition to this form of victory atonement, the civil rights movement and King's theology were inspired by Gandhi's philosophy of nonviolent resistance, which reflects the nonviolent theory of atonement.

J. Denny Weaver has developed the theory of nonviolence based on the *Christus Victor* theory of Aulen. He emphasizes the stark contrast between Aulen's *Christus Victor* theory and Anselm's satisfaction theory, arguing for a direct connection between satisfaction atonement and retributive justice, which dominates systems of justice in the Western world, especially the United States. Weaver characterized the retributive justice in the United States as "quid pro quo violence," which he asserts is "an evil deed involving some level of violence on one side, balanced by an equivalent violence of punishment on the other. The level of violence in the punishment corresponds to the level of violence in the criminal act."[30] In satisfaction atonement, the penalty of death for the sin of humanity is satisfied through the penalty of Jesus's violent death on the cross. Based on Weaver's theological presuppositions, satisfaction atonement represents the scandal of slaveholders in their contention that Christian salvation saved the souls of the enslaved, not their bodies. In other words, "it allowed white people to claim salvation while accommodating and advocating the violence of racism and slavery."[31] Ironically, Black theologian James Cone affirmed that within Anselm's satisfaction theory of atonement, God takes the place of humanity:

> The problem of sin is an alienation from God that is always connected with injustice and oppression. Thus the atonement of Jesus Christ represents God taking the place of the oppressed in history so that they might be given the freedom to create a new future as defined by the liberation struggle in history. Instead of black people having to accept the consequence of white oppression, Jesus takes our place and undergoes the depth of the pain of being black in a white racist society and thereby transforms the condition of alienation into the possibility and the actuality of reconciliation. Through his taking our place and

---

30. J. Denny Weaver, *The Nonviolent Atonement* (Grand Rapids, MI: Eerdmans, 2001), 2.
31. Weaver, *The Nonviolent Atonement*, 4.

becoming black in a white racist society, black people's existence is radically transformed *objectively*.[32]

Cone believed that Jesus became the Black Christ of necessity based on the satisfaction theory of the atonement for Blacks to overcome the violence of white supremacists against Blacks. Weaver concludes that in the modern era, Anselm's satisfaction theory does constitute contextual theology in the sense that it does reflect a particular context.[33]

The notion of a nonviolent atonement seems preposterous and irrational. Even Weaver conceded that at the heart of atonement theology is the act of violence, particularly the violent killing of Jesus to deliver salvation to humanity.[34] However, Weaver dichotomized violence and nonviolence, which proved effective in the formulation of his nonviolent atonement. Nonviolence constituted the preservation of the integrity of the human body. Violence certainly consists of bodily harm. Weaver's definition, however, transcends the generic meaning of violence. Violence constitutes that which violates the integrity of the human body physically, socially, spiritually, and psychologically. Similar to the view of the Boston personalists, sin was anything that violated and distorted personhood.[35]

Based on Weaver's presuppositions, the systemic acts of enslavement, racism, sexism, and economic oppression were not only sinful; these acts also constituted systemic violence. Ultimately, Weaver concludes that Jesus modeled nonviolent resistance and that violence, even within the atonement, was incompatible with the gospel of Jesus Christ.[36]

King's theological teachings epitomize the nonviolent atonement evident in the civil rights movement. King did not advocate for retributive justice against white supremacist enemies for the violence of racism and economic oppression. He advocated for nonviolent resistance and forgiveness through *agape* love, which he believed constituted the key ingredients necessary for the achievement of the Beloved Community, which would also include white supremacists through reconciliation. King believed that reconciliation could be achieved only between those who are equals since reconciliation would be an impossibility between an inferior and a superior.[37] He stipulated that white supremacists had to experience a transformation of heart, mind, and soul, and that they would have to experience regeneration for inclusion in the Beloved Community. Essentially, King believed that

---

32. James Cone, *God of the Oppressed*, rev. ed. (Maryknoll, NY: Orbis Books, 1997), 217–18.

33. Weaver, *The Nonviolent Atonement*, 6.

34. Weaver, *The Nonviolent Atonement*, 2.

35. Weaver, *The Nonviolent Atonement*, 8.

36. Weaver, *The Nonviolent Atonement*, 11.

37. Erskine, *King among Theologians*, 153.

nonviolence was the method of liberation through which reconciliation was achieved.[38]

Black Power

In the summer of 1966, James Meredith, who had integrated the University of Mississippi in 1962, initiated a march from Memphis, Tennessee, to Jackson, Mississippi, to promote voter registration for Blacks. On June 6, 1966, while marching peacefully, Meredith was shot in the back by a white supremacist. In reaction to Meredith's shooting, King and other civil rights leaders rallied activists to continue the march. The Student Nonviolent Coordinating Committee (SNCC), under the leadership of Stokely Carmichael, also known as Kware Ture, and the Congress for Racial Equality (CORE), under the leadership of Floyd McKissick, were determined to continue what they characterized as the "James Meredith March against Fear." The continuation of the Meredith march was the climax of the tension between the older and younger generations of civil rights activists. The members of SNCC and CORE were generally younger and constituted the new guard of the civil rights movement. They were also more militant and confrontational in combating the evil forces of white supremacy and oppression. When the old guard would chant "we shall overcome," the new guard would chant "we shall overrun." During the continuation of Meredith's march, as King was proclaiming "freedom now," Willie Ricks (Mukasa Dada) started proclaiming "Black Power," which gave birth to a new movement of the new generation of civil rights activists who threatened King's teachings specifically concerning nonviolence and civil disobedience.[39]

The Black Power movement was a repudiation of the philosophy and practices of the parent civil rights movement. Carmichael, the architect of the philosophy of the younger movement, claimed that the purpose of the Black Power movement was to reclaim Black history and Black identity from cultural terrorism.[40] He accused the civil rights movement of being ineffective and irrelevant, asserting that "the advocates of Black Power reject the old slogans and meaningless rhetoric of previous years in the civil rights struggle. The language of yesterday is indeed irrelevant: progress, nonviolence, integration, fear of white backlash, coalition."[41] He believed that the goal of the civil rights movement was to assimilate to the white American middle class, functioning as a buffer to control angry young Blacks.

---

38. Weaver, *The Nonviolent Atonement*, 155.

39. Whelchel, *The History and Heritage*, 217–18.

40. Stokely Carmichael and Charles V. Hamilton, *Black Power: The Politics of Liberation* (New York: Vintage Books, 1967), 34–35.

41. Carmichael and Hamilton, *Black Power*, 50.

Carmichael defined the Black Power movement as the reaction to the evil forces of White Power in America:

> The goal of black self-determination and black self-identity—Black Power—is full participation in the decision-making processes affecting the lives of black people, and recognition of the virtues in themselves as black people.... The goal of Black Power is positive and functional to a free and viable society. No racist can make this claim.[42]

Carmichael essentially accused the old guard of the civil rights establishment of doing the Black race harm and damage through its advocacy for nonviolence. He asserted that "those of us who advocate Black Power are quite clear in our own minds that a nonviolent approach to civil rights is an approach that Black people cannot afford and a luxury that white people do not deserve. It is crystal clear to us—and it must become so with the white society—that there can be no social order without social justice."[43]

The Black Panther Party

The most prominent product of the Black Power movement was the formation of the Black Panther Party for Self-Defense, founded by Huey P. Newton and Bobby Seale on October 15, 1966. Newton and Seale cultivated the Black Panthers to protect the Black community from the infectious disease of police brutality against Blacks in Oakland, California. They functioned as an armed Black citizens' militia to defend and promote the value of Black life through the teaching of Black self-worth based on the principles of the Black Power movement. Their ten-point platform included (1) the power to determine the destiny of our Black community; (2) full employment; (3) an end to the robbery of the Black community by the government; (4) decent housing; (5) real education; (6) all Black men to be exempt from military service; (7) an immediate end to police brutality and the murder of Black people; (8) freedom for all Black prisoners; (9) a jury of peers for all Black people on trial; and (10) peace and Black representation in the United Nations.[44] The Black Panthers implemented many of their objectives in Oakland and many other major cities through their policing of the police, providing daily free-breakfast programs for children, community health-care services, and educational programs through the development of the Black Panther Party Liberation Schools.

---

42. Carmichael and Hamilton, *Black Power*, 47–48.
43. Carmichael and Hamilton, *Black Power*, 53.
44. Jason Reynolds and Ibram X. Kendi, *Stamped: Racism, Antiracism, and You* (New York: Little, Brown and Company, 2020), 183–84.

Black Liberation Theology

In 1969, during the height of the Black Power movement, Black theologian James Cone published his groundbreaking work *Black Theology and Black Power*, in which he identified Black Power as Christ's message for America in the twentieth century.[45] Building on Carmichael's definition of Black Power, Cone defined it as "complete emancipation of black people from white oppression by whatever means black people deem necessary."[46] Historically, Black Power activists have been accused of being racists and of advocating Black supremacy to overcome and defeat the white oppression of Blacks. Cone correctly asserted that this accusation was an attempt by whites to alleviate their guilt for their perpetuation of white supremacy through acts of commission and omission. He claimed that "as long as whites can be assured that blacks are racists, they can find reasons to justify their own oppression of black people."[47] In the spirit of Black Power, Cone argued that integration was not the solution to the eradication of white supremacy, highlighting his view that integration on the terms of white people was an affirmation of Black inferiority.[48] Cone envisioned Black Power and Black theology working in tandem to eradicate white supremacy. He defined the role of Black theology as applying the liberating power of the gospel to Black people under white oppression and concluded that the sole purpose of Black theology is to emancipate the gospel of its whiteness.[49]

Cone was the first theologian to systematize Black liberation theology and is, therefore, celebrated as the father of Black theology, but he is not the progenitor of Black liberation theology. In 1898, Bishop Henry McNeal Turner caused great controversy when he wrote in an editorial that "God is a Negro." He argued that Blacks in America had come to believe that God was white and the devil was Black, and, therefore, asserted:

> We do not believe that there is any hope for a race of people who do not believe that they look like God. Demented though we be, whenever we reach the conclusion that God or even that Jesus Christ, while in the flesh, was a white man, we shall hang our gospel trumpet upon the willow and cease to preach. We had rather be an atheist and believe in no God, or a pantheist and believe that all nature is God, than to believe in the personality of a God and not to believe that He is a Negro. Blackness is much older than whiteness, for black was here before white.[50]

---

45. James Cone, *Black Theology and Black Power* (San Francisco: Harper & Row, 1969), 1.

46. Cone, *Black Theology and Black Power*, 6.

47. Cone, *Black Theology and Black Power*, 15.

48. Cone, *Black Theology and Black Power*, 17–19.

49. Cone, *Black Theology and Black Power*, 31–32.

50. Henry M. Turner, "God Is Black," in Mark G. Toulouse and James O. Duke, eds., *Sources of Christian Theology in America* (Nashville, TN: Abingdon Press, 1999), 328–29.

While Turner's claim was groundbreaking for Black theology, it was Dwight Hopkins who accurately formulated the origins of Black liberation theology in the spiritual experience of enslaved Africans in the "invisible institution." He argues that enslaved Africans have formulated their own theology of liberation using the elements of the brand of Christianity that they had formed. The European enslavers viewed enslaved Africans as foreigners to the Christian faith. However, the enslaved community possessed a pneumatic theology, and the circumstances surrounding their enslavement caused enslaved Africans to develop an ultimate concern, which was liberation.

In his systematic work, *A Black Theology of Liberation*, Cone identifies six sources and norms essential to engaging in Black liberation theology: (1) Black experience; (2) Black history; (3) Black culture; (4) revelation; (5) Scripture; and (6) tradition.[51] One of the major critiques of Cone's scholarship is his dependency on the theology of Karl Barth. Cone was attracted to Barth's Christology and the confessional nature of his theology, which Cone considered essential to the articulation of Black liberation theology.[52] Noel Erskine notes that, in addition to the influence of Barth, Cone's scholarship was also influenced by Paul Tillich's theology, but there was a theological point of departure with the methodology of the German theological tradition due to his emphasis on the sources of Black experience, Black culture, and Black history. These unconventional sources empowered Cone to ultimately transcend the theologies of Barth and Tillich because neither addressed the theological problem of white supremacy. In fact, Erskine asserts that "for Barth and Tillich, Black and third world people were invisible."[53]

Cone asserted that "there could be no black theology which does not take seriously the black experience, a life of humiliation and suffering."[54] Consequently, he addressed the theological issue of white supremacy through the dichotomy of whiteness and blackness and the dialectic between the oppressor and the oppressed, equating whiteness with the oppressor and blackness with the oppressed:

The focus on blackness does not mean that only blacks suffer as victims in a racist society, but that blackness is an ontological symbol

---

51. James Cone, *A Black Theology of Liberation*, 40th Anniversary Edition (Maryknoll, NY: Orbis Books, 2010), 24–41.

52. Erskine, *King among the Theologians*, 95.

53. Erskine, *King among the Theologians*, 84.

54. Cone, *A Black Theology*, 24. Barth and Tillich possessed fears about experience as a source for theological praxis, yet experience is primary in Black liberation theology, because it presupposes participation in the religious faith and encompasses the cultural and historical significance of Black people.

and a visible reality which best describes what oppression means in America. . . . Blackness, then, stands for all victims of oppression who realize that the survival of their humanity is bound up with liberation from whiteness. . . . Whiteness is the symbol of the Antichrist. Whiteness characterizes the activity of deranged individuals intrigued by their own image of themselves, and thus unable to see that they are what is wrong with the world.[55]

While blackness symbolized what is right with the world—the alleviation of oppression—Cone contended that, in the age of lynching, for Blacks to affirm blackness was suicidal.[56] His dichotomy of blackness and whiteness exposes the problem of white theology. One of Cone's contemporaries, New Testament scholar and CME bishop Joseph Johnson, argues that white theologians were ignorant of the Black experience and therefore were not qualified to formulate a theology for Black people.[57]

In his rejection of white theology and affirmation of Black theology, Cone claimed that white theology "preserved the integrity of the community of oppressors," and therefore, if white theology is the theology of the oppressor then Black theology must be the theology of the oppressed. Cone correlated Black theology with Christian theology, asserting that "Christian theology can only mean black theology, a theology that speaks of God as related to black liberation."[58] Therefore, Cone's solution to the problem of white supremacy and, by extension, white theology was to eradicate the whiteness embedded in white theology:

In order to be Christian theology, white theology must cease being white theology and become black theology by denying whiteness as a proper form of human existence and affirming blackness as God's intention for humanity.[59]

To justify his idea of Black theology as Christian theology, Cone de-emphasized the color of black skin and advocated for the ontology of blackness. From an ontological perspective, he concluded, being Black literally means being in solidarity with the oppressed.

Similarly, Johnson argues that the ideology of white supremacy embodied in white theology caused the opposition, exploitation, exclusion, and segregation of Blacks. Furthermore, the white church's image of Christ

---

55. Cone, *A Black Theology*, 8.

56. Cone, *The Cross and the Lynching Tree*, 11.

57. Joseph A. Johnson, "The Need for a Black Christian Theology," *Journal of the Interdenominational Theological Center* 2, no. 1 (1974): 19.

58. Cone, *A Black Theology*, 10.

59. Cone, *A Black Theology*, 10.

reflects an oppressor of Blacks, and the teachings of the white Christ are oppressive.[60] Womanist theologian Kelly Brown Douglas argues that slave-holding Christianity produced the white Christ, which demonstrated their ignorance of what Christ actually taught and practiced through his ministry to the poor and oppressed and emphasized what he did not do in the Scripture—reject and condemn slavery.[61] In her depiction of the white Christ, Douglas asserts:

> This Christ allowed for the maintenance of an oppressive social-economic system and freed the white ruling class to act in ways that benefitted them without fear for their salvation. Specifically, the white Christ provided for the religious justification of the chattel system, eliminated reservations about holding Christians as slaves, and obscured the tensions between Christian and the cruelty of slavery.[62]

Consequently, this white Christ had become the nucleus of the slaveholding religion of white supremacists, which necessitated that the enslaved African Christian develop the Black Christ. Douglas identifies three factors in this development of the Black Christ: (1) the intimate relationship between Jesus and enslaved Africans fostered through the enslaved interpretation of the cross of Christ as a symbol of life and death reflecting African spirituality; (2) the radicalization of enslaved Africans to fight for freedom; and (3) the enslaved African awareness of the contradiction between Christianity and the cruelty of slavery reflecting the hypocrisy of slaveholding white Christianity.[63] Finally, with formulating a Black Christian theology, Johnson emphasizes, comes the imperative of overcoming the offense and scandal of theological thinking in white Christianity.

Black Lives Matter

The Black Lives Matter (BLM) movement originated in the protests for justice surrounding the brutal murder of seventeen-year-old, African American youth Trayvon Martin at the hands of white supremacist George Zimmerman on February 26, 2012.[64]

After the election in 2008 of Barack Obama, the first African American president, many in the United States began to be deluded into thinking that

60. Johnson, "The Need," 23–25.

61. Kelly Brown Douglas, *The Black Christ* (Maryknoll, NY: Orbis Books, 1994), 15.

62. Douglas, *The Black Christ*, 19.

63. Douglas, *The Black Christ*, 20–30.

64. Keeanga-Yamahtta Taylor, *From #BlackLivesMatter to Black Liberation* (Chicago: Haymarket Books, 2016), 148. African American scholar and BLM activist Keeanga-Yamahtta Taylor has demonstrated the direct correlation between the death of Martin and the death of Emmett Till in 1955.

America had moved into a postracial society. However, the brutal murder of Martin shifted the mindset of even white people, who were naïve to the reality of white privilege and white supremacy in the United States. In this incident, the nation was reminded of Emmett Till, a Black boy, who was killed after being falsely accused of hissing at a white woman. Martin, a Black boy walking home from a convenience store in Sanford, Florida, was killed by George Zimmerman, a white supremacist, self-deputized vigilante, who determined that Martin was a misfit who did not belong in the neighborhood and was convinced that he was trouble based on the color of his skin and because he was wearing a hoodie.

Racial Profiling

The United States from its inception has had a very troubling history of racial profiling through which Black males are demonized and vilified as violent criminals, sexual predators, and subhuman savages. African American historian Barbara Ransby explains this reality in her historical analysis of Martin's death:

> In a sense, the explosion of protest in the wake of Martin's murder and Zimmerman's acquittal was a quarter century in the making, but more immediately the case underscored the precariousness that defined the lives of black youth in the United States, especially if they were poor and working class. . . . Black men and boys like Trayvon Martin had already been systematically criminalized, not by their individual actions but by their collective identity, their posture, their positionality, and sometimes even their fashion choices. They were typecast in popular culture and popular media as menacing, violent, and dangerous: bodies to be feared, contained, or even killed.[65]

Due to public outrage, Zimmerman was arrested and charged with the murder of Martin forty-five days after Martin's death. Unfortunately, not surprising to many in the Black community, Zimmerman was acquitted on all charges brought against him on July 13, 2013, after a trial in which Zimmerman was victimized and Martin criminalized. The acquittal was not shocking to Black people because of the unjust reality of two systems in the United States—one that has historically been unjust for people of color, and another that has historically favored white Americans with the benefit of doubt regardless of the crime. Taylor describes this reality clearly in the circumstances surrounding the brutal killing of Martin:

---

65. Barbara Ransby, *Making All Black Lives Matter: Reimagining Freedom in the 21st Century* (Oakland: University of California Press, 2018), 32–33.

There is a dual system of criminal justice—one for African Americans and one for whites. The result is the discriminatory disparities in punishment that run throughout all aspects of American jurisprudence. George Zimmerman benefitted from this dual system: he was allowed to walk free for weeks before protests pressured officials into arresting him. He was not subjected to drug tests, though Trayvon Martin's dead body had been. This double standard undermined public proclamations that the United States is a nation built around the rule of law.[66]

The BLM Movement

The moment of robust protests to achieve justice for Martin was transformed into a movement after Black community activist Alicia Garza posted the hashtag #blacklivesmatter on social media. The message of social resistance for social justice became the mantra and identity of this movement. Along with Garza, Black activists Patrisse Cullors and Opal Tometi launched the transformational BLM movement of social activism to achieve social change in American society.

The power of the BLM movement was activated when eighteen-year-old African American Michael Brown was murdered at the hands of white police officer Darren Wilson in Ferguson, Missouri, on August 9, 2014. After an altercation with Brown, Wilson fired twelve shots at Brown and killed him. Wilson thereafter claimed that he had shot Brown in self-defense, even though Brown had no weapons and no evidence has revealed that Wilson's life was in danger. The dehumanization and devaluation of Black lives by white America was evident in how Brown's corpse was treated following his death. His lifeless body lay in the streets for four hours before being properly removed from the scene of the crime. As did the murder of Martin, the Brown incident garnered national attention, with many protesters descending on Ferguson to join its Black citizens in protest. Brown's death brought to a climax the anger, frustration, and outrage of local Black citizens at the many years of white oppression of Blacks in Ferguson. Taylor notes vividly the Black residents' grievances against the city of Ferguson at the time:

Black protestors went to unmask the kleptocracy at the heart of municipal operations in Ferguson, revealing that the Ferguson police department, directed by the mayor and city council, were targeting the black population as the major source of revenue for the town. Black households were inundated with fines, fees, citations, tickets, and arrests to such an extent that the revenues were the town's second

66. Taylor, *From #BlackLivesMatter*, 150.

leading source of revenue. Court fines deriving from motor-vehicle violations were 21 percent of revenue accounting for "the equivalent of more than 81 percent of police salaries before overtime. Failure to pay or appear in court to respond to tickets instantly produced an arrest warrant.[67]

In response to the rebellion of local Black citizens in Ferguson and the protests in the wake of the brutal killing of Brown by an officer of the law, the Ferguson police department became a militarized police force equipped with tanks, machine guns, unlimited tear gas, rubber bullets, and batons. Taylor exclaims that "the Ferguson police department declared war on black residents and anyone who stood in solidarity with them."[68] The ultimate goal of the Ferguson protests, which occurred in three different waves, was to achieve a grand jury indictment of Wilson for the death of Brown. Unfortunately, and unsurprisingly to many in the Black community, the St. Louis County grand jury did not indict Wilson, and the justice system cleared him of any civil rights violations. Despite another failure of the unjust justice system, the BLM movement realized its organizing power in the fight for justice and protection of Black lives.

The incident that brought international attention to the BLM movement occurred on May 25, 2020, when the life of African American George Floyd was senselessly and unjustifiably taken in the custody of Minneapolis police officers. Floyd was arrested for allegedly passing a fraudulent twenty-dollar bill at a local convenience store. The officers involved in Floyd's arrest and impending death were J. Alexander Kueng, Thomas Lane, Tou Thao, and Derek Chauvin. While in custody Floyd complained that he was having difficulty breathing, and after being further restrained and his body positioned on the ground with his skull and face literally pressed into the concrete street, his cries and complaints for relief only escalated. Adding insult to injury, white supremacist officer Derek Chauvin strategically and forcefully positioned his knee on Floyd's neck for nine minutes and twenty-nine seconds, resulting in Floyd's death. The scene was so horrific, Floyd's cries so pervasive, and the demands from the surrounding crowd for Chauvin to take his knee off Floyd's neck so insistent that even the other officers asked Chauvin, their ranking officer, whether Floyd should be lifted from the ground and repositioned. Chauvin rejected these demands and even continued his inhumane and deplorable act until emergency medics arrived on the scene. Floyd's death and the demonic actions of Chauvin leading to his death were the catalyst for international outrage and massive protests

67. Taylor, *From #BlackLivesMatter*, 155.
68. Taylor, *From #BlackLivesMatter*, 154.

against police brutality in cities and towns across the United States and throughout the world. Many of these protests for justice over the killing of George Floyd were organized and led through the activist genius and auspices of the BLM movement.

In the wake of massive BLM protests demanding justice in the murder of Floyd and against the historic pervasiveness of police brutality, particularly at the expense of Black lives, criminal charges were brought against the officers. Chauvin was arrested and initially charged with third-degree murder and second-degree manslaughter. In the interest and pursuit of justice, Minnesota attorney general Keith Ellison increased Chauvin's charge to second-degree murder. Kueng, Lane, and Thao were arrested and charged with aiding and abetting second-degree murder and second-degree manslaughter.

Since protesting the murder of Trayvon Martin, BLM activists have been the standard bearers of justice for Black lives taken unjustifiably due to white supremacy through police brutality and civilian vigilantes.

12

Theological Solutions

Through this book, we have demonstrated the historical and theological trajectory of white supremacy that has plagued white Christianity and corrupted the Christian gospel. This theological scandal began with the Enlightenment, which fostered "racial othering," viewing Europe as culturally, racially, and spiritually superior to people of non-European territories, especially the "racial others" of African descent. Based on their racial othering, Enlightenment thinkers concluded that humans from colder climates were superior to humans from warmer climates and even characterized the latter category of humans as "subhuman."

The initial white Christian traditions complicit in the theological scandal and corruption of the Christian faith were the Puritans and Anglicans. In the Christian tradition, a divine covenant is an agreement made through divine grace. The covenantal theology of the Puritans was based on racial ideology rather than divine grace. The Reformed doctrine of election coupled with the idea that Europeans were racially superior resulted in the racialization of Puritan visible sainthood. New England Puritans demonized blackness as evil and made whiteness the prerequisite for Christian conversion. This religion of antiblackness even plagued the abolitionist New Divinity theologians such as Samuel Hopkins, who devised the Christianization-civilization-colonization process of the supposed virtue of Christian paternalism.

Parallel to the New England Puritans, Anglicans in the British colonies developed a theology of white privilege, which Rebecca Anne Goetz has characterized as "hereditary heathenism," whereby religious differences were transformed into racial differences. Katherine Gerbner bases this Anglican white privilege in Protestant supremacy. She argues that Protestant supremacy shifted Christianity from a religious to a racial category, and Protestant supremacy became white supremacy. Furthermore, white Christian slaveholders viewed slavery as a benevolent institution based on their false scriptural interpretations that portrayed slavery as righteous and providential.

233

Depending on the theology, resistance to this scandal differed. Black Calvinist evangelicals, including Phillis Wheatley, Jupiter Hammon, John Marrant, and Lemuel Haynes, epitomized the Reformed theology of Calvinism, which was the theology of the new American empire. While the Black Calvinist evangelicals were abolitionists, their Reformed theology caused them to condemn their motherland of Africa as a heathen land and motivated their belief that God intended for freed Blacks to return to Africa to evangelize their supposed heathen brothers and sisters still in the motherland.

Black Radical evangelicals such as David Walker and Nat Turner provided an adequate spiritual resistance to the institution of slavery. Their spiritual resistance stemmed from the possession of a liberative pneumatology. Walker declared that enslaved Africans were not the property of their slave owners but the property of the Holy Ghost. The influence of indigenous African spirituality and Turner's spiritual gifts reflected this liberative pneumatology.

The impact of the theological scandal and spiritual resistance is evident in the life and ministry of antebellum evangelicals. The revivalism of Charles Finney during the Second Great Awakening, specifically the inception of his "new measures" coupled with the perfectionist theology of Oberlinism, was pivotal to social reform in American society. Central to this activism for social change was immediate abolitionism. During the First Great Awakening, John Wesley promoted his theology of social holiness, which fueled his antislavery views and the abolitionism of early American Methodists. Northern Methodists remained committed to the spirit of abolitionism characteristic of social holiness despite the defection of the southern Methodists to the politics of social respectability. However, the northern Methodists practiced racial segregation, which led to the formation of the African Methodist Episcopal and African Methodist Episcopal Zion denominations in protest of white Christian supremacy. Prior to the Civil War, the American Methodists, American Baptists, and American Presbyterians experienced denominational schisms regarding slavery that were the theological precursors to the Civil War, which Mark Noll characterizes as "a theological crisis."

The impact of the theological scandal and spiritual resistance was also evident in postbellum evangelicalism. The Reconstruction amendments (Thirteenth, Fourteenth, and Fifteen Amendments) to the US Constitution coupled with other forms of civil rights legislation proved crucial to the full citizenship and enfranchisement of African Americans. The religious impact was evident in the Colored Methodist Episcopal denomination, which was formed through mutual agreement by the colored members of the Methodist Episcopal Church South. The political and social success of the Reconstruction era for African Americans horrified southern white supremacists and led to the atrocities of Jim Crow, including the lynching of Blacks, the enacting of Black codes, the practice of racial segregation, and the growth of sundown towns. Another major aspect of the southern white supremacist "whitelash" to Reconstruction was the mythical idea of Lost Cause religion, which represented the spiritualization of southern white supremacy. From this Lost Cause myth emerged the white Christian supremacist domestic organization the Ku Klux Klan.

The impact of the theological scandal continued into the twentieth century in the popularization of white American fundamentalism. As the progenitor of this movement, Dwight Moody held segregated revivals in the South and promoted the prosperity gospel, which fueled capitalism and had premillennial dispensationalism as its nucleus. Along with the influence of racial segregation, white American Pentecostals shifted away from the spiritual mandate of racial equality to denominational schisms based on racial differences. The same vile spirit of racial segregation corrupted Jerry Falwell and motivated his formation of the Moral Majority, which was instrumental in the success of the Reagan Revolution, which appealed to southern white Christian supremacists.

In its modern form, the theological scandal is most evident in the cult of Donald Trump, which can be traced to the racial motivations of the Tea Party, which planted the seeds of the birther movement. Both the Tea Party and the birther movement epitomized the spiritual hypocrisy of white evangelicals in the United States, which reached its zenith on January 6, 2021, when a mob of domestic white Christian supremacists supporting Trump invaded the US Capitol. Ironically, this insurrection took place on the day of Epiphany, which in the Christian tradition celebrated the manifestation of Christ to the magi. The domestic terrorist attack on the Capitol was, for some, an epiphany of the presence of white supremacy in the United States.

Our analysis of the theological scandal, resistance, and impact does present a way forward theologically through the social gospel and practically through social resistance. The social gospel emphasizes the kingdom of God, as demonstrated in the earthly life and ministry of Jesus. Walter Rauschenbusch, who represented the white social gospel, highlighted the ethic of love presented by Jesus in the Gospels to combat the kingdom of evil. The most significant critique of the white social gospel was its perceived preoccupation with the plight of the poor while ignoring the reality of white supremacy in the United States. The theologians of the Black social gospel, Mordecai Johnson, Benjamin Mays, and Howard Thurman, directly challenged white supremacy and advocated for its eradication through racial justice and nonviolence.

The theology of Martin Luther King Jr. fueled the social resistance of the civil rights movement and was influenced by the Black church tradition,

Black social gospel, and personalism. There was a stark contrast between King and his contemporary Billy Graham, who was often torn between the white fundamentalist quest for moral purity, which included racial purity, and the Black social gospel quest for love and justice as embodied in King's Beloved Community. The Beloved Community represented the earthly kingdom of God based on the ethic of love inherent in the holistic salvation of the body and soul of humans.

King's theology and leadership influenced civil rights activists who were committed to acts of nonviolent atonement. As a point of departure, the Black Power movement advocated Black liberation by any means necessary. In the modern age, protesters of the Black Lives Matter (BLM) movement have effectively challenged the systemic racism in the United States that has historically dehumanized and devalued Black bodies. BLM protesters are committed to the complete eradication of racial profiling, police brutality, and the unjustifiable killing of Black bodies.

Given this historical and theological trajectory of white Christian supremacy and corruption of the Christian faith, let us now propose some theological solutions. Theologian Katie Walker Grimes identifies white privilege and white supremacy as corporate vices and concludes that there is more emphasis on the discourse of white privilege than on the discourse of white supremacy.[1] She purports that the discourse of white supremacy is superior to the discourse of white privilege when both discourses are classified as corporate vices.[2] Grimes presents the dichotomy between the white/nonwhite binary and the Black/non-Black binary that informs her idea of antiblackness supremacy. Now, she defines white supremacy as white people, both as groups and individuals, who possess more power than people of color.[3] She defines antiblackness supremacy as non-Black people, both as individuals and as groups, who amass power due to the country's pervasive antiblackness.[4] She contends that antiblackness is the originating cause of white supremacy, which empowers and preserves the purity of whites. Certainly, the eradication of antiblackness supremacy is imperative, but in addition to white supremacy we must also acknowledge the reality of "neo-whiteness," which, in my view, represents the assimilation of nonwhites to whiteness.

Any nonwhite person, regardless of ethnic or cultural background, can assimilate to whiteness. However, neo-whiteness results in racial self-hate or internalized racism through which nonwhites are conditioned into

---

1. Katie Walker Grimes, *Christ Divided: Antiblackness as Corporate Vice* (Minneapolis: Fortress Press, 2017), xxiv.

2. Grimes, *Christ Divided*, xxiv.

3. Grimes, *Christ Divided*, xxiv.

4. Grimes, *Christ Divided*, xxiv.

believing the racial hierarchy that characterizes the white race as superior and nonwhite races as inferior. In his seminal work *Whiteness of a Different Color*, Matthew Frye Jacobson asserts that "racial categories themselves—their vicissitudes and the contests over them—reflect the competing notions of history, personhood, and collective destiny by which power has been organized and contested on the American scene."[5] Language is powerful, language matters, and language can have severe consequences. The binary understanding of the colors white and black has been the agenda of certain human beings seeking a status of human superiority.

Linguistically, the color white, on the one hand, is generally connected to having a good character, being upright, being fair, possessing innocence, being free from moral impurity, being favorable, and being fortunate. On the other hand, the color black is generally connected with someone or something being dirty, sinister, evil, wicked, sad, gloomy, hostile, angry, or a disaster. The black-and-white color binary is also ingrained in the spiritual and secular customs of American society. White is identified as the lightest of all colors. Black is identified as the darkest of colors. Angel foods are white and devil's foods are black. The White House is the residence of the most powerful person in the world, and the black market is a marketplace of illegal activity. A white lie is a harmless falsehood, and to be black balled means to be excluded and ostracized. White magic manifests blessings and healing, and black magic manifests evil. White is the color for weddings and baptisms because white symbolizes purity. And black is the color for funerals because black symbolizes darkness, sin, affliction, humiliation, calamity, death, and mourning. To eradicate antiblackness supremacy, we must end the perpetuation of this black/white color binary that favors whiteness and condemns blackness.

Another theological solution is decolonial love. Joseph Drexler-Dreis defines decolonial love as "love made concrete in history within struggles to reveal and shatter the structures of colonial modernity."[6] He builds his proposal for decolonial love on the literary work of James Baldwin. For Drexler-Dreis, Baldwin's decolonial love reveals and removes the American façade that legitimizes and perpetuates the matrix of colonial power.[7] It combats the colonialism and imperialism that gave birth to the white supremacy prevalent in American society. Moving forward with continual emphasis on the Wesleyan doctrine of Christian perfection, which stipulates perfect love of God and perfect love of one's neighbor, coupled with Drexler-Dreis's pro-

5. Matthew Frye Jacobson, *Whiteness of a Different Color: European Immigrants and the Alchemy of Race* (Cambridge, MA: Harvard University Press, 1998), 9.

6. Joseph Drexler-Dreis, *Decolonial Love: Salvation in Colonial Modernity* (New York: Fordham University Press, 2019), 4.

7. Drexler-Dreis, *Decolonial Love*, 105–6.

posal for decolonial love will prove most effective theologically in combating oppressive theologies with spiritual resistance mediated theologically through liberative pneumatology.

The most significant reflection of this spiritual resistance occurred during the BLM protests for justice following the murder of George Floyd. BLM activists would most assuredly disagree with my characterization of their protests as spiritual resistance. In fact, they are intentional in not associating the movement with any particular faith tradition or spiritual entity, even the Black church. BLM activists believe that the Black church has lost its prophetic voice and therefore is no longer effective in the cause of justice. Nevertheless, the BLM movement is very much a spiritual movement because the tremendous cultural and racial diversity of the protesters marching for the common cause of racial justice reflects the day of Pentecost outlined in the Book of Acts. Consequently, the BLM movement is a reawakening of Pentecost and the protests as a new Great Awakening in America. Only the Spirit of God can manifest the coming together of people from many different cultures and racial ethnicities in one accord for the cause of racial justice in the United States.

We began our journey with a quotation from Frederick Douglass, in which he noted the dichotomy between slaveholding religion and the Christianity of Christ. In 1973, Black theologian William Jones, in his quest to address the issue of divine racism, which he linked with ethnic suffering, particularly Black suffering, asked, "Is God a white racist?"[8] The god of slaveholding religion is indeed a white racist. When the white Christian supremacists invaded the Capitol and committed heinous crimes, including the taking of human life, they came together in prayer on the floor of the US Senate. Simultaneously, Representative Lisa Blunt Rochester fervently prayed for the protection of those in the Capitol as she sheltered with other members of Congress in the balcony of the House of Representatives. There is a stark contrast between Rochester's prayer and that of the domestic terrorists. There is also a stark contrast between Rochester's God and the god of the domestic terrorists. If we are ever to resolve the problem of white Christian supremacy, we have to condemn its beliefs and actions. The god of those domestic terrorists is a white racist. The God to whom Rochester prayed is the God who emanates from the Christianity of Christ, and this is the God who fuels spiritual and social resistance against all forms of oppression caused by the theological scandal that has historically corrupted the Christian faith.

---

8. See William R. Jones, *Is God a White Racist?: A Preamble to Black Theology* (Garden City, NY: Anchor Press/Doubleday), 1973.

In Memoriam

Trayvon Martin	Jamar Clark
Michael Brown	Clementa C. Pinckney
George Floyd	Cynthia Marie Graham Hurd
Dontre Hamilton	Susie Jackson
Eric Garner	Ethel Lee
John Crawford III	Depayne Middleton-Doctor
Ezell Ford	Tywanza Sanders
Laquan McDonald	Daniel L. Simmons
Akai Gurley	Sharonda Coleman-Singleton
Tamir Rice	Myra Thompson
Antonia Martin	Bruce Kelley Jr
Jerame Reid	Alton Sterling
Charley Leundeu Keunang	Philando Castile
Tony Robinson	Joseph Mann
Anthony Hill	Abdirahman Abdi
Megan Hockaday	Paul O'Neal
Eric Harris	Korryn Gaines
Walter Scott	Sylville Smith
Freddie Grey	Terence Crutcher
William Chapman	Keith Lamont Scott
Jonathan Sanders	Alfred Olango
Sandra Bland	Deborah Danner
Samuel DuBose	Ahmaud Arbery
Jeremy McDole	Breonna Taylor
Corey Jones	Jordan Davis

Index

Abbott, Lyman, and white social gospel, 198, 201
abolitionism, 47–50, 122–28
  Christian, 58
  and New Divinity movement, 49, 50, 80
  and Oberlin College, 121
  of Phillis Wheatley, 80, 81, 82
  and Second Great Awakening, 45, 46
  and Theodore Weld, 122
  See also Oberlinism
abolitionists, types of, 25, 26, 47
abortion myth, 168, 169, 170
Abyssinian Baptist Church (New York City), 133
"An Act for Encouraging the Importation of White Male Servants and the Preventing of the Clandestine Bringing of Negroes and Mulattoes" (1718), 48
affirmative action, 220
Affordable Care Act, 179
Africa
  as Dark continent, xvii, xviii
  return of Blacks to, in New Divinity movement, 49, 50, 90, 101
African Baptist Church of Williamsburg, VA, 132
African Episcopal Church of St. Thomas, 130
African Methodist Episcopal Church (AME), 129, 130, 144, 234
African Methodist Episcopal Zion Church (AMEZ), 130, 144, 234
African spirituality. *See* ecstasy, spiritual; enthusiasm; spirituality, indigenous African, and slaves

Africans, enslaved
  ancestral practices, survival of, 204, 205
  conversion of, 57–62
  knowledge of Christian faith, 58, 62
  prohibited from Puritan visible sainthood, 39
  prohibition against Christian conversion, 55, 56, 57
  as property of the Holy Ghost, 94
  and Second Great Awakening, 118
  washed in the white blood of Jesus, 37, 38, 39, 40, 92, 138, 139
  See also slaves
Allen, Richard, and African Methodist Episcopal Church, 129, 130
alt-right movement, in support of Donald J. Trump, 184, 185
America, as the "city on a hill," 9, 32, 33
American Baptist Churches USA, 132
American Baptist Home Mission Society (ABHMS), 131
American Baptist Missionary Convention (ABMC), 133
American Baptists, schism in, 131, 132
American Bible Society, and abolitionism, 123, 124
American Christian nationalism, 172
American Colonization Society, 27, 50, 100, 101
American exceptionalism, 9, 99, 172, 174
  and Puritanism, 31, 32
American Legislative Exchange Council (ALEC), and white supremacy, 179
American Missionary Association, and abolitionism, 124
American National Baptist Convention, 133, 134

241

American Tract Society, and abolitionism, 123, 124

Americanicity, xi, xii

Amistad, 124

Anderson, William, and one-blood doctrine, 137, 138

Andrew, Bishop James O., ownership of slaves, 128, 129

Anglicanism
and Black evangelical Christianity, 63–66
and blackness, 54, 71
and conversion of enslaved Africans, 57–59
and hereditary heathenism, 55–57
and proslavery paternalism, 62–63
and white privilege, 52, 53, 55, 56, 233
whiteness and white supremacy in, 53–55, 59–62
See also Christianity, benevolent; Whitefield, George

Anselm, St., and satisfaction theory of atonement, 221, 222

antiblackness, 35, 36, 39, 50, 51, 52, 126, 233
of ideal Christian masters, 95

anxious bench, 120

Aristotle
humanity as masters and slaves, 32
racial classification of, 5

armed resistance, to white resistance, 103, 104

Arminianism, 91, 118, 119, 121, 157

Assemblies of God (AG), 164, 165

Association of Regular Baptist Churches of Color in Ohio, 133

atonement
Christus Victor theory of, 220, 221
nonviolent, 221, 222, 223
satisfaction theory of, 221, 222

Aulen, Gustaf, and *Christus Victor* theory of atonement, 220, 221

Azusa Street Mission, and American Pentecostalism, 162–63

Bachmann, Michelle, views on slavery, 178

Bannon, Steve, and alt-right, 185

baptism, of Africans, 15, 56, 57, 59, 61. *See also* conversion, Christian

Baptist Association for Colored People (Amherstburg, Canada), 133

Baptist Foreign Mission Convention, 133, 134

beauty, general and particular, 41

Beloved Community, and Martin Luther King Jr., 212, 216, 217, 222, 236

Bernier, François, classification of races by, xvii

Bethel Bible College, 160

Bethel Healing Home, 160

Big Bethel AME Church, 141, 142

Birmingham bombing, and civil rights movement, 219

The Birth of a Nation (D. W. Griffith), 154

birtherism, xv, 175, 178, 180, 181, 183, 235

Black Baptist congregations, 132–34

Black Calvinist evangelicals, 75, 92, 93

Black Christ, 96, 222, 228

Black citizenship, 100–101

Black evangelical Christianity, 63–66
theological differences in, 64

Black liberation theology, 92, 225–28, 236

Black Lives Matter movement, 228, 230–32, 236, 238
governmental response to, 188, 189, 190

Black Methodist denominations, 129, 130

Black nationalism, 102–4

Black Panther Party for Self-Defense, 224

Black Panther Party Liberation Schools, 224

Black Power movement, 223, 224, 236

Black radical evangelicalism, 65, 94

Black root, and origins of Pentecostalism, 163

black skin
and enslavement, 137
and inferiority, 95

Black theology. *See* Black liberation theology

Black/non-Black binary, 236, 237

black/white, as colors, 237

blackness
Cotton Mather's view of, 37, 38, 39
as a curse, 34
in Enlightenment thought, 3–7
New Divinity theologians' view of, 101
Puritan correlation with evil, 36, 233
as symbol of subordination, 54

Varick, James, and African Methodist
    Episcopal Zion Church, 130
Voltaire
    and institution of slavery, 18
    racism of, 18, 19
Voting Rights Act of 1965, 220

Walker, David
    on armed resistance to white
        supremacy, 103, 104
    on Black citizenship, 100–101
    and Black nationalism, 102–4
    on moral superiority of Blacks, 102, 103
    on sinfulness of slavery, 100, 234
    spiritual resistance of, 98–104
*Walker's Appeal . . . to the Coloured Citizens
    of the World* (David Walker), 94, 98,
    99, 100, 103, 104, 112
Walters, Bishop Alexander, and Black
    social gospel tradition, 202
warfare, divinely sanctioned, in Nat
    Turner, 111, 112
Washington, Booker T., and Black social
    gospel tradition, 202, 211
wealth, as sign of the converted, 157, 158.
    See also prosperity gospel
Weld, Theodore, and abolitionism, 121,
    122, 123
Wells, Ida B., and Black social gospel
    tradition, 202
Welsing, Frances Cress, definition of
    racism, 7
Wesley, John
    condemnation of slavery and
        slaveholders, 125, 126, 234
    on identity and beliefs of Africans, 125,
        126
    opposition to American Revolutionary
        War, 126
Wesleyan Methodist Connection, and
    abolitionism, 127, 128
Wesleyan Methodists, 125–28
Wesleyanism, as foundation of Pente-
    costalism, 163
West, Cornel, on development of white
    supremacy, xvii
Weyrich, Paul, and the abortion myth, 168
Wheatley, Phillis
    benevolent treatment of, 75, 76

Calvinism of, 75, 76, 77, 234
on Christianity and enslaved Africans,
    69
influence of African spirituality on, 76
influence of George Whitefield, 79
influence of Selina Hastings, 79
proslavery theology of, 75–77, 80
religion of, 79
views on slavery, 80, 81, 82
"white as snow," as a curse, 138
white blood, of Jesus, 37, 38, 39, 92, 138,
    138, 139
white Christ, 96
white Christian evangelicals
    disenchantment with Jimmy Carter,
        167, 168
    spiritual hypocrisy of, 190, 191
    support for Donald Trump, 181–85
white supremacy (supremacists)/
        white Christian supremacy
        (supremacists)
    and American Christianity, 141
    as American religion, 53, 54
    as America's original sin, 184, 193
    and Christian supremacy, 30
    and cult of Donald Trump, 177
    definition, 30
    divine sanction for, xii
    and Ku Klux Klan, 153, 154
    and Lost Cause religion, 150–53, 193
    and lynchings, 146, 147
    obsession with Black male genitalia, 136
    origins in British colonial America, 95
    and Pentecostal movement, 164–65
    and presidency of Donald Trump,
        181–85
    and presidency of Ronald Reagan, 172,
        173
    religion and racial superiority, 30, 31
    and southern respectability, 183, 184
    and the Tea Party, 178
    and white social gospel, 201
White, Sampson, and American Baptist
    Missionary Convention, 133
white/non-white binary, 236, 237
Whitefield, George
    and benevolent Christianity, 70, 71
    and catechesis of enslaved Africans, 69,
        71

Whitefield, George (*cont.*)
    influence on John Marrant, 91
    revivalism of, 66–70
    views on slavery, 67–71
    work in southern colonies, 70
whitelash, against Barack Obama, 178
whiteness, xvii
    equated with Christianity, 56, 59
    and freedom, 60
    as idolatry, 54
    as quality of citizenship, 54
    and white supremacy, 53–55
Williams, Adam Daniel, and Black social
    gospel, 211
Williams, Peter, and Zion Church, 130
Wilson, Officer Darren, 230, 231
Winthrop, John, and America as the "city
    on a hill," 32
women
    African, rape by slaveholders, 136
    demeaning by Donald Trump, 182

    and Equal Rights Amendment, 169
    and Finney's revivalism, 120
    and interracial sex, 25
    as preachers, 46
    racist attacks against, by Ronald
      Reagan, 174
    and Second Great Awakening, 45, 118,
      120, 122
    in sexual ethics of Howard Thurman,
      206
Wood River Baptist Association of Illinois,
    133
Word of Faith movement, 158
work, and divine election, 34
worship in secret, and slave religion, 108

xenolalia, and Spirit baptism, 160

Zimmerman, George, 228, 229, 230
Zion Baptist Church (New York City), 133
Zion Church ("African Chapel"), 130